Table of Contents

UNITING
WORK
 and
SPIRIT

A CENTENNIAL HISTORY OF
ELIZABETHTOWN COLLEGE

by

Chet Williamson

Published by Elizabethtown College Press
One Alpha Drive
Elizabethtown, Pennsylvania 17022

Book design by ITP of USA, Inc.

Acknowledgements

Dr. Ralph W. Schlosser's 1971 history of the college proved an indispensable starting point for this work. The student-created centennial history, *Elizabethtown College: The First Hundred Years*, edited by Dr. David C. Downing, provided fresh insight into many events of the past century. Other valuable sources were the volumes on the history of the Church of the Brethren published by the Church itself, as well as Donald F. Durnbaugh's history of the Brethren, *Fruit of the Vine*, and Donald R. Fitzkee's *Moving Toward the Mainstream*, which skillfully and entertainingly records the changes in the Church throughout the twentieth century.

The author wishes to thank all those who graciously submitted to interviews and answered questions, the staff of the High Library, and especially Peter J. DePuydt (the friendly and helpful Cerberus at the entranceway into the Archives), the readers of and commentators on the early draft, the Centennial Steering Committee, Dr. Ted Long, and the book's editor, Edward A. Novak III, for his sound advice and patience over the course of a lengthy writing process. Any errors are my own rather than theirs.

The author's work is respectfully dedicated to the memory of G. N. Falkenstein, *primum mobile*.

Author's Introduction

When I was first approached by Elizabethtown College to write the centennial history of the school, I did not consider myself an ideal choice. Though I have lived in and near Elizabethtown my entire life, I am not an alumnus of the College. This, I was told, was not a problem, and indeed was actually preferable, as I would not be bringing any preconceptions to the work. Another concern was that, although I have been a professional writer for a quarter century, and a free-lance writer for fifteen of those years, my work has primarily been in fiction. Again, I was assured, this would be a strength, as the primary quality that the College wanted in the work was readability, rather than a straightforward, chronological account of historical data.

I decided that the best way to achieve this readability was not to write a history of a college, but a history of the people who created, sustained, and attended it. While characters in fiction can be spun from whole cloth, actual personages must be created from research, and that research was far more time-consuming than I had initially imagined. It was also more fascinating than I had ever hoped.

Although I conducted a number of productive interviews, no one is alive who recalls the College's earliest years, so I turned to the many contemporary documents which survive. I covered every page of every issue of *Our College Times/The Etownian*, from 1904 to the present, as I did nearly all college publications, from the first catalogue to the most recent yearbook. In these forums of college life I heard the voices of people who had died decades before, speaking out with passion about the subjects that concerned them. They speak just as clearly here, to our generations and those to come.

Another important source of information was the minutes of the meetings of the board of trustees, which, for the first half century, range from barely decipherable pencil scrawls to graceful and elegant calligraphy.

The writings of G. N. Falkenstein are the only lengthy contemporary account of the founding of the College, and it is on them that I have relied, along with surviving letters and documents by J. G. Francis and others. Many of these letters have never been published, and their appearance here casts a new light on the College's founding. Some readers may be surprised or even shocked by the intense feelings expressed by these men, but I found it refreshing to learn that these legendary church fathers and icons of the College were governed by the same human emotions that frequently burden and occasionally elevate the rest of us.

This discovery has made it easier for me to humanize these people, who most of us know only from stern portraits or idealized statues. At several points in the book, I went so far as to try and write from the point of view of some of these participants, a dead giveaway that a novel-writing barbarian has invaded the gates of the historians' city. Still, the effort is well intentioned, and has been undertaken in the spirit of historian Arnold Toynbee's words: "The definition of moral progress is the realization that other human beings are fully as human as oneself," a realization that should form the moral center of all non-fiction and fiction alike.

Nevertheless, I apologize in advance to those readers who find the device distracting, as I apologize to *all* readers for the book's as yet undisclosed sins. A volume that tries to cover a hundred years, thousands of characters, and tens of thousands of incidents is doomed in any attempt to be comprehensive, and such is the case here. Readers will find the major milestones in the history of the College, along with many stories and anecdotes that are worth recalling or resurrecting.

They are practically guaranteed, however, not to find the event or the person or the time that held the deepest meaning for them. These things are innumerable and individual, and can best be found in the histories of our own hearts, to be told to or be preserved on paper for those we love.

We are all our own finest historians of what truly matters.

Chapter 1

"A conference of representative brethren..."

It was not, thought George Falkenstein, the kind of day to under-take a new enterprise, particularly one as significant as planning a new school. The sun should be shining on such a venture. But instead clouds hung in the sky, gray reminders of the rain the night before, a rain so cold that at times it had turned to sleet, peppering the windows and keeping him awake.

The rain had melted much of the snow that a heavy storm had brought three days earlier, but it made the journey to Reading soggy and unpleasant. Falkenstein had taken the trolley to Wayne Junction from Germantown, where he served as pastor of the German Baptist Brethren Church. Then he had had to take a steam car to Columbia Avenue and the train to Reading before arriving at the church there with twelve minutes to spare.

It seemed odd that he and the other elders of the district should be there at all. The invitation from Jay G. Francis, pastor of the Green Tree German Baptist Brethren Church in Oaks, Pa., had come as quite a surprise. It had been dated November 17 of that year, 1898, and read:

> *Esteemed Brother — In the Reading meetinghouse, on Tuesday, November 29, beginning at 10 A.M., there will be a conference of representative brethren of our District to consider the practicability of establishing a Brethren's School in Eastern Pennsylvania. A somewhat extended session is anticipated. Dinner will be served by the Sisters of Reading. You, as an elder, are earnestly requested to be present.*
>
> > *Fraternally,*
> >
> > *Jay G. Francis*[1]

Falkenstein knew that Francis had been traveling throughout the Eastern District on his bicycle, drumming up interest in a Brethren school, but such a meeting was unanticipated. He replied to Francis:

> > *6611 G't'n Ave., Phila.*
> >
> > *11/21/98*
>
> *Rev. J. G. Francis*
>
> *Dear Bro.,*
> *Your rather startling announcement on a postal card, received this day. Give me a few particulars. I am anxious to know more about the matter. By whose authority is the meeting called? I should be glad to attend, but can not promise at this time. Is there hope of a profitable meeting? I am interested in the matter. We are well. I rec. Catalogs of Lordsburg College.*[2]
>
> > *Yours fraternally,*
> >
> > *G. N. Falkenstein*[3]

Falkenstein felt certain that he was not alone in his surprise, nor in his skepticism. Though he personally believed in both the need for and the value of a Brethren college, he knew there were many obstacles standing in the way.

He took another deep breath of the damp, chilly air, and walked up the steps toward the double doors of the Reading meetinghouse, passing between the pair of tall trees in front of the church. The weather had stripped them of their leaves, and they stood like stark sentinels, guardians of the traditions that could be both blessings for the conservative denomination and stones in its path to the future.

ఆ§—§ఴ

The German Baptist Brethren, as George N. Falkenstein's church was known at the time of the 1898 meeting in Reading, Pa., was the largest of the three major Brethren churches that had descended from the original Anabaptist movement begun by Alexander Mack in Schwarzenau, Germany in 1708. In the summer of 1729, Mack and his followers set sail for America, to escape both the religious persecution that plagued those who believed in adult baptism, and the poor economic conditions in which they lived. In the Germantown area of Philadelphia, they joined other Brethren who had migrated earlier, and Mack became the pastoral leader of the Brethren there.

The eighteenth and nineteenth centuries saw several schisms in the church, the most dramatic being the departure by Conrad Beissel to the famous Ephrata cloister, which he founded in 1728, and the 1848 formation of the less conservative Church of God, or New Dunkers. But by the early 1880s, disagreements had split the Brethren Church into three distinct groups. The most conservative was known as the Old German Baptist Brethren, and the most modern and progressive was simply called the Brethren Church.

The largest group was that which held the center. Though they were informally known as the Conservatives, they strove to merge the traditions of the church with a progressive vision as well. Legally, they retained the name of the German Baptist Brethren, but after 1908 they would be called the Church of the Brethren.

Combining both conservative and progressive attitudes often proved to be a difficult balancing act for the German Baptist Brethren, and so it was regarding their views on education. By 1898 there were a number of colleges successfully begun by Brethren, among them the Huntingdon (Pa.) Normal School in

1876, which became Juniata College twenty years later, as well as Ashland College (1877), Mount Morris College (1879), Bridgewater College (1880), McPherson College (1888), Manchester College (1889) and La Verne College (1891).

These colleges had come into being partly as a result of an educational movement begun in the United States around the time of the country's centennial celebration in 1876. The last quarter of the nineteenth century, known as the Gilded Age, seemed to be gilded with new colleges. Between 1875 and 1900, literally hundreds of private, church-related colleges were founded in the East and Midwest United States.

The Brethren of eastern Pennsylvania, however, were more conservative than those in areas that had already established colleges. Brethren were supposed to practice nonconformity to the rest of the world, and higher education was viewed by many as a threat to that way of life. There were even some who still felt the way that the father of famed Brethren scholar Abraham Harley Cassel did, that children should be raised in "Pious Ignorance," and that "If you give a child learning then you fit…him for Forging, Counterfeiting, or any other badness that he may choose to do, which an unlearned or ignorant one would not be capable of doing."[4]

Most of the arguments against higher education were not as radical as the elder Cassel's. Still, many Brethren were concerned that their children might leave the faith should they be exposed to teachings outside the home. As for living *away* from home, the dangers only multiplied. Colleges were often viewed as hotbeds of sin and worldliness, so much so that the 1870 catalogue of Salem College, a failed Brethren school in Indiana, listed the activities that were forbidden, activities implicitly understood to be *de rigueur* at other, worldly colleges. They included:

> *Indecent and profane language, rude and boisterous conduct, tippling; frequenting taverns, inns, beer houses, places of mere idle amusements and resorts of bad company, gambling, betting, games of chance, smoking tobacco within the college enclosure, or*

*carrying concealed firearms or deadly weapons, and
every other species of vulgar and immoral conduct...*[5]

That certainly seemed to cover it, although smoking outside
"the college enclosure" seems to have been permitted, and there is
no specific mention of one of the prime bugbears of college life, fraternities, which were considered secret societies, and thus to be
shunned.

Besides the aforementioned perils, there was also the danger
of students getting "above their raising." A Franklin County elder
predicted that students who attended the new Juniata College
would "come home from college dressed in fine broadcloth, wearing a high bee gum hat, swinging a little cane, and acting like
dudes."[6] Though this would seem on the surface to be more a
question of sartorial style than religious orthodoxy, it must be
remembered that even clothing was proscribed among the
Brethren, and the plainer the better, so that such a change in dress
would signify a much deeper change in spirit and philosophy.

Those Brethren who favored education had equally strong
arguments. Many of their children wanted to further their education, with a view to teaching in the public schools, or going into
the ministry or mission fields. If they were going to go to college
anyway, why not a college conducted under the auspices of the
church? That way, baleful outside influences could be decreased,
and the young scholars would be "surrounded by a Christian environment, free from atheistical and other influences that tend to
make shipwreck of their religious life...such as intercollegiate athletics, hazing, students' fraternities, class rushes, etc."[7]

There was another reason to establish Brethren colleges, however. The times called for it. The last decades of the nineteenth
century were an era of huge entrepreneurial growth in America.
Fortunes were being made overnight, and Robber Barons flourished. It was the time of the Gilded Age and "The Four Hundred,"
and even stern German Brethren were not immune to its call. The
earliest Brethren schools, rather than being fully supported by the
church, were set up as business propositions and established as
joint stock companies, their money coming from stock sold to their

shareholders. As Donald F. Durnbaugh points out in his history of the Brethren, the church leaders who founded these colleges, often bankrupting themselves in the process, "meant to do good but also hoped to do well."[8]

There is no record of whether or not Jay G. Francis, who called the meeting in November of 1898 to discuss the possibility of a Brethren college in eastern Pennsylvania, had any eye toward profit. That he wanted to establish such a school, whatever his motive, is beyond doubt. Francis traveled many miles on a bicycle, visiting church leaders to bolster support for his vision. Though the story has taken on a mythic quality, records indicate that his travels took him as far west as Waynesboro, as far north as Allentown, and as far east and south as New Jersey and Maryland.

It is almost certain that not every church leader he visited gave him the warmest of welcomes, for Francis was viewed with suspicion by many of his fellow Brethren. He had studied under the controversial figure, Charles A. Briggs, at Union Theological Seminary, a believer in higher criticism of the Bible, who was actually tried for heresy by the Presbyterian Church. This association in itself might have been enough for many conservative Brethren to dismiss Francis out of hand. Add to the equation Francis's youth, energy, and what many could have seen as arrogance, and it comes as no surprise that the visits from this brash young man, still in his twenties, brought about no such initiative for the start of a college from the church proper.

Instead, the initiative would have to come from individuals who were part of the church, and it was to these elders that Francis finally addressed his November 17th, 1898 postcards. The card called for "representative brethren," possibly because Francis realized that he could not hope to gather a quorum that could have officially represented the church. Indeed, the turnout was disappointingly small, and if every one of the twenty-two men and twelve women who attended that meeting had immediately voted for the establishment of a school, it would have held no official imprimatur. These elders were present as individuals only, concerned for both their church and for the young people who were its members.

that I am not complaining or criticizing nor apologiz-
ing for lack of accomplishment. I am writing the stern
facts of history and history is nothing if not facts.[19]

Again we find the mention of the "crisis," but not a further
definition. He goes on:

> *First, it has always been a matter of deep regret*
> *that a number of our teaching ministers were not at*
> *that "Educational Meeting" at Reading to help when*
> *helping was needful.*
> *Second, The Committee on Location lost two of its*
> *most important members by resignation.*[20]

As for the first regret, this is the only time it is recorded. That
the teaching ministers were not present may be due either to the
fact that they did not respond to the invitation, or that they never
received invitations at all, in which case J. G. Francis was at fault.
Over a hundred years later, there is no way of knowing.

Similarly, there is no way to know why Elder J. H. Longenecker
resigned, although John Herr's resignation was due to ill health,
which Falkenstein places in quotation marks, a stylistic device possibly designed to raise the suspicions of those who, as we are
advised to do, "read between the lines." Longenecker's resignation
was never accepted, and Elizabethtown College President D. C.
Reber, in his 1912 essay on the founding of the college, states that
"the reason seemed insufficient to grant it."[21] It seems possible,
then, that both resignations were made under a cloud.

Falkenstein's next "stern fact" is a more personal one:

> *Third, The "Committee" saw fit (maybe of neces-*
> *sity) to hand the major part of the work over into the*
> *hands of the Secretary who was already overloaded*
> *with multiplied duties of pastoral responsibilities and*
> *much other church work. I have no doubt this over-*
> *loading in time and strength was a distinct handicap*
> *to the progress and development of the work for the*
> *time being, and led to my ultimate breakdown.*[22]

That breakdown would not come until the autumn of 1902, after three more years of stretched schedules and overwork, which included weekdays spent teaching at Elizabethtown College and weekends serving his Germantown pastorate. From all evidence, Falkenstein's description of his overwork on the committee is not exaggerated, and that work load would not diminish, so it is obviously not a private "crisis" to which Falkenstein refers.

There were, however, even greater obstacles than overwork:

> *Fourth, then there were those persons, who, for reasons best known to themselves, did everything possible against this educational movement, some from within, some from without. Of the two, I think, the force from within is most to be feared.*
>
> *Well, perhaps, in the end, this opposition, within and without, had but little permanent effect, but for the time being it added to the burden of the secretary in his tremendous, single-handed struggle.*[23]

There is no further clue as to who these people are, though it might be imagined that the outside opposition came from very conservative Brethren who found any advanced education a threat to their way of life. As for those who worked against the movement "from within," Falkenstein records neither their names nor their actions, but does suggest that they eventually had a change of heart:

> *Even if there were those discouragements, there was a measure of success, for the effects of my struggles were cumulative and when such results became apparent some were anxious to scramble into the bus when it was ready to go.*[24]

The above passages would seem to indicate that the path toward a Brethren college in eastern Pennsylvania was neither an easy nor a happy one, at least not for those who, like Falkenstein, were deeply involved in the process. What was to come next would be, in Falkenstein's words, "the hardest struggle of all."[25]

❧—❦

The April 5th meeting was both the end of the Committee on Location, and the beginning of an even more earnest attempt to plan for the new college. It was held in the Elizabethtown German Baptist Brethren Church on Washington Street, now the site of the parochial school of St. Peter's Roman Catholic Church.

Falkenstein had sent a notice of the meeting to every Brethren church in Pennsylvania's Eastern District, and although the attendance at the 9:30 A.M. start was small, the attendance was far greater than that of the first meeting the previous November. The first order of business was to choose officers of the meeting: Samuel R. Zug and Samuel H. Hertzler, both of Elizabethtown, became Moderator and Treasurer, and Falkenstein was once again chosen to be Secretary. The remainder of the morning was spent hearing reports on the six considered sites.

It was not until the afternoon session that the decision was made to proceed with the college, although not before a great deal of discussion and several timely questions ensued. The first question was from George Bucher, pastor at Mechanic Grove Church, and a self-educated man who read Greek and who was said to have "the finest collection of books in lower Lancaster County."[26] He asked, simply and flatly, "By what authority is this meeting called?"[27]

It was a logical question, though odd that Bucher should have asked it, since he had attended the first meeting in November.[28] Still, it was a question that must have been on the minds of many of the newcomers. Did the meeting have the backing of the Eastern District? Had a number of pastors gotten a quorum together? Perhaps Bucher was simply presenting the question so that one of the members of the original Committee on Location might judiciously answer that a number of interested elders, spurred on by the needs and desires of their fellow Brethren and their children, had decided to look into the matter of a Brethren school.

Whether anyone attempted to answer in that manner is not recorded. What is a matter of record is that J. G. Francis, the man who initiated the first meeting, took full credit for it by saying. "It originated in my mind."[29]

It may have been said as a simple statement of fact, for, after all, it was the truth. It may have also been said sacrificially, to take the blame if any was to be laid. Or it may have been said in a peremptory and slightly arrogant manner. None of those who heard it recorded the tone with which it was uttered, although Falkenstein's history, both histories of the Eastern Pennsylvania Church of the Brethren, and Dr. Ralph Schlosser's 1971 history of the college feature it prominently.

If it was indeed Francis's ego that spoke, the remark did little toward stifling the discussion. After a number of positive comments concerning a college, George Bucher moved that those of the district establish a school. The minutes have no record of the fate of Francis's similar motion made at the first meeting.

More talk followed about the kind of school it should be, and finally George Falkenstein made a motion:

> That we establish a school of such a character
> that compares favorably with any of our schools,
> including Bible, academic, and collegiate departments
> — a school to be at the same time a home and a
> church.[30]

The motion was passed. A committee of ten was then appointed, fully authorized to select the site, and directed to draft a constitution and by-laws for the new college. This time J. G. Francis was a member. The others were H. E. Light, S. H. Hertzler, George Bucher, Jesse C. Ziegler, Samuel R. Zug, Abram H. Royer, Benjamin Hottel, and William H. Oberholtzer. At the April 20th organizational meeting, Light became Chairman, Hertzler Treasurer, and Falkenstein again reprised his role as Secretary.

Of that momentous Elizabethtown meeting, Falkenstein wrote that it was:

> ...altogether in a different spirit. It was not cau-
> tious in the approach to the tremendous problems
> involved and it was not conservative in deciding
> things that must concern generations to come. Was it
> a courageous bravery because of things already accom-

plished, or was it a desperate determination to do the things that should be done. I will not say. That there were some who had courage, I do well know, and visions also. Neutrals counted with the majority. The unanimity in decisions was striking, and that impression has lasted forty years.[31]

Falkenstein's observation that most people were neutral is not surprising, nor is the fact that unanimity ruled, as it would in most of the decisive votes to follow. The Brethren knew the importance of erecting a solid front, and if any personally felt a move was unwise, once the vote was on the table they apparently stood with the majority, not only at this meeting but later as well.

Another example of this united front occurred at the May 24th meeting, which took place during the church's annual conference in Roanoke, Virginia. Seven of the ten committee members (H. B. Hollinger had replaced Oberholtzer, who had resigned) met in a small white house on Patterson Avenue to make a final decision on the location of the college.

Six towns were in the running, though only Elizabethtown and Ephrata had submitted sealed offers. The committee considered the qualities they deemed important: accessibility by rail, the practical questions of water and drainage, the financial aspects, and the support likely to be given by the local church.

The first three ballots were split among Elizabethtown, Mountville, and Pottstown. Though Falkenstein does not state who spoke in favor of Pottstown, J. G. Francis had earlier been promoting that town, much closer to his home than Elizabethtown. Still, neither Francis nor the unidentified supporters of Mountville dug in their heels. Brethren unanimity came to the fore, and on the fourth ballot all seven men present voted for Elizabethtown.

The committee then appointed a subcommittee of Falkenstein, Ziegler, and Francis to write the constitution and by-laws of the new college. Falkenstein had been on every committee since the start of the process, and the strain was beginning to tell. "I was not only tired," he says of those weeks, "but at times bilious and dull and disinclined to work and disqualified for work."[32]

In spite of that fact, he set to with a will, preparing for another public meeting and arranging to meet with Francis and Ziegler on June 1st at Ziegler's house in Collegeville. There they spent a long day preparing the drafts of the constitution and by-laws.

At this point in his history, between this meeting with Jesse Ziegler and J. G. Francis and the June 7th public meeting, Falkenstein again tantalizingly hints at "tremendous problems" in the form of "unexpected opposition from within" that, although it did not stop the progress by a single day, "did make the going more difficult."[33] Again, he gives no further details as to who or what furnished the opposition, though the events of the next day may suggest an answer.

On June 6th, the day before the next public meeting, eight members of the ten-man locating committee gathered at Elizabethtown in a meeting that must have deeply frustrated those who had thought the choice of location was concluded. On the contrary, they seemed to be back at square one.

First, a formal protest was lodged from Ephrata, almost certainly from Abram Moyer, who had been absent from the Roanoke meeting. The argument was that, since Ephrata had not been properly represented there, the committee should disregard their previous decision and reconsider the location. J. G. Francis, seeing a door opening, added an informal protest in behalf of Pottstown, upon what grounds is not known.

At this point a protest from Pittsburgh would probably have been considered. All the careful thought and deliberation that had taken place at the previous meeting was suddenly for naught. A motion was made to reconsider, and it passed, but the majority, who undoubtedly favored Elizabethtown, decided to make the meeting finite by permitting each representative only three minutes to state his case.

And state their cases they did. Royer pleaded Ephrata's cause, Zug gave a brief exhortation for Elizabethtown, and even though all of these men except Royer had already unanimously voted for the Elizabethtown site, J. G. Francis took the opportunity to pitch Pottstown, and H. E. Light even made one final stand for Mountville. This unforeseen demonstration of chauvinism and division may very well be what Falkenstein refers to as the "unexpected opposition from within."

When the surreal series of one-on-seven inducements, with a constantly shifting cast of characters, ended, a vote was called for. Once again, it took several ballots to reach full agreement. On the third ballot, the dissenters, seeing that Elizabethtown had a strong and unbreakable majority, surrendered and gave the committee the unanimity that would be expected of them at the next day's public meeting.

The question at last was settled, at least in the matter of location, but other decisions remained. First was the question of which of the two sites in Elizabethtown was the better. Following a meeting with a citizens' committee, all of whom had their own vocal opinions on the subject, the committee finally decided on the tract southeast of town, on farmland belonging to Benjamin G. Groff. Then the committee went over the constitution and by-laws, making some minor changes.

The next area of contention was the school's name. Falkenstein, Ziegler, and Francis had come up with one, but no one else liked it, not even Francis, who suggested naming the school Mack College after Alexander Mack, the pioneer of the Anabaptist movement. George Bucher objected to naming the college after a single man, no matter how important to their faith, and suggested Conestoga College.

But H. E. Light felt that Conestoga gave the school too local an appellation. This was, after all, a school for the entire Eastern Pennsylvania district. Jesse Ziegler, in logical reaction, offered East Penn College, and the reaction was positive enough that it was brought to a vote, but didn't pass, and it was finally decided to go with "Conestoga College" after all.

That name, however, remained for only one night. The next day, at the third and last public meeting, it was "completely knocked out,"[34] as Falkenstein puts it. After much discussion, a large majority of the assembled Brethren decided that "Elizabethtown College" was the right choice, and the college now had a name.

The Constitution and By-laws were just as scrupulously discussed and examined, but very few changes were made, and those mostly minor. George Bucher wanted to include a clause prohibiting instrumental music at the college, but it was decided to leave that decision to the trustees.

It was a question that would arise in the future, for many Brethren believed that musical instruments were soulless and unfit for the worship of God. Just the previous year, an article in *The Gospel Messenger* affirmed that "Musical instruments are the usual accompaniments of wars. They are found at feastings and revelings. Even today our saloon-keepers take advantage of music instruments to allure the young into the saloon."[35] It must have been hard for the liberals to argue in favor of something that contributed to both warfare and drunkenness.

Trustees were selected next. The Locating Committee presented the names of seventeen men as nominees for the Board of Trustees. Although five of the nominees were from the committee itself, J. G. Francis was not among them. The nine men elected by ballot by both the men and women present included Hertzler, Light, and Ziegler, all of the Locating Committee, as well as J. H. Rider, Nathan Hoffman, M. R. Henry, P. C. Nyce, T. F. Imler, and L. R. Brumbaugh. The ninth man, and one of the three with a full three-year term, was the overworked George Falkenstein, who naturally was elected Secretary.

The meeting adjourned at last, and the new college was born. The Constitution and By-laws consisted of a great deal of organizational and legal boilerplate, including the overriding provision that the college would remain under the control of the German Baptist Brethren Church, and that the trustees would be representative members of that church. But within its clauses were spelled out the objectives and values that would eventually turn Elizabethtown College from something that existed only on paper into a world class institution.

In fact, the first items in the Constitution after the name of the school are the "Object" and the "Character," which states that although the college is basically intended for the education of children of the Brethren Church, it is open to all who wish to attend. The actual "Object" of the school "shall be such a harmonious development of the physical, mental, and moral powers of both sexes as will best fit them for the duties of life and promote the spiritual interests of its patrons."[36]

It was an idealistic goal, but one worth struggling for. In the coming years, the objective would be met over and over, but the struggles had only begun.

1 *History of the Church of the Brethren of the Eastern District of Pennsylvania, 1915–1965*, p. 189

2 later La Verne College

3 *History of the Church of the Brethren of the Eastern District of Pennsylvania, 1915–1965*, p. 189

4 *Fruit of the Vine*, 246

5 *Fruit of the Vine*, 253–54

6 *Fruit of the Vine*, 251

7 *History of the Church of the Brethren of the Eastern District of Pennsylvania, 1708–1915*, p. 622

8 *Fruit of the Vine*, p. 262

9 *The Organization and Early History of Elizabethtown College*, p. 15

10 Ibid.

11 Ibid.

12 op. cit., p. 16

13 Francis, born in 1870, was only 28 at the time, far younger than the other founders. In contrast, Falkenstein was born in 1859, Jesse Ziegler in 1856, Samuel Hertzler in 1853, and Samuel Zug in 1832.

14 Ibid.

15 op. cit., p. 17

16 op. cit., p. 17

17 op. cit., p. 25

18 op. cit., p. 27

19 Ibid.

20 op. cit., pp. 27–28

21 *Our College Times*, November 1912

22 *The Organization and Early History of Elizabethtown College*, p. 28

23 Ibid.

24 Ibid.

25 Ibid.

26 *History of the Church of the Brethren, Eastern Pennsylvania, 1915–1965*, p. 244

27 op. cit., p. 190

28 A brief history of Elizabethtown College by Elizabeth Myer, which appeared in the January 1907 *Our College Times*, states that George Bucher was added to the first Committee on Location as a replacement member. This is incorrect, along with her statement that S. R. Zug and T. F. Imler were original members of the same committee.

29 *History of the Church of the Brethren, Eastern Pennsylvania, 1915–1965*, p. 190

30 *The Organization and Early History of Elizabethtown College*, p. 32

31 op. cit., p. 33

32 op. cit., p. 36

33 op. cit., p. 37

34 op. cit., p. 38

35 Joseph Studebaker, "Vocal Versus Instrumental Music for Worship — No. 1," *Gospel Messenger*, June 18, 1898, pp. 371–372, cited in *Moving Toward the Mainstream*.

36 *Constitution and By-Laws for the Government of Elizabethtown College*, 1899

Chapter 2

"The winding ways through which we must yet pass..."

Elizabethtown College now had a name and a site. It had a Constitution and By-laws, a board of trustees, and the promise of Brethren students.

What it did not have was a single building, teacher, or a cent of money. At the first meeting of the Board on June 16, 1899, nine days after the final public meeting, plans got underway to rectify that situation. The first thing that occurred at the meeting, held at the home of Nathan Hoffman in Pottstown, was the election of George Bucher to take the place of P. C. Nyce, who had resigned. The next order of business was the election of officers. When the ballots showed a tie between Jesse Ziegler and another member for President of the board, the matter was settled by casting lots. It seems a delicious irony that a group of men who frowned so on wagering elected the president of their new college board through chance. Ziegler was elected President, T. F. Imler Vice-President,

S. H. Hertzler Treasurer, and Falkenstein officially became Secretary
of yet another board.

After appointing members to write a charter and design a seal
for the school, the board got down to financial business. Each member was assigned a number of churches to solicit for funds. Several
of the subscription books used still exist, and show the signatures of
the subscriber with the amount promised next to the name. The
amounts ranged from $500 all the way down to a single dollar,
which in 1899 still had the buying power that twenty-six dollars
would have today.

Times were different in other ways as well. The next evening,
after a Brethren Lovefeast at Mingo, George Falkenstein spent the
night at board president Jesse Ziegler's house. Sleeping in the same
room, they talked until after midnight, when they were forced to
arise and herd the cows that had broken out of Ziegler's pasture
field. "College trustees," Falkenstein said, "should make good on
any emergency."[1]

At the next board meeting on August 16, the trustees added up
their pledges and found that they had a total of $4815, $3150 of
which had come from Elizabethtown. Falkenstein himself had had
little luck in the Philadelphia area, where he had met with some
opposition to the school. Other trustees had fared equally poorly,
partly due to poor congregations, many of whom still had debts on
their houses. Also, Lancaster County was the heart of the
"Pennsylvania Dutch" country, and these German (or *Deutsch*) farmers who were being solicited were notorious for their conservatism
in both financial and social matters. Even those who agreed with
the "Progressives" who wanted to found the College would be reluctant to contribute any money toward it.

There were no contributions, nor promises of any from Ephrata
whose residents were apparently unhappy that their town had not
been chosen as the site. The winds of division quickly grew into
a gale.

On September eighth, Falkenstein writes in his diary:

> *I received a shameful letter from J. G. Francis. He*
> *is bitterly envious and jealous at my activity with*

> *Elizabethtown College work and he is working to start*
> *a second movement to establish a College, viz: "Mack*
> *College." I should call it "Beissel College" because it is*
> *the spirit of Beissel and not Mack.*[2]

Falkenstein's comment refers to the schism in the Brethren Church when Conrad Beissel split from Alexander Mack and his followers to found the Ephrata Cloister. Even the parallel of locations is apt.

The "shameful" letter was not quoted in Falkenstein's diary or his history, but it still exists, and reads as follows:

> *Dear Bro., —*
>
> *An invitation is herewith extended to you to*
> *attend the school meeting in Mentzer's Hall, Ephrata,*
> *Pa., 10 A.M., Tuesday, Sept. 12.*
> *Before leaving home inflate yourself well, so as to*
> *impress the meeting with a due sense of your great*
> *importance. Also, for a pretense be ready to make a*
> *long prayer to the effect that we may not be self-seek-*
> *ing. It might also be well to oil your lying machinery.*
>
> > *Fraternally.*
> >
> > *Jay G. Francis*
>
> *P.S. It might be well to extend an invitation to your*
> *congregation.*
>
> > *J. G. F.*[3]

Three days later, Falkenstein visited Jesse Ziegler, who had also been invited to the same meeting, in Ephrata to discuss the proposed "Mack College." Although Ziegler wanted Falkenstein to join him, possibly as another dissenting voice, he declined, possibly telling Ziegler what he states in his diary: "It is a bold, audacious, shameful, malicious move to crush Elizabethtown College."[4]

The next few days were full of apprehension for Falkenstein and the College for which he had worked so hard. It was not until

Friday that he received a letter from Samuel H. Hertzler telling of the Ephrata meeting. It read in part:

> *Whatever there was of "Mack College" is <u>not</u>.*
> *What I half suspected was that Mack College was 9/10*
> *Francis & so we found it to be. Only a few of the*
> *Ephrata members knew anything about it.*
> 　　*So far as we could learn Bro. Francis was the*
> *author of the constitution, "Elected" the trustees &*
> *advisory board, made arrangements to receive into*
> *trust the Mountain Springs property "which under the*
> *providence of God is for sale" at $50,000.00 & sent out*
> *the notices to trustees & Elders who were or are inter-*
> *ested. Bro. Francis stated that the object of the meeting*
> *was for the purpose of taking steps to reconsider the*
> *location of the College. When we told him that it was*
> *a <u>very</u> peculiar way of getting at it he said, "It will not*
> *do to be too <u>simple</u> when you deal with <u>craft</u>."[5] He*
> *claims that there was some scheming done to get the*
> *location at Elizabethtown. He however exonerates Bro.*
> *Jesse [Ziegler] & me from any unfair act. I can not tell*
> *you all that transpired, but the outcome of the matter*
> *was that a vote to drop the whole "Mack College" proj-*
> *ect was carried without a dissenting vote. And Bro.*
> *Francis confessed to me that he was wrong & this*
> *move was possibly the result of brooding over the mat-*
> *ter. He is very much hurt at the thought of being out*
> *of the College project. I <u>pity</u> <u>him</u>. I hope he will apolo-*
> *gize to you and Bro. Zug for the very ugly thrusts he*
> *has made. So that the whole unpleasantness may be*
> *buried never again to be resurrected.[6]*

After Falkenstein received Hertzler's letter, he noted with relief in his diary:

> *Mack College "failed." (I suppose it might be said*
> *it was "still born.") Well, it is best it did not live, for it*
> *had very poor generation.[7]*

Fifty years later, J. G. Francis still was brooding over the way he felt he had been treated. In a 1949 letter to L. D. Rose, he accuses some in Elizabethtown of accepting positions with the College as bribes for their support, and says:

> ...the instigator of the School [Francis] had been set at naught by those doing things at Etown...Jesse Ziegler head of your Board...claimed to have put the instigator of your school out of the ministry. Did he not put himself out of the ministry of Christ?[8]

Falkenstein remained equally bitter. Forty years later, he still referred to Francis's attempt as "mischief-making trickery,"[9] a label given even more credence by Francis's further refusal to accept the reality of Elizabethtown College.

For J. G. Francis had one last trick up his sleeve, though that he truly believed it would be effective is beyond credulity. At the trustee meeting on October third, Jesse Ziegler presented to the Board a petition he had received from Francis. It stated that the undersigned desired the site of the College changed from Elizabethtown to Ephrata. Once again the "Beissel spirit" had raised its head, lending further credence to Brethren historian Donald F. Durnbaugh's description of Francis as "talented but erratic."[10] Accompanying the petition were some letters from its signers.

The petition was Francis's last stand, and it didn't take long for the Elizabethtown College Board of Trustees to dispose of it. The recent meeting to establish a school in Ephrata had been a dismal failure, and the board considered it completely impractical to entertain any change in location. So the petition and the idea of a college in Ephrata (and presumably any involvement of J. G. Francis) were permanently dropped.

At this point, Francis vanishes from the history of the College to reappear only twice, the first time in 1908, when he was a guest speaker at the January Bible term. He spoke of service to mankind and to the church, and concluded by saying that:

> I hear it said that you have need of another building. I should be very glad to see another building

erected. I hope that the work will go on and that you will be educated for service.[11]

Only once more is there any record of J. G. Francis returning to the campus. On October 20, 1950, the Zug Memorial Library was dedicated. That year was the fiftieth anniversary of the founding of Elizabethtown College, and J. G. Francis, now in his late seventies, gave the scripture reading at the ceremony. He read from the twenty-eighth chapter of the Book of Job, which included these words:

Whence then cometh wisdom? and where is the place of understanding?
Behold, the fear of the Lord, that is wisdom; and to depart from evil is understanding.

There is only one statue of a founder on the campus of Elizabethtown College, and it stands between Alpha Hall, the first building erected, and the High Library. It is a full-sized bronze of the young J. G. Francis, his bicycle and camera leaning nearby.

Once J. G. Francis's petition was disposed of, there was other work to occupy the trustees at that October 3, 1899 meeting, not the least of which were the plans for a college building. After it was decided that a building should be erected at a cost of not more than $10,000, George Falkenstein displayed a front elevation of the proposed building. He had drawn it, his first attempt at architecture, several days earlier, and refers to it as "a twin building,"[12] probably because of the two front entrances.

The trustees settled on a size of 48 by 84 feet, with the first and second stories to be nine feet high, and the basement and third floor eight feet. The other prerequisite was that it have a mansard roof.

Another topic of discussion, one that had so far not been officially considered, was the appointment of the president of the new college. On October 10, Board president Jesse Ziegler discussed with George Falkenstein the possibility of Falkenstein's filling the position, though this seemed premature.

During informal meetings and conferences, plans proceeded for the physical plant of the College. Architects were considered and rejected; discussion continued about heating and ventilating, the installation of a fireproof vault in the College president's office, and the physical placement of the building on the land. The trustees wanted to place the initial building in a location that would allow them to systematically arrange future buildings around an open court.

And still talk of the presidency continued. Of his chances, Falkenstein wrote: "I am willing to be led, as the Lord seems to direct, or lead. The Lord will direct in due time."[13]

That time would not come for quite a while. Months passed with little apparent progress, though money slowly continued to be solicited and raised. George Falkenstein and his wife lived in suspense, not knowing whether the presidency would be offered to him or not, but having reason to suspect it might: "Brother Ziegler told me he hadn't any doubt but that I would be called upon to organize the school and take charge of it. He would have presented the matter [at the December 14th trustee meeting] if there had been any time."[14]

Falkenstein's credentials stood him in good stead, as did the prodigious work he had already done for the school. He had attended Juniata College for three and a half years, graduating in 1882, and went on to study Latin and Greek at Oberlin College and mathematics, German, and biology at Mount Morris College. He was then offered the chair of the Department of Sciences there, and entered the University of Michigan, devoting himself solely to the sciences in preparation for his Mount Morris position. He taught at Mount Morris for four years until the General Mission Board called him to the pastorate of the Germantown Church, a signal honor, since it was the home church of the German Baptist Brethren in America.

But as Falkenstein would learn, credentials and hard work were not necessarily the only considerations: "the winding ways through which we must yet pass, we little dreamed of, and the severe tests of faith left many by the wayside."[15]

There was a four-month gap between the December 14th board meeting and that of April 12, 1900, when the trustees finally entered an agreement with the ultimate architect of their first building, A. A.

Richter of Lebanon, who was to deliver the plans in three weeks' time.

Other decisions were reached as well. The trustees decided to open Elizabethtown College for classes the following fall and then discussed possible teachers. Among those considered were John J. John, the son-in-law of trustee George Bucher, and D. C. Reber, the first person ever to receive an A. B. degree from Juniata College. Another man whose name surfaced was Isaac Newton Harvey Beahm, a forty-year-old educational pioneer.

Beahm was born in 1859 to an itinerant Virginia preacher and schoolteacher who had married one of his students. He was the fifth of fourteen children in a family that found solace in religion. Young Isaac took to it, and was elected to the German Brethren Baptist ministry in 1881. The Beahms lived only a few miles east of Bridgewater, home of the Brethren Bridgewater College, where Beahm enrolled in 1884, and received his bachelor's degree as valedictorian in 1887.

Brethren schools tried to get their best and brightest students into the teaching harness, and Beahm was no exception. At Bridgewater, he taught nine subjects, including elocution and rhetoric, and somehow found time to marry one of his students, as his father had before him, in 1890.

Later that year in nearby Daleville, Virginia, a number of Brethren families wanted to start their own school, and Beahm helped them to found Botetourt Normal College. He both managed the College and taught classes for four years, after which he spent two years as a travelling evangelist, amazingly enough in order to lessen the strain of work and restore his overworked body to health.

Life on the road, however, was interrupted by the good folk of Brentsville, another Virginia town ripe for a Brethren school. There Beahm was instrumental in the founding of Prince William Normal School in 1897, remaining until 1899, when still another college requested his aid, this time in California. His health began to fail again, and, thinking the drier weather might improve his constitution, he moved his family to Lordsburg (later La Verne) College, accepting its presidency. After only a few months under the California sun, he found that his strength was starting to flag.

A continent away, at the April 1900 board meeting, T. F. Imler moved that I. N. H. Beahm be elected Principal of Elizabethtown College, if the terms could be agreed upon. S. H. Hertzler seconded, and the motion passed. George Falkenstein records no discussion concerning the motion, but the choice must have made sense to the majority. Falkenstein had a far more impressive education than Beahm, but Beahm had served as midwife to two Brethren colleges, was currently the president of a third, and had taught in a total of four. He was a natural.

Still, Falkenstein could not help but be disappointed by the outcome. He was not the kind of man to promote himself, and if Jesse Ziegler, with whom he had discussed his possible presidency (or principalship, as it was now called), did not champion his cause, it is unlikely that he would have himself. The vote on Beahm came directly before adjournment, and Falkenstein's comments on the minutes reflect his regret:

> We often lacked time when our meetings were secondary to some other meeting, and sometimes we ... passed on big questions without due consideration in order to rush business while we had a quorum. I often much regretted this whole matter and what I regret most of all that we did business some times when we were not ready, but someone wanted to get things off hand.[16]

The juxtaposition of this observation with the account of the preceding vote leaves little doubt that one of these "things" was the principalship of the College. If it was indeed a decision made in haste, it would be repented at the little leisure had by those who voted on it. The truth was that I. N. H. Beahm was neither physically nor mentally fit to become a college principal, being on the brink of a total nervous breakdown.

At the next meeting on May second, A. A. Richter delivered the architectural plans, but the larger concern was with Beahm's health, which he had apparently written of in his official correspondence with Falkenstein. Despite his ill health, the trustees decided to keep their offer on the table, but added the contingency that if Beahm was physically unable to teach, he should receive $300 for organizing and managing the school. They had no contingency plan for what might happen should even that be beyond his powers, but that was precisely what happened.

The meeting closed with a plan to place a full-time solicitor in the field to solicit both money and patronage. The trustees were far-sighted enough to see that they would need plenty of both in the months ahead.

They would need plenty of energy too. To attend the next board meeting on June 11, Falkenstein left his home at 2:15 in the morning to arrive at Broad Street Station in Philadelphia for the 4:25 A.M. train so that he could arrive at the 8 A.M. meeting on time. The need for an early starting hour was indicative of the large number of vital issues that would be dealt with that day.

First on the docket was I. N. H. Beahm's agreement to accept the job of organizing the College for an annual salary of between $300 and $350. Along with the hiring of the College's first president was the hiring of its first teacher, a decision that would bring to the school one of its true legends, Elizabeth Myer.

That this first teacher should be a woman set a template for Elizabethtown College. Myer was the first of a long line of strong female personalities who would prove instrumental in shaping the school. Her father, Samuel R. Myer, had been a minister of the German Baptist Brethren Church, the only English-speaking one for miles around, so that young Lizzie, the fifth child of twelve, grew up speaking both English and German.

She also grew up spending most of her time alone and apart from other children. Part of this solitude may have been due to the fact that Lizzie was different: from birth, she had sight in only one eye, which made her carry her head oddly. For this, and for her habit of speaking very distinctly and walking strangely, other children frequently teased her. This did not prevent her from exhibiting an innate ability to learn quickly, and a compulsion to read everything she could lay her hands on. She also became a stern mentor to two of her younger sisters, so that her mother described her as "a disciplinarian in embryo."[17]

Her parents quickly recognized Lizzie's abilities, and sent her to the district school, where she excelled in her studies. She entered the State Normal School at Millersville in 1885, but the following year she "came under conviction," deciding to be baptized in the German Baptist Brethren faith. This created a major problem with the State Normal School. For many years, public school boards across the state had made it a policy never to hire teachers who wore the "plain" garb associated with the Anabaptist and Pietist groups. No religious garb was to be worn by a teacher in a public school classroom, a practice that became a legal restriction in 1895 with the passing of the "Garb Law" (PL 395-S.L. Sec. 4801).

Though that law was not yet on the books, Elizabeth Myer became a test case. No one wearing plain garb had ever enrolled in a state normal school, for common practice insured that no one in plain dress would be permitted to teach in the public schools. Elizabeth was convinced that she would have to leave Millersville. However, she received a pleasant surprise when B. F. Shaub, president of the College, told her that because of her high academic achievements he wanted her to remain at the school and continue her studies. He added, "I shall see to it that you have every opportunity to live out your convictions."[18]

On July 7, 1887, Elizabeth Myer became the first "plain" woman to graduate from a state normal school, giving the salutatorian address. Elizabeth Gibbel McCann, who served as Assistant Dean of Women for eleven years at Elizabethtown College, attended that commencement:

> *No one knew what the audience reaction might be. When Elizabeth, dressed in a pearl gray simple dress with a rose bud on her bosom and her prayer veil covering her soft hair, began her salutatorian's address, a holy quiet fell over the audience and prevailed throughout her speech.*[19]

For the next fourteen years, Elizabeth Myer taught in the Lancaster County public schools, gaining a reputation as a superb teacher and a firm disciplinarian. She was sent to one school in which several previous teachers had been literally thrown out of the building by the big and rowdy male students, a dozen of whom formed a gauntlet for their new, frail, little teacher to pass through on the first day of school. According to reports, she walked briskly past them, smiling and saying, "Good morning, gentlemen," and entered the building. They followed obediently, causing no more trouble.

This was the wise, witty, and caring woman whom the Board hired to teach at Elizabethtown College at a salary of forty-five dollars a month. Over the years, it would prove to be one of the finest investments that the College ever made.

An offer was made that day to another prospective teacher. George Falkenstein was finally going to see the possibility of financial remuneration for his tireless work on behalf of the new Elizabethtown College. He was asked to leave the room; he returned to discover that he had been elected to the faculty. When asked what salary he would require, Falkenstein replied that he could not accept a post for less than $600 a year, a figure the other trustees found acceptable.

"The matter came as a complete surprise and therefore could not accept, desiring to consult Eva (who is visiting her mother in Ohio),"[20] Falkenstein wrote in his diary. He was given ten days to accept, which the trustees pressed him to do. He also received a persuasive letter from I. N. H. Beahm, who fully realized what a benefit Falkenstein would be on the faculty of the new college.

With a principal and two faculty members nearly in hand, talk turned to the College building. Bids had been received based on the architect's plans, but all exceeded the initial $10,000 target, ranging from $14,000 to $18,000. The trustees then conferred with fellow Brethren Benjamin G. Groff of Elizabethtown, who had submitted a $15,000 bid, and asked him if he could reduce the amount. He agreed to donate $750, bringing his final bid to $14,250, which the Board accepted.

Even more progress was made at the next board meeting on August 16. In the interim, Falkenstein had accepted the teaching position, and had also agreed to help Beahm with the organization of the College. Construction of the new building was underway and the basement nearly completed.

Newly appointed principal I. N. H. Beahm was present for at least part of this board meeting, but his appearance was far from reassuring. In fact, Falkenstein's diary states, "I am almost discouraged with him. He seemed to have settled down to the conviction that he is an invalid. He is almost helpless. He walks with much difficulty on two canes. When the principal should be the embodiment of tremendous energy, I pity him and the principalship."[21]

Despite Beahm's frailty, he was appointed to the committee to plan the school's catalogue, textbooks, printing, and stationery, along with Falkenstein, Ziegler, and Elizabeth Myer. Another teacher, J. A. Seese, was hired on Beahm's recommendation, at a salary of thirty dollars a month.

As for the physical plant, decisions were made to drill a well to furnish the College with water, and to wire the building for electricity. Benjamin Groff, the builder, so wanted white keystones placed above each window that he offered to pay twenty-five percent of the cost, and the board agreed, as long as the total did not exceed sixty dollars, a bargain considering that the front of the building alone required thirty-four stones, not to mention the additional work in laying the irregular brickwork around them.

The Board decided to appoint Mrs. Beahm as matron of the College, with her reimbursement in the form of room and board for the family of six, who would live in one of the large recitation rooms. Beahm's sister-in-law would be the cook at a salary of two dollars a week.

Falkenstein and Jesse Ziegler spent the entire following day working on the College catalogue, a task that also demanded two full days the following week, delaying Ziegler's threshing duties. Beahm, despite being on the committee, was unable to help at all. But shortly after the noonday dinner on August 21, the first catalogue was completed.

A digest-sized document of sixteen pages with blue covers, the catalogue is a masterpiece of concision. The first page lists the trustees, and the second the faculty of five: Beahm, teaching Bible, psychology, and pedagogy, as well as serving as Principal; Falkenstein, teaching sciences, civil government, history and classics; Myer (misspelled "Meyer"), teaching mathematics, elocution, and English; Seese, teaching commercial and mathematics; and J. Kurtz Miller, who had been hired as a teacher of the special Bible term. Myer and Seese were named in charge of the Ladies' Hall and Gentlemen's Hall, respectively. S. H. Hertzler was Business Manager, and Mary Bucher Beahm was Matron.

A calendar follows, with the six-week fall term starting November 13, 1900, followed by a thirteen-week winter term and a twelve-week spring term. The copy states: "The town is up-to-date in modern improvements; well-paved streets, excellent water-works, electric lights, etc. The people of the town and surrounding country are noted for their industry and thrift; and a healthy religious sentiment prevails."[22]

The history is naturally brief, giving the reason for the College's existence: "a growing conviction on the part of many members of the German Baptist Brethren Church that the educational wants of their children are insufficiently provided for..."[23] The College Building is touted (long before its completion) as "a model in its plans and arrangements for school purposes," but gives us the first glimpse of how the structure, still standing as Alpha Hall, would be used:

> *The basement contains the dining room, kitchen, store room, laundry, and heating plant.*
>
> *On the first floor are the chapel, four recitation rooms, the book room, office and reception room. The second floor contains the library, day students' study room, teachers' rooms and dormitories. The third floor is devoted entirely to dormitories.*[24]

A statement of the school's purpose follows, as well as a brief paragraph about its teachers and the statement that, "Additional teaching force will be employed as the development and needs of the different departments may demand."[25]

Then comes the section that must have taken Falkenstein and Ziegler the most time to put together, the educational departments and courses of study. In only three small pages are outlined the classes that a student would be able to take in the three years' work required for the Teachers' or Literary courses offered. The Scientific and Classical courses would be outlined, it was promised, in the next catalogue. Along with such predictable classes as United States History, Grammar, and English Literature, were such subjects as Mental Arithmetic, Vocal Music, Map Drawing, and the relatively new subject of Psychology.

The classes of the two-year Bible course were also listed, and included such subjects as Lives of the Apostles, History of Missions, Moral Science, and others. There was also the possibility of courses in Commercial Work and Agriculture, should students desire them.

Next came a listing of the expenses. Full tuition was $1.00 per week, room and board $3.00. Light and fuel were $2.50 per term, along with a fifty-cent library fee. Ladies' rooms had free carpeting, but men were charged fifty cents per term.

For a winter term of thirteen weeks, then, a male student in a carpeted room would pay $55.50, and $134.50 for the entire school year. It was a substantial amount at the turn of the century, when the average worker earned less than ten dollars per week. There would also be the expense of textbooks and stationery, available in the College book room.

A two-page "Miscellaneous" section followed, dealing with rules of behavior and practical issues. Students were expected to bring a Bible and attend Sunday-school, church services, and chapel exercises. Brethren students were requested to bring their certificates of membership and to conform to church doctrines of dress and deportment. As with colleges today, students were expected to supply their own soap, towels, and blankets. Parents were advised to require a written account of their child's expenditures, and "the use of tobacco," the catalogue affirmed, "is absolutely forbidden in the building and on the grounds."[26]

The document concludes with "Our Needs," a section explaining that Elizabethtown College was not a stock company, had no endowment as a source of income, and so was dependent on "friends of the enterprise."[27] But while money was needed, so were other things, tangible and intangible: books for the library, specimens for the museum, apparatus for the laboratories, but also sympathy, patronage, and "young men and women with high ideals and noble purposes, who are ready to avail themselves of the opportunities that this school affords."[28]

Now that the catalogue existed, it had to be distributed. Falkenstein and the other trustees traveled about the surrounding counties in the following weeks, advertising the College, giving the catalogue to parents with students of college age, and striving to raise both funds for and recognition of the fledgling school.

Still, by October 2, the date of the next board meeting, the College had received only $3300 from those solicited, while it owed $4400. The trustees decided to increase the energy of their solicitations, and see where they might be able to find "the largest amount at the lowest rate."[29] The loan needed to finish the College building would be secured by mortgaging the ten acres of land and the building as it now stood. Unfortunately, it did not stand very tall, for the construction had experienced frequent delays and was far behind schedule.

If every other source became exhausted, the trustees decided to borrow on their own responsibility. This was the first time, but would not be the last, in which those involved with the College would put their money where their hearts were.

And those hearts would have to be strong. There they were, six weeks away from their opening day, with an invalid principal, a building that had no chance of being completed in time, and a debt of $1100. George Falkenstein spoke for all the trustees when he confided to his diary, "So many things to do and think about. I am struggling somewhat as a man who is beyond his depths. I hope I may soon be able to wade again."[30]

---

1 *The Organization and The Early History of Elizabethtown College*, p. 48
2 *The Organization and The Early History of Elizabethtown College*, p. 54
3 Letter, J. G. Francis to G. N. Falkenstein, September 7, 1899.
4 *The Organization and The Early History of Elizabethtown College*, p. 55
5 It is obvious that Francis uses "craft" here to mean cunning or deceit.
6 Letter from Samuel H. Hertzler to G. N. Falkenstein, September 15, 1899.
7 *The Organization and The Early History of Elizabethtown College*, p. 55
8 J. G. Francis, Letter to L. D. Rose, October 26, 1949.
9 Ibid.
10 *Fruit of the Vine*, p. 261
11 *Our College Times*, February 1908, p. 8
12 *The Organization and The Early History of Elizabethtown College*, p. 57
13 op. cit., p. 64
14 op. cit., p. 66
15 op. cit., p. 68

16 op. cit., p. 73

17 *History of the Church of the Brethren: Eastern Pennsylvania: 1915–1965*, p. 321

18 op. cit., p. 322

19 op. cit., p. 322

20 *The Organization and The Early History of Elizabethtown College*, p. 75

21 op. cit., p. 78–79

22 *First Annual Catalogue: Elizabethtown College: 1900–1901*, p. 5

23 Ibid.

24 op. cit., p. 6

25 op. cit., p. 7

26 op. cit., p. 13

27 op. cit., p. 15

28 op. cit., p. 16

29 *The Organization and The Early History of Elizabethtown College*, p. 84

30 Ibid.

Chapter 3

1900–1910

"The beginning of the actual work — small and yet very auspicious..."

The water was destined to get much deeper before George Falkenstein would be able to wade again. The weeks before the opening were spent in correspondence, choosing textbooks for the students' minds and furniture for their bodies, planning and gathering books for the library, and dozens of other preparations.

Due to I. N. H. Beahm's illness, most of the work fell on Falkenstein's shoulders. In a small back room of his house, lit by one window by day and a coal oil lamp by night, he wrote the necessary letters, committee reports, and program for the opening day, kept the school's records, and conducted the affairs of his Germantown church. At the same time, he was finishing work on his book, *History of the German Baptist Brethren.* Saturday, November 3, 1900, saw him making several visits, including one to Beahm, arranging for a place to hold the opening day exercises, going to Lancaster to have the programs printed, and visiting the *New Era* office to discuss his forthcoming book.

On November 12, the day before the College was to open, there was one more emergency. Since the school building was still unfinished, classes were to be held at the home of Joseph H. Rider on Washington Street, the parsonage of the German Baptist Brethren Church. However, Rider's house was not yet ready for classes to be held there the next day. Though some thought the opening would have to be delayed, Falkenstein immediately made arrangements to hold classes in the same building where the opening exercises were to be held, the A. Heisey building on the corner of South Market and Bainbridge Streets.

A hundred people attended those exercises in the third floor meeting hall of that building the following afternoon at two o'clock. There were six students enrolled, who in time came to be called "The Faithful Six." Two, John K. Boll and Willis S. Heisey, were from Elizabethtown. The others were Warren H. Ziegler, Walter A. Kittinger, Kurwin D. Henry (Falkenstein's nephew, considered the "First gentleman student of the College"[1]), and Rufus P. Bucher, trustee George Bucher's son, who would later become chairman of the board of trustees, a post he would hold for fifteen years.[2] The four out-of-town students roomed with the two male faculty members in the home of W. A. Withers[3], the six of them sharing two rooms, and had their meals at the Beahms' home.

At a board meeting held that night it was reported that the College could receive a loan of up to $8000 on their building and property at five percent interest, but instead the Board voted to make a loan of only $2000 "on the personal paper of Brethren Rider and Hertzler."[4] In another financial arrangement, the Board voted to allow Walter Kittinger credit toward his tuition "for such work as he can do in case of fires and sweeping, etc."[5] thus creating the first work/study program at Elizabethtown College.

They also decided to enter a protest against Benjamin G. Groff for taking so long to erect the College building. Perhaps the sting of the Board's disapproval goaded Groff and his workers, for the building was ready for occupancy seven weeks later.

In the interim, however, classes had to begin, and they did so the next day in Heisey Hall, opening with chapel exercises and examinations to see how proficient the students already were in the subjects to be taught. Although J. A. Seese, Elizabeth Myer, and Falkenstein were all in attendance, I. N. H. Beahm was unable to take any part, and Falkenstein performed all the duties of principal.

At the end of that first day of classes, Falkenstein wrote in his diary:

> This is the beginning of the actual work — small and yet very auspicious. The Lord knows the end from the beginning. We do not, but I desire 75 students enrolled before the close of the school year, — Bible and all, and I ask the Lord for the same here and now! Lord Grant it![6]

Not until the spring session of 1904 was Falkenstein's prayer for seventy-five students answered, but there was rapid growth in the College. The second annual catalogue of the College lists twenty-seven full-time students in the Literary Department, including the first woman student, Anna Brenneman of New Danville, and lists well over a hundred people who attended at least one meeting of the special three-week Bible term in the spring. There would not, however, have been room for such multitudes in Heisey Hall, where the students and faculty spent the week. By Friday, Falkenstein was pleased with what he saw:

> Things are getting in fair shape in our school work. It begins to look like school and feel like it. Sister Myer is proving herself to be an excellent teacher.
> The boys are settling down to good work, and most of them are going to be good students, in conduct and work.[7]

Along with his other duties, Falkenstein apparently did what he could for the prostrate Brother Beahm, including "massage treatment and surface rubbing."[8] The work took its toll, and Falkenstein's diary states that he was very tired most days. That his double life exhausted him cannot be doubted, but he continued to see the humor in it.

The following Sunday in Germantown, "I preached twice, as usual," he states, "and people would not have suspected that I organized a College during the week, 87 miles away."[9]

There was little respite for anyone involved with the school the following week, for on Monday, November 19th, the Rider house was at last ready to accommodate classes. After the day's lessons, everyone carried the furniture and books down two flights of stairs, and loaded them onto Rider's two-horse hardware wagon. The move took a total of three trips to Washington Street, but Falkenstein still had sufficient stamina to end the day by giving Beahm further massage treatment.

The next day saw more moving before chapel, but the new location offered a far more efficient physical layout. The front room of the house served as the book room, office, and library; the next room doubled as chapel and recitation room; another served as a study and a second recitation room, and the back room functioned as both cloakroom and storeroom.

There was a janitor too, in the person of student Walter Kittinger, whom Falkenstein naturally supervised. Along with his duties, Falkenstein also talked with Kittinger about his smoking, and the boy promised to give it up. Demon Tobacco might have had the upper hand, however, for Kittinger's name does not appear among the students or alumni after the 1900–1901 school year.

Though the Rider house may have been "sufficient unto the day," the day would not be long in coming when the tiny college would outgrow it. Brothers Hertzler and Falkenstein, fearful of further delays in the completion of the College building, spoke to Brother Groff, the contractor, about adding additional plasterers to the two already on the job. Groff demurred, saying that plasterers were currently hard to get, but Falkenstein suspected that the small size of the crew was due to the fact that Groff had to supply the heat for his workmen, and he wished to wait until the building's heating plant was installed. Hertzler and Falkenstein prevailed, and Groff promised to secure ten more plasterers as quickly as possible. For one time, at least, urgency trumped Pennsylvania German thrift.

Though Benjamin Groff may have tried to save a dollar here and there, his generosity to the young college was abundant. He donated nearly a thousand dollars of contract work to Alpha Hall, served as superintendent of the grounds and buildings, and erected all the College buildings until his death in 1907.

In the following months, Falkenstein and Hertzler closely monitored the building process, viewing the rooms as they were completed, and measuring them for carpet, furniture, and equipment. Falkenstein continued to teach, run the College, and give Beahm massages, as well as experiment with another contemporary medical fad. In his diary for November 28, Falkenstein states:

> *Gave Brother Beahm magnetic treatment (by clasping his ankles in my hands) hoping to be rejuvinated (sic) by my overflow of vital fluid...I had no faith in it, but I was interested in him and was anxious to help him if I could, even though it seemed utterly useless.*[10]

Those first few months were a trial, not only for Falkenstein, but for the other teachers as well. Elizabeth Myer offered further evidence of the difficulties facing them in her early "History of Elizabethtown College":

> *It might be well to say right here that at the time of the opening, the Principal, Prof. I. N. H. Beahm, now President of our College, was confined to his bed with nervous prostration, and Prof. G. N. Falkenstein was obliged to perform the duties of Principal and teach besides. Those of you who have been pioneers in any kind of work can imagine the arduous duties and discouraging conditions which Prof. Falkenstein and his corps of workers were obliged to meet perseveringly.*[11]

Work continued on the new building, made possible by a loan of $9000 on January 8, 1901 from the Lancaster Trust Company. On Tuesday, January 22, the first month of the new century, the members of the College moved their belongings out of the Rider house and over to College Hill, into what would later be known as Alpha Hall. The building was not yet fully completed, and finishing work went on during the next few weeks, but the professors and students found themselves in a fully functional college building.

In the basement were the heating plant, the kitchen and dining room, and a science laboratory. The first floor contained offices, the library, the chapel, a bookstore, and three classrooms. The second floor was made up of dormitory rooms, with the west end for the women and the east end for the men. The unfinished third floor would later be used for more dormitory space.

Those who had planned the building had looked to the future. It had such amenities as steam heat, electric lighting, indoor bathrooms, and an electric "program clock" to regulate the school schedule.

Shortly after the building was completed, a dedication service was held on March fourth, with sermons and addresses by G. N. Falkenstein, S. R. Zug, T. F. Imler, Jesse C. Ziegler, and Elizabeth Myer. A month later, at the Board of Trustees' meeting of March 28th, the building was accepted from Benjamin G. Groff at a final cost of $14,318.71. At last Elizabethtown College had a home.

It wasn't long before attempts were underway to beautify that new home. Since College Hill had formerly been farmland and had long been denuded of trees, April 6, 1901, was declared a campus improvement day. Donors were sought to pay for two hundred Norway maple trees and fifty fruit trees which were planted on the campus, along with shrubbery and flowers. The day dawned fair, but a heavy rain arrived during the planting. Undismayed, the students, teachers, and other volunteers worked through the downpour until the planting was finished. The vast majority of the maple trees, planted at right angles under the methodical direction of T. F. Imler, survive to this day, although the original chart showing who donated each tree has been long lost.

The new college quickly became a part of the community, thanks in part to a special four-week "Bible Term," first held in the spring of 1901. This consisted of both day and evening classes in Bible study. While the day classes were well attended, the evening talks drew even more of the townspeople, many of them members of the local German Baptist Church. Thus a further bond was formed between the townspeople and the students and faculty of the College.

The Bible Term proved to be highly successful, with the number of people in attendance far greater than the number of full-time students. In 1901 the Bible Term attracted 115 attendees, compared with 27 full academic students; the 1902 session boasted 173 Bible Term students, and in 1903 the number increased to over 200.

In those early years, however, the number of faculty did not grow proportionately with the number of full-time students. As a result, there was little relief to the "arduous duties" mentioned by Elizabeth Myer. The first year's faculty/student ratio was 1/9, the second year was 1/13, the third was 1/22. Miss Myer's workload significantly increased, with her appointment as Superintendent of the Model School, which opened in September 1901. Its purpose was to place future teachers in a classroom setting. Three of the Falkenstein children as well as others from town were enrolled. Fortunately for Miss Myer, she was relieved of this office several months later.

In the fall of 1902, two new faculty members arrived to assume their duties. Daniel C. Reber was hired to teach mathematics, foreign language, and pedagogy, and also appointed Vice-Principal, while Henry K. Ober taught math and commercial subjects. Both young men would eventually become President of Elizabethtown College. For Daniel Reber the responsibility was not long in coming.

In October of 1902, only a month after the arrival of the new teachers, G. N. Falkenstein's tireless schedule had finally caught up with him. He and his family had moved to Elizabethtown in February of 1901, and he had been elected Principal of the College for the 1901–02 school year, rather than serve as Acting Principal, as he had done the previous year. He, his wife, and their four children now lived in two recitation rooms of Alpha Hall, and took their meals in the College dining room.

In order to augment the annual salary of $600 that was paid him to teach pedagogy, psychology, and Bible (and later history and science) as well as run the College, he opened a small bookstore early in 1902. Added to his extremely heavy teaching schedule, his administrative work, and his church duties, the workload proved too great, and he fell ill at the beginning of the 1902 fall term. He resigned as principal, and shortly thereafter as a teacher, stating to the board of Trustees:

> *In severing my connection with Elizabethtown*
> *College, I feel keenly that I leave a work that was close*
> *to my heart and I earnestly must pray for its future*
> *greater success under God's blessing.*[12]

Falkenstein continued to serve as secretary of the Board for five more months, then turned his attention to his bookstore. Beside books and stationery, the store also sold music, candy, wallpaper, and dress patterns. The primary source of profit, however, was the sale of picture postcards. This tremendously popular fad began to fade in the mid-1910s, and by 1915 the bookstore was forced to close.

G. N. Falkenstein would not be seen again in Elizabethtown, or at the College, for many years. His departure left the position of principal open, and a month after his resignation, the Board of Trustees appointed one of the new teachers, Vice-Principal D. C. Reber, to the post of Acting Principal.

Daniel Conrad Reber was born on February 20, 1872, on his family's farm in Berks County. Reber was the first of three brothers to attend Juniata College, the result of a Juniata professor canvassing for students, a frequent activity at the time. Only sixteen when he entered college, he became so desperately homesick that he left Juniata after six weeks and returned home, spending the rest of the winter teaching in a one-room schoolhouse. Through his teaching and by studying ahead of his older pupils, he gained enough self-confidence to return to Juniata for the following fall term.

There D. C., as his friends called him, earned the school's first baccalaureate degree and became a full faculty member. Later he met Anna Kauffman, whom he married in June 1900. The newlyweds set up housekeeping in Brooklyn, N.Y., where Anna kept house in a flat above the Brooklyn Mission while D. C. studied for his doctorate at Manhattan's New York University on a scholarship. Instead of using public transportation, Reber economized by walking across the newly built Brooklyn Bridge both morning and evening. He made hundreds of trips, saving hundreds of nickels, until he received his doctorate in 1902. It was also in Brooklyn that Reber received his ordination as a minister of the German Baptist Church.

He had been finishing his doctoral work when the invitation to teach came from Elizabethtown College. However, Reber's faculty advisor counseled the young man to decline. These small, church-related, liberal arts colleges, Reber was warned, would die aborning. Still, he and his wife had always wanted to bring up their children in the atmosphere of a church-related school, and he accepted the offer. It started a relationship that would last nearly two decades.

Reber and his wife built a house on the edge of the campus, where their four children were born. The care of the family fell largely to Anna, as Reber energetically stepped into the footsteps of Falkenstein, both teaching a heavy course load and administering the day-to-day workings of the College. He unfailingly left his house at seven in the morning, and the lights in his office often went out only when the ten o'clock retiring bell rang for the students.

The College's necessity for strict economy can readily be appreciated in Mrs. Reber's sacrifice of a new dress that she had been planning to make. Instead, the cost of fabric helped to purchase fifteen chairs with writing arms for a classroom, so that the students would no longer need to carry chairs back and forth between the dining room and the classroom.

The end of D. C. Reber's first year with the College saw another milestone, the first commencement. It was a modest affair with only three graduates, all of them in the commercial course, a program that would prove the most popular course of study for several more years. All three graduates were women: Bessie M. Rider of Elizabethtown, Lizzie M. Eby of Lancaster, and Luella G. Fogelsanger of Woodbury, N.J. None of the "Faithful Six," the first to enroll in the College, ever graduated, not even Rufus Bucher, who served as a trustee for many years.

The 1903–1904 school year found I. N. H. Beahm still in ill health, so Reber served another term as Principal, with H. K. Ober as Vice-Principal. Beahm had recovered suffiently, however, to become Business Manager of the College.

It had been a difficult period for the Beahms. Beahm had spent a year in a sanitarium, and, in his absence, his wife Mary had run their home as a boarding-house, charging fifty cents per day for room and board. But by 1903, Beahm "recovered his youthful resiliency, in the main; and he learned to stay clear of the danger line."[13] He learned so well, in fact, that he lived to the age of ninety-one, his death occurring, not from sickness, but in an automobile accident.

On March 14, 1904, near the end of that school year, Elizabethtown College took its first tentative step away from direct control by the German Baptist Church. Until that time, the actual operation of the College was nominally in the hands of the Board of Trustees. Beahm, Reber, and Ober presented the Board with a proposal which would put that responsibility into the hands of an "Administrative Committee of the Faculty."

The Board agreed, naming the three faculty presenters as the committee, giving them a raise in salary for the increased duties, and essentially placing the functioning of the school under their control. Any hiring of teachers was to be approved by the Board of Trustees, and the treasurer of the Administrative Committee (Ober) would also be made acting treasurer of the trustees.

Provision #14 left no doubt that the College was indeed an investment, however much a shaky one. It stated that, at the end of each school year, "...if there is a balance in favor of the College ...the Board of Trustees shall receive 25% of said balance, and the Administrative Committee the remaining 75%."[14]

I. N. H. Beahm's recovery seemed complete, and he was given the new title of President for the 1904–05 school year, during which he also taught psychology and ethics. The number of faculty and students continued to increase, and among these early teachers were many individuals who would help to build the College in other ways besides teaching.

In 1905, two graduates of the Elizabethtown Class of '05 joined the staff. Jacob G. Meyer, who would later become president of the College, taught history and geography, and Jacob Z. Herr, who would serve as treasurer and business manager for many years, taught commercial studies. A year later Lewis Day Rose arrived; he would be the College librarian from 1907 to 1911, and from 1921 to 1940. Another future president, Ralph W. Schlosser, began his teaching career at the College in 1907, after completing two courses of study there as a student.

With the increase in both students and faculty, it wasn't long before the single (and as yet unnamed) college building proved too small to house all the activities of the campus. How far the College had come can be gauged by the fact that only three weeks after solicitation of funds began for the new building on April 7, 1905, over twelve thousand dollars was already received in cash and pledges. Elizabethtown College had achieved a broad base of support in just six years of existence.

The new building, erected at a cost of $14,347, was dedicated on March 4, 1906. It housed the library, a "physical culture" room, and a new chapel, as well as many classrooms. The new building also boasted a bell tower, which was the scene of many pranks during the school's early years.

Joseph H. Rider, who served as vice president of the board of trustees, made a large donation to the cost of the building, but modestly declined the College's offer to name the building after him. Instead, it was called Memorial Hall, becoming Rider Memorial Hall after the donor's death. The naming of this second building raised the question as to what to call the first, so the day after the dedication of Memorial Hall, the trustees voted to name the earlier building Alpha Hall.

At the start of the 1906–07 term, I. N. H. Beahm once again withdrew from the activities of the president. This time, the hiatus was not due to his state of health, but to the fulfillment of a lifelong dream. Because of his knowledge of classical and biblical lore, he was named what might be best termed a cultural attaché to guide American travelers on a tour to the Holy Land. Beahm's expenses were paid as he accompanied and enlightened the party from Damascus to Egypt, writing letters back to Elizabethtown, where they were published in *Our College Times*, the College magazine.

D. C. Reber, the vice president, temporarily assumed Beahm's duties as he had before and would again the following year. In 1908, Beahm was elected as the "nominal" president, while Reber became the "acting" president, managing the affairs of the College during Beahm's absence.

Beahm now taught only during the annual Bible term, devoting the rest of his time to preaching and representing the school in the field, serving essentially as a goodwill ambassador, recruitment officer, and fund raiser. He was certainly fit for such a task. Despite the ill health which had dogged his early years and the bad investments that would eventually leave him and his family pushed "from pillar to post,"[15] he remained indefatigably gregarious, blessed with a grand sense of humor. He also had a wide knowledge of literature and remained an omnivorous reader throughout his life, quoting Shakespeare and the Bible at the slightest provocation.

Perhaps the qualities which made him so valuable to Elizabethtown College in its early years were his utter determination to clearly express his ideas and beliefs of the worth of the College, and his reputation as a conservative to whom unity was more important than mere tradition. As a church history described Beahm's thinking, "It is more important to keep the church united than old-fashioned."[16] More than one parent of prospective students must have thought to themselves, *If Brother Beahm thinks Elizabethtown College would be good for my children, then it must be so.*

While Beahm was giving Elizabethtown College its warm and public face, D. C. Reber set to the far more arduous task of building the academic reputation of the College. As S. Z. Sharp said of Reber in his book, *The Educational History of the Church of the Brethren*, "It was the policy of the president to make this school a college in fact as well as in name."[17]

A classical course of study, first offered in 1907, began to attract students who had finished the pedagogical course. In 1907, several Elizabethtown students attended the summer term at Ursinus College, from which Reber would receive his Master of Arts degree in 1909. Ursinus was the first of many colleges to accept Elizabethtown's work. Within the next few years, Juniata, Lebanon (now Lebanon Valley), State College (Penn State), Oberlin, Franklin & Marshall, and the University of Pennsylvania would all accept Elizabethtown students without requiring entrance examinations.

Another area that flourished under Reber was the music department, although acceptance of music at the College had been a struggle. George Bucher, who originally wished to have the College's

Constitution state that instrumental music would not be allowed, was not alone in his feelings. No German Baptist Brethren churches used instrumental music, and many churchmen thought the same principle should extend to church-related colleges.

The first request for instrumental music came in 1903, when students requested the Board grant its permission for them to receive piano instruction. The trustees proved themselves on the liberal side of the music question when they hired a teacher of vocal *and instrumental* music for the following school year, and approved purchase of both a used piano and a used organ for a total of $175. However, when students asked for the piano to be used during chapel, the faculty refused the request. Indeed the trustees made certain that the administrative committee would move cautiously in allowing *any* use of instruments in college programs, including those of the Keystone Literary Society.

Still, more instruments appeared. By 1908, there were four pianos on campus, and the trustees finally voted to approve piano music during the Keystone Literary Society's sessions. In spite of the widespread prejudice from church members against instrumental music, B. F. Wampler, head of the music department from 1905 to 1911, somehow succeeded in minimizing this criticism. By the decade's end, Elizabethtown College had a strong piano and organ course, a harbinger of the healthy music programs to come.

Music, or the lack of it, was not the only area in which the influence of the church was felt. The students were to be given as few opportunities for temptation as possible, so their conduct was rigidly circumscribed. Permission was required for students to leave their rooms during study hours, and no female student could leave the campus with any man unless chaperoned by a faculty member. In order to attend church services in Elizabethtown, female students were required to walk there and back in a group, chaperoned, of course.

The church's hand was also felt in the administration of athletics on campus. When, in 1904, students requested to play against teams from other colleges, I. N. H. Beahm wrote a policy statement that the Board then approved and published. It stated that "the modern match games of base-ball, foot-ball, etc. with outside teams are not in accord with Christian virtue and true education."[18] Along with this statement printed in *Our College Times* was a quotation from Dr. Charles W. Eliot, President of Harvard and compiler of the *Harvard Classics*, that famous "five-foot shelf" intended for every civilized home: "The breaking up of College work for the individual student by frequent absence to play games at a distance from Cambridge is an evil which ought to be checked."[19]

The stand against intercollegiate sports was given further support by the comment of the *Our College Times* writer, in all likelihood Elizabeth Myer or another faculty or administration member:

> *It is a strong stand, and it will be welcomed by the sturdy, substantial citizenship of the country. It will be especially welcomed by those who are interested in the progress of true, Christian education, and the plain, simple, yet glorious doctrines of the New Testament.*[20]

It was a stand, however, that proved unpopular with many students, some of whom formed teams to play clandestine games with outside groups. The official ban remained in effect for nearly a quarter century, and continued to generate controversy and discussion, if *Our College Times* can be trusted as a barometer of student opinion. In 1905, a short essay titled "Glad to Say" states: "A number of students are in Elizabethtown College primarily on account of the position taken against intercollegiate match games."[21] The claim seems exaggerated. Though some parents may have considered such a ban a positive measure for their children, it would hardly seem to provide a deciding factor.

One cannot help but feel that many of the anti-intercollegiate articles are administrative and faculty attempts to put out small fires of protest lodged by students. This is not to deny that some students strongly agreed with the stand. "Physical Culture" by C. M. Neff, a junior, supports "the management" by affirming that: "We are here trying to cultivate our *mental* abilities, and this can be done well only by excluding as much excitement as possible." Many college men, Neff claims, "do not think of exercising and developing their brains, but only their sinews. They think only of excelling in sports, and with that comes rowdyism. ...Elizabethtown College is an advance agent on inter-collegiate athletic reform."[22]

Still, athletics could be found on the campus. Baseball proved popular, and the first team was formed in 1905 (with C. M. Neff at second base). Nor did the College policy stop many students from playing on other teams in Elizabethtown, Maytown, Columbia, and Hummelstown. Students played basketball in the basement of Memorial Hall, and also engaged in gymnastics. Football, always officially frowned upon, was banned altogether in 1910.

There were other activities in the College's first decade. The Keystone Literary Society was the earliest of the school's organizations, founded in 1901. Its purpose was "the improvement of the mind by literary culture, the ability to express thoughts with power and eloquence, readiness and skill in debate, and a familiar acquaintance with the rules and usage of deliberative bodies."[23] In short, the members engaged in writing, debate, and the committing to memory of large portions of *Roberts' Rules of Order.*

As dry as it may sound to today's students, the society was an enormous success, so much so that in 1909 the members petitioned the trustees to allow a second society to be formed. The board granted the request, allowing the organization of a "junior society."

Another literary activity in which students could participate was writing for *Our College Times*, the monthly college magazine begun in 1904. At its inception, the magazine was little more than a platform for administration policies, as can be seen by the earliest masthead. The editor-in-chief was I. N. H. Beahm, and the associate editors were D. C. Reber, Elizabeth Myer, and I. E. Shoop, all faculty members. Two students, however, were listed as "special editors"; as the years passed, more of the writing was done by students.

Along with the expected stories about academia and student activities, a number of other stories show another side of Elizabethtown College and its connection to the German Baptist Brethren Church. This is the sense of tolerance of the beliefs and convictions of others. In a 1904 issue of *Our College Times*, a brief essay called "Every Denomination" states that "the doors are...open to everybody, regardless of creed, and they are not to be intimidated on account of their honest, religious convictions."[24] There follows a list of the nine denominations represented at the College, including Roman Catholicism.

Another piece a year later reiterates this idea by stressing the idea of *lenity,* meaning the quality or state of being mild or gentle, particularly toward others. It is a word and, unfortunately, a concept seldom used today, but the sense of lenity pervades the early years of *Our College Times* as certainly as it did the College itself:

> While [Elizabethtown College] is loyal to its immediate fraternity, yet no one on account of his religious convictions, shall in any way be embarrassed while making his sojourn with us; but that he shall always feel at liberty to hold his honest religious convictions, even though they may in some degree be at variance with others.[25]

Simply looking through the old magazines indicates at least a willingness, if not a desire, to be exposed to different ideas, creeds, and even races. In 1907, the Library Committee sponsored a lecture on the African-American poet, Paul Laurence Dunbar, and two years later Rev. Z. A. Jones, "a cultured and courteous colored man," spoke on the need for "Education of the Negro."[26]

Both students and faculty seemed to be very much aware of the happenings in the non-academic world. Though sheltered to a certain extent, discussions often centered on current world affairs. By 1907, the library was subscribing to *Scientific American*, and the encyclopedia used was *The Americana*, published by *Scientific American* as well. At the 1907 graduation exercises, among the orations was one by senior Amos G. Hottenstein calling for "a supreme court of international justice" to be established at the second Hague Tribunal, which was to open several days later, "so that right, and not might, shall prevail."[27]

In that first decade of the College's history, however, there were two *causes célèbres* that commanded the attention of both faculty and students. The first, and shorter-lived, was the Garb Law, the state statute forbidding a teacher to wear religious garb while teaching in a Pennsylvania public school. The law was put to the test when Lillian Risser, a graduate of Elizabethtown College and a

Mennonite, was hired by the school board of Mount Joy Township, which, upon receiving complaints, refused to dismiss her because of her "plain" Brethren clothing. A taxpayer of the township then filed suit against the school board for violating the statute.

It was an incident that was bound to draw the interest of the College. Many students wore "plain" dress, and many of those wished to teach in the public schools when they were graduated. The events were closely followed by those on campus. Faculty and students could not help but be relieved when the President Judge of the Lancaster County Court declared that the law was contrary to the Bill of Rights, unconstitutional, and therefore null and void. It was a decision that was guaranteed to please the vast majority of his religiously conservative Lancaster County jurisdiction. Still, funds were solicited by *Our College Times* in order to further test the case in Pennsylvania Superior and Supreme Courts.

The second and more far-reaching concern was the issue of temperance. Alcoholic beverages had been frowned on for many years by the church. In 1908, the year in which the German Baptist Brethren Church took the name of Church of the Brethren, it was actively fighting alcohol as a moral and social evil. At the church's annual conference that year, a proposal to form a "permanent temperance committee" stated that, "it is the duty of Christians to endeavor to suppress all forms of evil that imperil the morality of the people, as well as the sacred interests of the visible church."[28]

Elizabethtown's Church of the Brethren already had a temperance committee, of which several members, such as Elizabeth Myer and G. N. Falkenstein, had strong college connections. They requested the Eastern Pennsylvania District to petition the state legislature to enact a "Local Option Law," which would give local municipalities the right to ban the sale and manufacture of alcohol within their jurisdiction. Under such a law, it was felt that many towns within Lancaster County would have gone "dry."

The district accepted the request, and I. N. H. Beahm was chosen to present the petition and speak before a committee of the legislature in Harrisburg. Despite the pleas of Beahm and other temperance speakers from the Women's Christian Temperance Union and the Anti-Saloon League, the local option law was defeated by a wide margin, since the state legislature represented the entire state, and not just the bastions of conservatism, of which Lancaster County was a prime example.

This represented, however, only the first shot in a battle that the faculty and students of Elizabethtown College would fiercely wage for the next fifteen years, with *Our College Times* as the primary sounding board.

⋘—⋙

The College magazine, besides being a soapbox, proves an excellent time machine to observe what day-to-day college life must have been like in that first decade. For example, students would have heard President Beahm addressing them on such topics as swearing ("Do not use language that you would not use in the presence of your mother"), smoking ("If they are able even to buy a five or ten cent cigar and hold it up at an angle of 45 degrees while they puff, they think that is manly, that is a farce"), the need for sleep ("If I were starting to go to College now, I would have my time to go to bed — ten o'clock"), and health ("Take care of your stomachs, as the stomach is a very important organ").[29]

They would have attended the annual "Musicale," and heard such offerings as "Come to the Gay Feast of Song," "Who Knows What the Bells Say," "While the Dew is on the Lilies," and the highlight, Liszt's "Rhapsodie Hongroise No. 2," played by Leah M. Shaeffer, a graduate of the four year piano course. "At times we were carried away," says the reporter, "in a veritable storm of chromatic progressions."[30]

In the pedagogical department, future teachers might have been studying Dewey's *School and Society*, or learning about modern schoolhouses, hygienic furniture, diseases prevalent among school children, fatigue and its remedy, and motor activity as an educational factor.

Science students might have been examining the new Trippensee Planetarium, or making field excursions to collect various species of insects and small animals, classifying and mounting them.

Sophomores in the Classical Course would have been deep in the study of medieval Europe, contrasting Roman laws with those of the Teutons. They also studied the fall of the Roman Empire and the rise of the papacy, using Robinson's *History of Mediaeval Europe* as a text. The same period was being studied in English Literature, looking at how the union of the Celts and Teutons "formed the earnest, vigorous, courageous, courtly, cultured, art loving English race — the most capable race in Europe." Classical students also were studying the origin, nature, and transmission of the Bible, the Protestant Reformation, the history of the Brethren, and, keeping with the medieval theme, medieval missions.

Commercial students would be immersed in Sadler, Rowe Office Practice: "The student secures his knowledge almost entirely by practice, continually handling and disposing of such business papers, of all kinds, as are used in leading business houses today."

Latin students were reading Caesar, Virgil, Livy, and Ovid, and many students were battling the bane of college life, "a general lack of muscular tone which often results in a flat chest and drooping shoulders, familiarly known as 'the students' stoop,'" by taking physical culture classes.[31]

There were other amusements besides the "marches and free hand movements" that made up much of the physical culture exercises and drills. Holidays were celebrated merrily when students were present, and the Dickensian Thanksgiving Day of 1909 boasted a menu of "chicken well browned and richly seasoned, filling, sweet potatoes, mashed potatoes, gravy, cranberry-sauce, celery, pickles, chocolate cake, and lemon custard," served in a dining hall decorated by chrysanthemums, geraniums, and other plants. The festivities were punctuated by numerous toasts, and climaxed by an impromptu program that included music, reminiscences, and speeches. "Spirits bubbled over with joy and hearts were happy. The true spirit of thankfulness prevailed."[32]

There were also picnics and sleigh rides. One of these snowy outings served an educational purpose, when the Bible department teachers and students visited two schools in Rapho Township to observe classes. They stopped to socialize at several homes on their return, one of which belonged to a Dr. Becker. "As it was St. Valentine's Day, Mr. A. P. Geib very obligingly let the ladies look at his heart through Dr. Becker's x-ray apparatus."[33]

꠸—♋꠸

By the end of the decade, Elizabethtown College had transformed itself into an institution with six different departments offering sixteen courses of study ranging from a single term to four years, even though the emphasis was still on teacher training and commercial education. The 1909–10 catalogue was able to boast of 5000 square feet of cement walkways, a compound microscope, "abundant slate blackboards, six typewriters, with more to be installed early, organ, five pianos, laboratory stand and fixtures, three hundred and fifty dollar science cabinet...and numerous other items of interest."[34]

There were seventeen faculty members, nearly two hundred students enrolled, and a hundred alumni. In 1906, these graduates had formed an alumni association, whose activities were still overseen by the faculty and board of trustees. Chaperonage extended to even post-college life, with the requirement that a faculty member be on the program committee of any alumni reunion, "and no meetings to be held at any summer resorts nor followed by banquets."[35] When the request was made in 1908 to hold an alumni supper, it was denied, but two years later the trustees granted the request, "provided such supper be held not later than 7 o'clock P.M. and that the menu be submitted to the Faculty for approval."[36]

While old rules were loosening ever so slightly, the next decade would see an even closer attachment to the Church of the Brethren. It would also see, under the administration of D. C. Reber, a vast improvement in the actual quality of education students received at Elizabethtown College. Though physical growth would be minimal, intellectual growth would thrive through a decade that would plunge the world into war, and harvest the finest young lives of the age.

---

1 *Second Annual Catalogue of Elizabethtown College*, p. 23

2 The first issue (May 1904) of *Our College Times* places five of the six: Henry was teaching in rural schools, Bucher had been elected to the ministry, Ziegler was teaching in Freeman, Pa., Kittinger was working in Philadelphia for the Electrical Supply Co., and Heisey had become a merchant in Elizabethtown.

3 Schlosser's *History* gives this name, revising Falkenstein's possibly erroneous assertion of the name, "Wittles." William A. Withers was a resident of Elizabethtown at this time.

4 *The Organization and the Early History of Elizabethtown College*, p. 91

5 op. cit., p. 92

6 op. cit., p. 91

7 op. cit., p. 93

8 Ibid.

9 op. cit., p. 94

10 op. cit., p. 96

11 "History of Elizabethtown College," *Our College Times*, January 1907, p. 2

12 *Minutes, Elizabethtown College Board of Trustees*, September 30, 1902

13 *History of the Church of the Brethren: Eastern Pennsylvania, 1915–1965*, p. 211

14 *Minutes of the Board of Trustees, Elizabethtown College*, March 15, 1904

15 *History of the Church of the Brethren: Eastern Pennsylvania, 1915–1965*, p. 212

16 op. cit., p. 213

17 *The Educational History of the Church of the Brethren*, p. 262

18 *Our College Times*, July 1904, p. 10

19 Ibid.

20 Ibid.

21 *Our College Times*, November 1905, p. 10

22 *Our College Times*, May 1907, p. 16

23 *History of Elizabethtown College: 1899–1970*, p. 55

24 *Our College Times*, July 1904, p. 9

25 *Our College Times*, November 1905, p. 9

26 *Our College Times*, April 1909, p. 4

27 *Our College Times*, July 1907, p. 8

28 *Annual Meeting Minutes*, 1909, quoted in *Moving Toward the Mainstream*, p. 177

29 *Our College Times*, October 1907, p. 9

30 *Our College Times*, July 1908, p. 3

31 *Our College Times*, October 1908, pp. 8–10

32 *Our College Times*, January 1909, p. 13

33 *Our College Times*, March 1910, p. 4

34 *Elizabethtown College: Tenth Annual Catalogue, 1909–10*, p. 8

35 Board of Trustees Minutes, February 7, 1908.

36 Board of Trustees Minutes, May 19, 1910.

Chapter 4
1910–1920

"A movement on foot to transfer the College to the Church..."

When young Charles Abba Baugher stepped onto the grounds of Elizabethtown College in April of 1914, it already looked like a sturdily established, if not ancient, institution. The two main buildings were surrounded by trees, some of which nearly reached to the top of their second stories. A cement walk ran the length of the campus, and as Charles looked at the students walking up and down its length, many of them dressed in the plain garb of his own Church of the Brethren, he was surprised at how young some of them appeared.

He was about to become a twenty-one year old freshman, and was even more apprehensive since he was two weeks late for classes, which had begun on March 23. It was not the first time, however, that Charles had been behind when it came to his education, though he had always caught up and surpassed those whose circumstances had allowed them to pursue a more orderly schedule.

Instead of a straight, unbroken series of courses in elementary and high school, the line of Charles' education resembled a series of ascents and plateaus, but one that moved always upward. He was determined to get an education, the desire due not only to his innate intellect, but to the encouragement of his parents. His father, Aaron, was the schoolmaster in the small village where they lived on the Pennsylvania-Maryland border, and loved books dearly. His mother, Lydia, a refined and genteel woman, also valued learning; she and her husband saw that young Charles attended school when he was five.

Charles loved to practice his writing, especially his own name. Even when very young, he began to write his name with his initials reversed, and even today some of the walls of the outbuildings on the old Baugher farm bear the name, "A. C. Baugher." Perhaps he felt it sounded more dignified. Certainly early photographs show a young man of dignified mien, with handsome, delicate features, and wavy, upswept hair.

Up to this point, it had been an effort for Charles to continue his schooling. He had had to walk six miles a day to attend high school, which meant rising every morning at 4:30. The venture was made even more difficult by the fact that each day after school he would work on a neighbor's farm until 9:30 in the evening. Still, he graduated with top honors from Glenville High School in 1913, and gave the commencement oration for his class.

He had taught school for a short time after his graduation, but his desire for a Christian education gave him no peace, and he decided that he could find it at Elizabethtown College. He knew tuition would be a problem, but he was willing to work, indeed, to take any kind of job to help him earn enough money to get the education he so desperately craved.

As he walked up the steps of Alpha Hall to register for classes, he stopped at the top and looked down. From there he looked out over the small campus, and down toward the town in the distance. For a moment he paused, admiring the view, hoping that he had made the right choice.

Then he felt peace come over him at last, and knew that this *was* the right place for him to be. His ever present confidence surged once again. Perhaps, he thought, I can do as much for this college as it can do for me. "He can who thinks he can," he whispered to himself. He smiled his soft smile, and then, for the first of what would be tens of thousands of times, A. C. Baugher walked through the doors of Alpha Hall.

He had come home.

⊷§—§⊶

A. C. Baugher would be the champion of Elizabethtown College for nearly a half century. The Elizabethtown College to which he had come was indeed becoming more firmly established as a center of learning. D. C. Reber, in his years as acting president, had organized and developed the curriculum so that it was now far more attractive to those seeking to teach, or to experience a four-year college course.

So it was only natural that when I. N. H. Beahm resigned as president on June 30, 1909, the Acting President should be his successor. In 1908, Beahm had been instrumental in opening a Christian school in Nokesville, Pennsylvania, called Hebron Seminary, and had built a house nearby. Nokesville had become his home base, and it was to the seminary that he now decided to dedicate his time.

Reber became president of Elizabethtown College in the 1910–11 school year, with H. K. Ober as his Vice President. He would hold that office for the next eight years. Though they would not be years of physical growth, they would see unprecedented intellectual growth in the number of students, the quality of the faculty, and the courses offered.

During these years, the internal event of greatest import was the transfer of ownership of the College. Ever since its beginning, Elizabethtown College had actually been owned by the people who had contributed the funds to establish it. Though definitely church-related, it was not church-owned; this process of transfer would eventually take place over four years.

The impetus for this change seems to have come from the College trustees themselves, possibly as the result of pressure brought to bear upon the College by the more conservative members of the church. They had counseled to "Be ye separate," particularly in such things as the absence of instrumental music, intercollegiate sports, liquor, tobacco, gambling, hazing — all the things that many students were exposed to in most other colleges. Elizabethtown was to be different, a college which would represent the highest virtues of the Church of the Brethren. If this was to be the case, the logic presumably went, then why not have the College completely owned by the church in order to preserve these virtues?

So in April 1913, at the church's Eastern District Conference, the Ephrata church asked the district to consider the question of the church's assuming ownership of the College, and to form a committee to consult with the College's present owners. Apparently it was not regarded as a matter for haste, since the committee was asked to report back a year later.

The three-person committee met in July 1913 with trustees and officers of the College in what seems to have been a "fact-finding" mission. However, no decisions were reached until the following January, when representatives from the Southeastern District joined those of the Eastern District and met with college trustees and faculty. Caution and deliberation seemed to be the order of the day, for the conclusion was simply that the transfer might be productive. That resolution was to be further considered for at least a year, during which time church members would be acquainted with the general educational movements in the church, and specifically with Elizabethtown College. Thus a decision was put off until 1915, at the earliest.

The College trustees acted much more quickly, trying to hasten the situation. Less than a month later, on February 17, 1914, they passed a recommendation that the College be taken over by the church, and be placed under the supervision of its General Education Board. But at the District Conference in April, the only action taken was a request for further study.

More months passed, and in July 1915, the College trustees tried again, voting to "Take steps to have S.E. Penna and Southern Pa. Districts express their attitude toward the proposition of taking over Elizabethtown College."[1] It seemed a step backwards. While the recommendation of the trustees a year before was that the church take over the College, now they were merely asking for the districts to "express their attitude" about the prospect.

A history of the Church of the Brethren in Eastern Pennsylvania published in 1915 mentions that "there is a movement on foot to transfer the College to the Church as the property of the two state districts."[2] The author's choice of words was telling: "on foot" was indicative of the speed at which the movement was progressing.

At the Eastern Pennsylvania District Meeting in April 1915, the takeover proposal brought up the year before was discussed. It was decided to defer even *considering* taking over the College until the next district meeting. It was also recommended that the College trustees try to ascertain the attitudes of the Southeastern and Southern Districts.

Amazingly, the trails to the takeover grew even more labyrinthine. A long nine months later, on January 11, Jesse C. Ziegler reported to the College trustees that the Southeastern District "did not give very much expression as to their views." Furthermore, they had decided "to defer the question until E. Pa. makes its final decision."[3]

On the brighter side, Ziegler and S. H. Hertzler had learned that the Southern District was amenable to the transfer, and had appointed two members to discuss the possibility with the trustees. This was enough positive feedback for the Board to compose a formal plan of transfer of the College to the Eastern and Southern Districts, leaving the reluctant Southeastern District out of the equation for the time being.

The plan called for the acquiring districts to also assume any indebtedness of the original "contributors," and that the future trustees of the College would be members of and elected by the districts. A final clause stated that the new trustees would have no authority to levy or assess any taxes on the churches for the College's upkeep without the consent of district meetings, which was unlikely to occur.

The transfer made sense for all the parties involved. The original contributors would be free of debt, the church could determine exactly how conservative it wanted the College to be, and the clause against taxation ensured that the church districts would suffer no undue financial pressure.

Another April, that of 1916, came around, and the District Meeting finally hosted a lengthy discussion of the plan to transfer Elizabethtown College to the church. Again, it seemed that the Southeastern District evinced little interest in the College, showing more concern for another Brethren school, Juniata College in Huntingdon, Pennsylvania. The Southern District, on the other hand, again expressed its interest in and encouragement of Elizabethtown.

At last the plan of transfer written by the College's trustees was considered, and again the proceedings came to a dead stop. The delegates voted to defer final action for a full year.

That year had to have been a trying one for the trustees and faculty of the College. Every argument against the transfer was heard again and again from the more conservative church members: *the Church of the Brethren doesn't need to get involved running colleges; it's going to cost the church too much money; colleges are against many things the church stands for; there's no real need for higher education at all.*

The debate didn't stop at the annual District Meeting on April 25, 1917, where the vote was finally taken on the transfer plan submitted by the College trustees the year before. Before that vote, however, the more conservative delegates were successful in changing the section about levying college taxes upon the churches with the consent of the District Meeting.

The conservatives refused to have their churches taxed by the College, even if a majority of delegates agreed they should be, so the section was changed to state that a church could be taxed by the College and the District only if the individual church ratified such taxation. This, in effect, meant that any donations to the College would be purely voluntary, and each church in the participating districts would have the option to contribute or not.

Still, the proposal passed by a vote of 46 to 30, which meant that a full 40 percent of the delegates were against it, even if it required no financial support on the part of their individual churches. It was a less than solid victory, but a victory nonetheless. Finally, after four years, Elizabethtown College would become the property of the Church of the Brethren.

But though the transfer seemed assured, all the pieces were not yet in place. By the time of the next annual district meeting in April of 1918, after another year had passed, the Southern District had finally voted in favor of co-owning the College, so it elected four trustees and the Eastern District elected eight. Their terms of office began on January 1, 1919, and at the board meeting on January 2, the new board, for the sake of formality, formally requested the president and secretary of the College to deliver a deed for all real estate held by the College. At last the transfer was complete and total.

To further appreciate, or perhaps stand in awe of, the tremendous caution and deliberation of the Brethren during this decision-making process, it may be instructive to note that in comparison, the thirteen disparate American colonies required less than a month from the first proposal of autonomy to the unanimous signing of the final Declaration of Independence. But then, they were already at war.

There seems to have been no abrupt change in policies with the advent of the new board, most of which was made up of previous board members. Samuel H. Hertzler, who had been chairman of the board, remained so. Amos G. Longenecker, secretary since 1908, retained his office, and I. W. Taylor remained as treasurer. They were all Brethren elders, and they knew the operations of the College well, so there was no need for change.

❧—❧

The relaxed pace at which decisions were made seemed to influence the College's physical growth, or lack thereof, during the next decade. Meanwhile, around the College, the community of Elizabethtown itself was quickly expanding. Reflecting the changes that were transforming much of Lancaster County from an agrarian to an industrial economy, the town gradually changed from a farm community to a manufacturing center. From 1900 to 1910, Elizabethtown's population increased by 75 percent. By 1920, it had more than doubled, due primarily to the influx of workers required in the new factories, among them the A. S. Kreider Shoe Manufacturing Co. and the Klein Chocolate Company. The building of the Masonic Homes, beginning in 1911, brought still more people to the community.[4]

The College's growth, however, was slower than that of the town and county. Among its most pressing needs was a new science building. Alpha Hall offered only limited laboratory space, so in 1915 the faculty requested that the Board approve a new facility. As always, discretion was the better part of valor, and the Board deferred the plans to a later meeting.

A year later, J. G. Meyer, who had been teaching science courses at the College since 1911, presented the Board with a sketch of plans for the building. This demonstration of serious concern convinced the Board to select a committee to present more specific plans at a later meeting.

In the next few years, the committee not only presented the Board with detailed architect's drawings of a four-story science building, but also with requests for an auditorium-gymnasium, a heating plant, a new library, and a women's dormitory. The science building was estimated to cost $50,000, but it is indicative of the precarious financial state of the College in those early years that construction would be postponed until 1927.

Jacob Gibble Meyer was typical of the faculty who taught at Elizabethtown during the Reber presidency. He came from farming stock (the farm on which he was raised had been deeded to the Meyer family by William Penn), and his father and grandfather had both been elders in the Church of the Brethren. He had taught in the public schools after he had completed his secondary education, and in 1905 he graduated from Elizabethtown with a degree in pedagogy. After teaching science in the Elizabethtown Academy, he received his A. B. from Franklin & Marshall College in Lancaster in 1910, and returned to Elizabethtown to teach physics and chemistry.

Meyer was one of sixteen faculty members at the College at the start of the decade. Those sixteen, under the supervision of D. C. Reber, strove to meet the basic needs of three types of students: those who wanted to become teachers, those who wished to complete a four-year high school course, and those seeking a commercial education.

In 1910, an agricultural course was added, since so many students came from farming families. H. K. Ober, then Vice President of the College, took charge of the program. The listing in the catalogue of 1910–11 confessed that "For several years we have catalogued an Agricultural Course, but up to this time we have had only one regular student enrolled in this course." It went on to state that "we mean to push this department along practical and progressive lines....An orchard of 400 fruit trees, 2,000 strawberry plants, currants, raspberries, grape vines, blackberries, is all at the hands of this department for practical instruction."[5]

The three-year course prescribed classes in mathematics, bookkeeping, and sciences, along with agronomy, botany, dairying, animal husbandry, rural economy, and three hours per week of "actual work on the ground, in experiments, cultivating, planting, budding, grafting, etc."[6]

In the spring of 1911, *Our College Times* reported that the College had gone into the chicken business, erecting a poultry house, as well as a hog stable. A dozen pullets and three White Rocks were donated by local church members. Another elder donated 3150 strawberry plants, and thirty students, under Ober's direction, planted them on Saturday, May sixth. "When the work was finished, all those who helped were treated to lemonade and cake by our efficient matron,"[7] Mrs. Reber.

The agricultural course proved to be of more than merely educational benefit to the school. The following December, the College sold one of its hogs, which weighed 347 pounds dressed, and another was ready for sale:

> *In the College hog sty are 9 nice flourishing shoats which ought to make real nice porkers by next March...The College aims to raise all the plants it needs by next spring, such as, tomatoes, cabbage, celery, redbeets, sweet potato, sprouts, etc. The grapevines have made very nice growth...The corn is husked and fodder is being turned into manure. It is the ambition of those in charge of the Agricultural Department to make the orchard and truck patch a very helpful source of income to the College.*[8]

"Agricultural Notes" remained a feature of *Our College Times* throughout the decade, reporting on the number of hogs sold, the frequency of the truck patch's manure treatments, and the size of the crops harvested. The summer of 1915 provided enough peaches for the College to sell $125 worth, preserve fifty quarts, and can 730 quarts. "There have also been peaches in the College dining room at least three times a day."[9] That same year a dry-house was erected to dry fruits and vegetables, and an addition was built on the south side of Alpha Hall with bins to hold a thousand bushels of potatoes.

Despite its tremendous financial success, the agricultural program had one insurmountable problem — not enough students signed up for it. It seemed that most of the male students who came to college did so not only to gain a Christian education, but to have a ticket off the farm as well. In the roll of alumni of the 1915–1916 catalogue, professions are listed behind each individual name. Of all those who had attended Elizabethtown College from 1900 to 1915, only five listed their post-college occupation as farming. Four of those had been in the commercial course, and one in the agricultural course. By 1917, only three students had actually graduated in the agricultural course, and by the end of the decade, no students at all were registered.

Although the farming heritage from which many Lancaster County students had come was suffering, most of the other values of the Church of the Brethren were not. On the contrary, Elizabethtown College continued as the bastion of proper behavior, with a strong emphasis on religious exercises. All students were still required to attend the morning chapel service every day, furnishing "a favorable environment for the moral welfare and the spiritual growth of the students."[10]

"Be ye separate" was still the watchword. Debating had proven a popular activity at Elizabethtown College, but intercollegiate debate was still prohibited. When, in 1917, Elizabethtown students wished to have a three-cornered debate with students from Blue Ridge and Daleville Colleges, the board of trustees responded that the decision was up to the faculty. A conflict in scheduling the prospective debate prevented the faculty from taking any action, but their response probably would have been similar to their reply to another request at the same meeting. The seniors wished to debate with Brownstown High School students, and were denied, for fear of establishing a precedent.

The definitive policy came on October 1, 1917, from the Committee on Literary Societies, which was made up of four faculty members. It stated:

> *We have carefully considered the advisability of entering upon intercollegiate debating contests and are unable to recommend same because of the fact that all students eligible are already overcrowded with work. The committee suggests, however, that all students eligible to such work concentrate their efforts on oratorical contests now held so that the standards of these contests may be maintained or advanced.*[11]

In short, be ye separate.

The administration's continuing response to the request for intercollegiate athletics reflects the same desire for separateness, along with the additional motivation of keeping Elizabethtown students away from "rowdyism" and possible exposure to not only poor sportsmanship, but also physical danger.

It was hard enough to keep students from such influences even at Elizabethtown, according to student Andrew Dixon. In an *Our College Times* article, he observed that basketball was "now the main athletic attraction at our college. ...It is almost impossible to keep it within the bounds of clean sport. ...the enthusiasm aroused sometimes leads to rough tactics in which brute strength and weight predominate over skill. ...Let your slogan be, 'We want clean basket ball.'"[12]

Such ungentlemanly displays were no fault of the administration, which had established firm rules of behavior at basketball games for both spectators and players. Male or female players on one side were to be designated by a sash, men and women could attend each others' games as spectators only once a week, enthusiasm was to be expressed by *gentle* applause, and street clothes rather than gym clothes were to be worn. This sartorial rule remained for years, and was made official in 1917, when the Board of Trustees felt it necessary to explain that the ban on gym suits had been made "On account of probable adverse criticism on the part of the constituency of the College and added expense to the students."[13]

If the prospect of gym shorts and overly enthusiastic basketball were daunting, the mere idea of football at Elizabethtown College was anathema. A faculty paper condemning the game said, "What human(e) person will not shudder at the list of fatalities which occurred in the year 1909, due to the brutal game of foot ball? During the season just closed, seven young men have been killed and ninety-three crippled."[14]

The administration attitude toward sports may be glimpsed in an *Our College Times* editorial titled "Athleticism," written by Ralph W. Schlosser in 1914. Schlosser taught English, Latin, and French, and would later serve as president of the College. During his presidency, Elizabethtown would finally participate in intercollegiate sports, but one would be hard pressed to find such leniency in Schlosser's early article.

He first defines athleticism as "sports, or athletics, gone to seed. …The man who is so devoted to this frenzied zeal for athletics is possessed of the system of athleticism." Schlosser praises physical exercise as necessary to keep the body healthy, but states that "home athletics" are in the better interests of the students than are intercollegiate athletics, which he considers part of the dreaded athleticism:

> *Sport may be tolerated when it is for sport's sake,*
> *but when it tends to professionalism, and virtually*
> *becomes the business of anyone, it becomes a menace*
> *to Christian manhood. No man has a moral right to*
> *make a sport of any kind his profession.*[15]

It is a vast leap from the intercollegiate sports of the time to the professional arena, but Schlosser seems to find any explanation unnecessary. He makes the further points that only a skillful few can play in intercollegiate games, and that "in a system of athleticism those who least need physical training get most of it, and those who need the most training get the least." Football is once more condemned:

> *We cannot, we must not, we dare not sanction*
> *this slaughter of our youths under the name of*

Christian education. Were one student killed by another in a fight before twenty thousand people, the slayer would be hanged, but yet a talented young man is frequently killed by foul play in a game of football and his slayer is allowed to go scot-free. And all this is termed by Christian education as an accident! O the morals of athleticism! The scenes of the Coliseum are still to be found in America, civilized America, and the verdict of Christian Education is "Thumbs down!"

Another problem Schlosser had with "athleticism" was that the tension of intercollegiate games made students lose their concentration, creating "inefficient class-work" and cheating the student in preparing him for life, which is not a series of games. Further objections were that it was unfair to judge what should be an educational institution on the basis of its athletic record, that colleges often nominally (and unethically) enrolled "professional athletes," and that the "undue" popularity that came to the hero of a game "often gives a young man a false notion of himself."[16]

Unknown to most at the time, Schlosser was deeply familiar with the temptations of the sporting life. In an interview with the College newspaper conducted over forty years later, the elderly Schlosser confessed that while he was a student at Elizabethtown College, he had played for various local baseball teams under an assumed name. Pitching was his area of expertise, and in Lancaster he pitched an exhibition game against the Lancaster Tri-State League team and struck out eighteen men. "I pitched an out-drop ball," he said in 1957. "It dropped away from the batter, and if the ball was hit, it seldom went out of the infield." He received several offers to play professional baseball, but declined for a life of education and ministry.[17]

He speaks then, in this 1914 essay, as one who has known both the joys and temptations of the game. As a result, his objections take on even more validity and sincerity. There was enough agreement with them that intercollegiate sports would be taboo at the College until the late 1920s.

The limitations on instrumental music also remained in place throughout the 1910s. The yearly cantatas were rendered a cappella, since the Church of the Brethren still did not use pianos or organs in their services. A minor breach was made in 1917, when the trustees decided that:

> *A piano might be placed in the Chapel in Rider Memorial Hall for practice, and used during special occasions such as literary society meetings, musicals, etc.; however, it is not to be used during chapel exercises, religious services, or during commencement programs.*[18]

Such caution was not ill-placed. Although the Southeastern District of the Church of the Brethren was not adverse to using musical instruments in their services, they were not co-owners of Elizabethtown College. The Eastern District, the "majority owner," was still firmly set against the use of instruments in worship. In 1914, district elders of the Harrisburg First Church closed an urban mission because its leader had used musical instruments. Even by the mid-twenties, the subject would be too controversial to discuss in Harrisburg.[19] The Southern District, the College's other owner, was similarly inclined against instruments.

Since the church was also anti-tobacco, it followed that the College should continue to be so as well. Although some Church of the Brethren members grew and sold tobacco as a crop, any member who did so (or used tobacco in any form) could not be elected as a delegate to district and annual conferences. The use of tobacco had always been forbidden on the grounds of the College, but the College catalogue of 1917–18 went further by stating that any student using tobacco would be suspended and would not be graduated from the school.

The influence of the church was also found in the two phrases which became the official mottoes of Elizabethtown College. In 1915, D. C. Reber and H. K. Ober were asked by the trustees to select mottoes, one to be placed in Alpha Hall and the other over the rostrum in the Rider Hall chapel. The President and Vice

President selected "MAKE JESUS KING," which was placed on the arch above the pulpit.

The second motto chosen, and the one that still appears on the College seal (along with *Deus, Lux et Veritas*, or God, Light and Truth), was "EDUCATE FOR SERVICE," quite fitting for all the graduates who went into teaching, the ministry, and the mission fields. First handwritten in chalk on a slate panel on the front wall of the chapel, it was later lettered more permanently.

More student activities were established as part of that education, including in 1911 an advanced literary society. Though the Keystone Literary Society was open to all students, the new Homerian Society was intended for students in the classical course and seniors in the pedagogical and piano courses. It was also open to the faculty, provided there was room. According to the 1911–1912 college catalogue, the organization "aims to foster a higher grade of literary work than the Keystone, and lays special emphasis on argumentation, oratory, literary criticism and parliamentary practice."[20]

The year 1916 saw the birth of another student society, the Student Volunteer Band. It had nothing to do with music, but was a distinctly religious organization made up of students who had decided to dedicate their lives to religious work. There were similar chapters in all of the Brethren colleges, and the joiners were asked to sign a declaration of purpose and intent that ended, "I hereby dedicate myself to special missionary service in whatever way God may direct, at anytime, in any place, and at any cost."[21]

"Missionary service" was defined as working as a home or foreign missionary, a preacher, a child rescue worker, a city mission worker, or a teacher in a Brethren college or a similar church-related school. At weekly meetings, members would pray together, offer their good thoughts or a passage of scripture, and would plan their outside work. These activities might consist of teaching in Sunday schools, visiting the sick and shut-ins, with whom the volunteers would pray and sing, and sending flowers to the sick.

There were other activities, both connected and separate from course work. *Our College Times* gives an account of a 1912 trip of the "'local division of the Geographical Survey of E'town College'" to the Susquehanna River. The party consisted of six female students and two professors serving as chaperones. It seems to have been a combination geography field trip and picnic, interrupted only by "horrifying screams, a method the girls used to announce the sudden appearance of that terrible creature, the turtle."[22]

Our College Times of June 1914 reviews an "arbutus outing," remarking on the way the participants would get out of sight of each other on the walk: "This peculiar difficulty is accounted for, when we remember that man is prone to wander (especially if there's a woman along)."[23]

There was another arboreal excuse for walks in the woods. In 1916, the annual chestnut outing was held on October 14. The students, accompanied by Professor H. A. Via, principal of the commercial department, his wife, Jennie Miller Via, head of the vocal music department, and Elizabeth Myer, walked three miles to Tea Hill. There they hunted for chestnuts, enjoyed a picnic lunch, and played games.

Socials hosted by the faculty for the students were common. One of these on October 31, 1913 provided the students with memory games, refreshments consisting of apples, chestnuts, peanuts, stuffed dates, pretzels, pumpkin pie, and coffee, along with musical solos, recitations, and speeches by various faculty members. By 1916 the Hallowe'en social had become even more lavish. The dining room had been decorated with pumpkins, leaves, and crepe paper, Miss Myer served as toastmistress, Professor and Mrs. Via sang a duet, and Miss Gertrude Miller got the crowd into the Hallowe'en spirit with a recitation of James Whitcomb Riley's "Little Orphant Annie," while still expressing the spirit and motto of Elizabethtown College:

> You better mind yer parents, and yer teachers fond an' dear,
> An' cherish them 'at loves you, an' dry the orphant's tear,
> An' he'p the pore an' needy ones 'at clusters all about,
> Er' the Gobble-uns'll git *you*
> > Ef you
> > > Don't
> > > > Watch
> > > > > Out![24]

The times were becoming more frightening, and Elizabethtown College, sheltered as it was, was not immune to the "Gobble-uns" that haunted that decade, a decade that had begun with so much optimism, and ended with hundreds of thousands dead from war and disease.

⋘—⋙

The College community, like those at every other educational institution of its time, were very much aware of the outside world. The College seemed determined that this should be so, for in order to have a good education, students should be exposed to the controversies and questions that were a part of society and of life.

Although *Our College Times* dealt primarily with the activities of the College, many essays were published about world and national events, written both by students and faculty. These essays also reflect values and feelings toward their subjects that most likely echo the feelings of other students and faculty. An essay by Tillman H. Ebersole entitled "The Negro in America (A Theme in Rhetoric)" deals with the "color line" and the difficulties facing African-Americans. It finds hope in the increase in literacy among the group and ends: "The American Negro's ability to rise in the scale of civilization is, in a large degree like the white man's, unlimited."[25]

Another racial minority dealt with in the magazine's pages was the American Indian. George Capitanios's "The Origin and Traits of the Indian" is filled with cliches: "…proud and reserved, serious if not gloomy…brave and fond of war…fond of gambling and drinking…indifferent to pain…revengeful and cruel almost beyond belief to those who have given offense." Yet the essay is compassionate as well, ending with a flattering description: "The old time Indian had courage, dignity, self-respect, and hospitality, and not one of these qualities has entirely disappeared from the Indian of the present day."[26]

Positive depictions of racial minorities were not the only socially liberal views held by *Our College Times* writers. Woman suffrage was a subject frequently dealt with, always with a goal to its establishment. "Resolved, That woman should have the right to vote," was a frequent debate topic of the literary societies, and an unsigned article in 1911 stated that "Suffrage for women is a question of ethics. If it is right for women to vote, let the franchise be granted and trust the future to prove that women in general will show themselves as adaptable and efficient in this as in other matters."[27]

That same school year an article by Anna M. Wolgemuth appeared entitled "Women's Sphere in the Business World," and a 1912 article titled "National Blessings" states: "...the fact that California voted in favor of woman's suffrage shows that the United States has respect for woman which is indeed a blessing to our country."[28] Another major article, Orlena Wolgemuth's "Some Arguments for Woman Suffrage," appeared in 1917, and the championing of the cause continued until the nineteenth amendment to the U. S. Constitution, granting women the vote, was ratified in 1920.

The raising of campus voices over woman suffrage, however, was puny next to the cry for the passage of what would, in 1919, become the eighteenth amendment, prohibiting the manufacturing, sale, and transportation of alcoholic beverages. The official stance of the College, like that of the Church of the Brethren, was anti-alcohol, and both editorials and articles in *Our College Times* strongly supported prohibition.

The June 1914 issue's "Sic Semper Tyrannis" gives a plot for dispatching the tyrant, "King Alcohol." Ryntha B. Shelly's "The Christian's Duty Toward the Saloon" bewails the existence of "250,000 saloons in which the poison is sold which turns men into demons, causes them to commit outlandish acts, become insane, and otherwise pollute themselves."[29] The lead article in a 1918 issue is critical of the eighteen Pennsylvania representatives who had not yet voted for prohibition. The writer, Orlena Wolgemuth, suggests, years before the Religious Right would wed politics to morality, that the people of Pennsylvania "vote for no candidate for office unless he declares publicly that he is in favor of ratification."[30]

Indeed the College had established a Temperance League of which Professor Ralph Schlosser was president. At a 1916 meeting in the chapel, a guest speaker identified the "Thieves of Society" as "the gambling den, the white slave traffic, and licensed saloon."

The cause contributed its share of hyperbole. An editorial entitled "Vodka" in the March 1915 issue praises Czar Nicholas II for banning "all traffic in strong drink throughout Russia." The writer, presumably editor-in-chief Jacob S. Harley, says that "the elimination of vodka has transformed society as if by magic," and goes on:

> *The efficiency of labor has been increased fifty per cent. Even the poorest are respectably clad and adequately fed. The town meetings which had degenerated into disgraceful orgies are now in charge of the more intelligent class of peasants who discuss soberly the interests of the community. Husbands have ceased to beat their wives and remain at home to discuss domestic affairs with their families. Children ask their mothers, "Will papa always be as he is now?" Wives and children of former drunkards are invoking Heaven's blessing upon the government which has abolished vodka.*[31]

The prose smacks more of a temperance tract than of reality. Russia was now at war with Germany, and by May of 1915, its series of triumphant advances had ceased. By September, an English nurse on the Russian front wrote in her diary of "internal disturbances," and the shortage of bread: "In some parts famine already threatened to engulf the masses. The thousands of refugees swarming into the cities and towns were followed by pestilence and crime."[32]

It was a far cry from the alcohol-free utopia depicted in *Our College Times,* and that government upon which grateful families were "invoking Heaven's blessings" would be overthrown in another two years. It was, however, the tragic events of the World War, rather than a ban on vodka, that would lead to that demise.

The war was an ever present reality to the students and faculty of Elizabethtown College. World topics were frequently discussed, both in the classroom and in the pages of the College magazine. There were articles on political change in China, the internal conflicts in Mexico, and by 1914, what was then the European War.

The Church of the Brethren had affirmed the policies of non-violence and non-resistance for almost two centuries. Still, they were becoming more involved in politics, primarily as the result of the temperance movement. In January of 1915, Martin G.

Brumbaugh, a member of the church and a former president of Juniata College, a Brethren-owned school, was affirmed (rather than sworn in) as governor of Pennsylvania.

Still, the Church sought ever for peace. Before, it had tried only to keep its members from becoming parties to armed conflict, but now, on the eve of the First World War, it became more active, as it had with the temperance issue. It sought to keep governments from warring upon each other, and attempted to play a reconciliatory role.

In 1916, the Annual Brethren Conference wrote and delivered to President Woodrow Wilson a resolution stating their disapproval of war as a method of settling disputes, and requesting that their members be treated as conscientious objectors, should the United States become involved in the current war. The Eastern District, co-owners of the College, held that enlisting in the armed services forfeited membership in the church, and in 1915 removed a young man from membership because of his enlistment in the Navy.

It was only natural that the view of Elizabethtown College should be equally pacifistic. The first article to deal with the war in *Our College Times* appeared in December, 1914, and reported on a speech made at the College by a Dr. Driver on "The Present Situation in Europe." It accurately enumerates the causes of the war, but is too optimistic in predicting its eventual end. At no time is any mention made of the possible involvement of the United States.

That possibility, however, was always present. Only two months later, Owen Hershey's article, "The World's Beacon-Light," urges America to become a light to the world by maintaining absolute neutrality. In a similar article in June, "The Beacon-Light of the Centuries," Hershey says, "Let us strive to be a nation too upright for war, too righteous for murder."[33] The same issue contains Mary G. Hershey's "Lost Treasures." The treasures of the title are the human lives lost in the current war, and she urges America to flee the conflict.

All was not serious talk about war, however. These earnest articles are followed by "Class Yells:"

> Straw-berry short-cake, huckle-berry pie,
>
> V-I-C-T-O-R-Y,

Are we in it? Well, I guess,

E'town, E'town, Yes! Yes! Yes!

Chica-laca, Chica-laca, chow, chow, chow.

Boma-laca, Boma-laca, bow, wow, wow,

Chica-laca, Boma-laca, Cis, Bom, Bah,

Seniors, Seniors, Rah! Rah! Rah![34]

The official desire for victory, however, did not extend beyond the confines of the campus. Still, concerns about the war mounted. Another anti-war article appeared in November 1915, along with a report on the Homerian Literary Society's debate on whether or not America should increase its armaments. The meeting's tone was lightened by unmarried professor Elizabeth Myer's protest when one of the debaters used the term, "old maids." "A better way of expressing this," she said, showing the dry humor that made her a campus favorite, "is unclaimed blessings."[35]

Further articles appeared on "Preparedness," not for war, but for a life of service, "The Path to Universal Peace," "The Mission of America," and others, most of which were sincere but naïve, assuming that it was always possible to gain peace without waging war.

Even President Reber, in the introduction to the June, 1917 "Senior Number" of *Our College Times*, which served as a yearbook, stated: "You enter the arena of life in a world crisis. How will you meet it? How will you answer the call to duty?"[36] By then, the United States had entered the war, and Pershing's men had landed in France.

The change in the attitude of the College to the war was abrupt. There were no more calls from students for neutrality. Instead they wrote articles like "Good Marksmanship," in which freshman Philip Greenblatt praises the shooting abilities of American soldiers. "Our fore-fathers who were utterly unfamiliar with all military movements, but who were sure death as shots were able to overwhelm much superior forces of the best-drilled soldiers of Europe, and the truth of those facts have not changed."[37]

Greenblatt's paean to riflemen seems almost Gandhian in comparison to "The Mission of United States" by senior Aaron Edris:

Is there one so cowardly among us, as to allow this noble nation to die in cold blood? Fellow-citizens, arise to service. The man who does not serve his country is not worthy of a country.

If, to-day we will not clasp the sword to preserve democracy, to-morrow we will take up arms to defend aristocracy.… Never let us for one moment forget the high and holy mission with which we entered this war, no matter what it costs. …Give me democracy or give me death.[38]

This was a strange, if not shocking, piece to appear in a journal officially published by a Church of the Brethren college. Edris was not talking about non-combatant service, but about "clasping the sword."

It was most definitely not the position of the Brethren Church. Several months before, on January 9, the church's General Conference, meeting in Goshen City, Indiana, declared that "…war or any participation in war is wrong and utterly incompatible with the spirit, example, and teachings of Jesus Christ."[39] This "Goshen Statement" further urged Brethren not to enlist in the service, wear a military uniform, drill, learn any of the arts of war, or do anything that would contribute to war.

In July 1918, several church leaders were called to Washington, D. C., and were ordered to withdraw what the government considered the treasonous advice not to drill or wear uniforms. Threatened with imprisonment, they agreed.

Many young Brethren, including some Elizabethtown College students, went into the service, where they accepted mostly non-combatant duties. *Our College Times* of October 1917 shows three former students, Alfred Eckroth, Raymond Gephart, and Paul Burkholder, in military training camps. In November of 1918, just before the war ended, the magazine began to run "Khaki Column," which included extracts from letters from those in the service. David Markley wrote from the hospital at Camp Meade, where he worked along with three other former Elizabethtown students.

According to S. Z. Sharp's 1923 *Educational History of the Church of the Brethren*, college attendance was reduced 40 percent by the war, even though "the College management took a firm stand against military training, and the principles of non-resistance were strictly carried out."[40]

Nevertheless, ten names are listed in *Our College Times* as serving in France, and over forty servicemen's names and addresses are given, including such familiar names as Falkenstein, Ober, Via, and Reber. Only one death of a serviceman is listed, that of Walter Forney Eshleman, Class of 1912. His death at Camp Dix on October 2, 1918, was not combat related, but was caused by the disease known as Spanish Influenza.

The influenza that struck in 1918–1919 would eventually kill twenty million people worldwide, and half a million in the United States. More American soldiers in France died from influenza than from enemy fire. The same issue of *Our College Times* that reports Eshleman's death begins with an article by Professor Jacob S. Harley. Its title, "Separate and Aloof," tells of the recent quarantine of the College, not to keep the influenza in, but to keep it *out*.

Although "the borough of Elizabethtown is being ravaged by the influenza," the College itself was so far untouched. "There is not a healthier community anywhere," says Harley. To keep the influenza at bay, the College made an arrangement with the Board of Health that those who lived on campus would confine themselves there, and the College would be closed to the public:

> We have withdrawn from the multitude for fear of contagion; here is our refuge from the scourge that is sweeping the country; this is an oasis in the desert... The great outside world bears the yellow label of disease — we are clean of the plague....
>
> If we steer clear of the epidemic, for at this writing there is scarcely a trace of illness of any kind, should we not regard it as an intervention of Providence, and should we not pour forth our hearts in Te Deums of gratitude? "A thousand shall fall at thy

side, and ten thousand at thy right hand; but it shall
not come nigh thee."[41]

Harley's hope for divine intervention met with no better result
than did the self-preserving hubris of Prospero in Poe's "The
Masque of the Red Death." Only a month later there was a report
that several students had contracted influenza. "We have been
greatly grieved that the epidemic claimed three of our students.
They were not sick however when they left College Hill, but suc-
cumbed to the disease in their homes."[42]

The same issue, under "School Notes," lightly asks:

> December already!
> Christmas is coming!
> Did you have the Flu?[43]

If not, most of the students would probably contract it and
survive. The College closed for four weeks during the height of the
epidemic. The following June, *Our College Times* had an "In
Memoriam" page edged in black that listed the names of ten students and alumni whose lives had been taken by influenza.

D. C. Reber did not have to deal with the influenza epidemic, at
least not as President of Elizabethtown College. He had been offered
a teaching position at Manchester College in Indiana. Since the
classroom had always been his first love, he left his administrative
duties at Elizabethtown behind with some relief.

The natural person to fill his position was Henry Kulp Ober, the
man who had been his Vice President for so many years. Reber and
Ober had done more than merely work side by side at the College.
In the first decade of the school's growth, the "horse and buggy
days," as Ober later called them, he and Reber had traveled together
all over the area, working to spread the word of the College and
raise money for its well-being. Harry, the strong and lanky bay horse
that pulled Ober's buggy, was well known to Brethren for many
miles around.

From the accounts of all who knew him, Ober was enthusiastic,
energetic (if his "half-run" walk was any indication), and possessed

of a sincere warmth. His personality was magnetic, as described in the *History of the Church of the Brethren, Eastern Pennsylvania: 1915–1965*: "In his sermons, his stories, and his manner of speaking and gesturing he held a rapt attention. In his benedictions he developed a crescendo which could best be described as having a heavenly ring which hearers just could not forget."[44]

At the same time, he could be a shrewd businessman. He had served as acting treasurer and business manager of the College from 1904 to 1911, and was successful in both private business matters and in the early endowment campaign of the College.

Ober was born to a thrifty, Pennsylvania German family on January 2, 1878, near Elizabethtown, and resided in the area his entire life, though he traveled widely, ranging as far as Japan. He received degrees from Millersville State Normal School, Franklin & Marshall College, and Columbia.

His teaching career began in rural schools, but in 1902 he came to Elizabethtown College, with which he was associated until his death. His tenure as president, from 1918 to 1921, and from 1924 to the beginning of 1928, would be filled with efforts to make Elizabethtown a full-fledged college, especially in the field of the sciences.

One of his first steps toward that goal was to insist that the College begin a major building fund and endowment campaign to take care of both current and future needs, and primarily to become accredited. Although students received diplomas from Elizabethtown College upon graduation, they could not receive baccalaureate degrees, and had to transfer their credits to a "standard" college, one that had received academic standardization. There, after taking a required number of courses, they would eventually receive a baccalaureate.

In January 1919, the faculty requested that an effort be made to standardize Elizabethtown College, and the Board agreed. The state requirement was that the applying college have a minimum of six full-time professors, and Elizabethtown had more than twice that number. The challenge was a financial one.

The state required a standard college to have a total of $500,000 in buildings, equipment, and endowment. Although Elizabethtown had been in existence for nearly twenty years, it fell dishearteningly short of that goal. Still, everyone directly involved with the College felt it was attainable, and it was decided to raise an endowment fund of $250,000, with the surplus placed in a building fund until the half a million dollar total was met. The first buildings added were to be a women's dormitory and a science hall.

Ralph W. Schlosser was put in charge of the campaign, along with three trustees. The one who would become most involved was Isaac W. Taylor, the College's treasurer, who was relieved of his duties so that he could work more closely with Schlosser on raising the needed money. The fund was named the Jesse C. Ziegler Memorial Fund, after the first chairman of the Board of Trustees, who had served for eighteen years and had died only several months before.

Now Elizabethtown College began undertaking in earnest what would become one of the primary activities of colleges in the twentieth century, soliciting funds. Schlosser and the trustees first went to individual churches and congregation leaders, and generally received a positive response, so that by July, $80,000 had been received in gifts and pledges from southern Pennsylvania churches.

Such an auspicious beginning called for a further investment, and Schlosser and Taylor were given permission by the trustees to buy a car to use on solicitation trips. In January 1920, they purchased a used, red, Model-T Ford for $400. With this car, Schlosser, Taylor, and a number of elders, G. N. Falkenstein among them, drove from house to house, asking for contributions and pledges from members of various Church of the Brethren congregations.

Articles in *Our College Times* cited the reasons for raising endowment money, with H. K. Ober's "Why Elizabethtown College Should Have an Endowment Fund" (April 1919) being the most detailed explanation. *Our College Times* also began to run a lengthy section every issue entitled "Endowment Campaign Notes," which told both amusing and inspiring anecdotes concerning the campaign.

One woman decided to contribute because "This last year I gave more to the church than during any year, but it is also a fact that my chickens never laid better."[45] There is a story of a washerwoman with a daughter in the mission field giving twenty-five dollars, and a tale of a solicitor's pen running out of ink, making it necessary for the donor to sign in Bixby's Shoe Polish.

There are also negative examples, with quotations followed by comments about the speakers:

"'I can't give anything to our church schools.' She spends twenty cents a week for chocolate candy."

"'I have no children to send. It will never do me any good.' He runs a Cadillac and owns four houses."

"'I can hardly make ends meet.' He chews three packs of tobacco a week."[46]

As is apparent from the above comments, many people were reluctant to donate. Some had trouble understanding the terms of the endowment, particularly the fact that their pledges, to be donated over a ten-year period, bore interest at four percent in order to make it the equivalent of cash. They felt that they would be paying interest on their own money for ten years.

Others were still wary of higher education, just as they had been twenty years earlier when the College was founded. It was not an altogether irrational sentiment, considering the history of the Brethren. As J. G. Meyer pointed out in an *Our College Times* article, many Brethren had forgotten that the church had a long history of education and scholarship. Half a million volumes had come from the church's press before the American Revolution. Instead, they recalled only their persecution in Europe at the hands of those controlling the universities.

But, Meyer stresses, perhaps the greater problem was that many Brethren had become farmers, moving into rural sections where higher education was absent, and where any education was difficult to find.[47] The anti-education faction used biblical injunctions to support their argument, and such faith-held beliefs were hard to shake.

Still, there were a greater number who supported "their" college in Elizabethtown, and in July of 1920, a year after the campaign began, *Our College Times* ran the following dramatic paragraph:

> At first thought the task seemed IMPOSSIBLE. The solicitors are now over more than half the field and have found the task DIFFICULT. But judging from the

*success of the work on the whole thus far it is evident that **the task will be DONE**.*[48]

At that point, thirty-five congregations made up of nearly seven thousand Brethren had received house-to-house canvasses, and had contributed almost $270,000, a third of which had already been paid. Over a third of the congregations had surpassed their quotas, and there were still five thousand Brethren to be solicited.

Despite the ravages of a world war and a worldwide epidemic, Elizabethtown College was entering the 1920s in a position of strength and financial security that it had never known before. Its situation would continue to improve, and the next decade would be one of unprecedented growth, both physically and in terms of educational quality, before the 1930s brought the darkest hours of all.

1 Minutes, Elizabethtown College Board of Trustees July 29, 1915
2 *History of the Church of the Brethren of the Eastern District of Pennsylvania*, p. 640
3 Minutes, Elizabethtown College Board of Trustees, January 11, 1916
4 *Elizabethtown: The First Three Centuries*, p. 167.
5 *Eleventh Annual Catalogue of Elizabethtown College, 1910–1911*, p. 33
6 Ibid.
7 *Our College Times*, June 1911, p. 12
8 *Our College Times*, January 1912, p. 21
9 *Our College Times*, September 1915, p. 13
10 *Eleventh Annual Catalogue of Elizabethtown College, 1910–1911*, p. 46
11 *Committee of Literary Societies Report to Faculty*, October 1, 1917.
12 *Our College Times*, February 1912, p. 7
13 Minutes, Elizabethtown College Board of Trustees, January 11, 1917
14 *Our College Times*, January, 1910, p. 3
15 *Our College Times*, March 1914, pp. 15-18
16 Ibid.
17 *The Etownian*, October 28, 1957, p. 1
18 Minutes, Elizabethtown College Board of Trustees, July 24, 1917
19 *Moving Toward the Mainstream*, p. 266
20 *Twelfth Annual Catalogue: Elizabethtown College, 1911–1912*, p. 40
21 *Our College Times*, November 1916, p. 12
22 *Our College Times*, June 1912, p. 21-22
23 *Our College Times*, June 1914, p. 21
24 James Whitcomb Riley, "Little Orphant Annie"
25 *Our College Times*, June 1910, p. 9
26 *Our College Times*, November 1913, p. 12
27 *Our College Times*, April 1911, p. 4
28 *Our College Times*, January 1912, p. 15
29 *Our College Times*, June 1915, p. 17
30 *Our College Times*, June–July 1918, p. 8
31 *Our College Times*, March 1915, pp. 10–11

32 Florence Farmborough: *Nurses at the Russian Front, A Diary 1914–18*, Constable, London, 1974
33 *Our College Times*, June 1915, p. 28
34 *Our College Times*, June 1915, p. 45
35 *Our College Times*, November 1915, p. 17
36 *Our College Times*, June 1917, p. 7
37 *Our College Times*, December 1917, p. 16
38 *Our College Times*, April–May 1918, p. 13
39 *Annual Conference Minutes*, 1920, pp. 11–12, cited in *Moving Toward the Mainstream*
40 *Educational History of the Church of the Brethren*, p. 265
41 *Our College Times*, November 1918, p. 3–5
42 *Our College Times*, December 1918, p. 12
43 Ibid.
44 *History of the Church of the Brethren, Eastern Pennsylvania: 1915–1965*, p. 224
45 *Our College Times*, Volume XVI, No. 1, p. 6
46 *Our College Times*, Volume XVI, No. 5, p. 5
47 *Our College Times*, April 1919, p. 6–7
48 *Our College Times*, Volume XVI, No. 10, p. 5

Chapter 5

1920–1930

"A constantly threatening deficit in the current expenses..."

The red college Ford continued its travels, and the College's coffers continued to fill. By December 12, 1920, $385,000 had been raised. By February 1921, Elizabethtown Borough had donated another $30,000, and the final total in cash and pledges reached $420,000. Added to the College's inventory, the grand total was $550,000, which was $50,000 more than the amount required for the state to standardize it.

The board had anticipated success, and on January 4, 1921, had made an application for a charter giving the College the right to grant degrees. The bureaucratic procedures were followed in due course: a petition to the County Court of Common Pleas on February 17, the amendment of the charter on June 25, and the endorsement by the State Council of Education on December 19 and sealed on December 23, 1921, "granting to such corporation the privilege of conferring degrees of art, pure and applied science, philosophy and literature, and theology, but not including law and medicine, do approve the same."[1] The county court approved the amended charter on January 14, 1922, and at last Elizabethtown College could officially grant baccalaureate degrees.

The Class of 1922 would be the first to benefit from the accreditation. A. C. Baugher was the first of twelve students to receive their baccalaureates that June, even though he had earlier received a non-standardized degree from the College.

Standardization opened a number of academic doors to Elizabethtown students. In December 1923, Herman V. Ames, Dean of the University of Pennsylvania, wrote to President Meyer, saying, "the graduate school is willing to admit your recent graduates namely, those who received degrees since the State Council of Education granted the College the privilege of conferring the baccalaureate degree."[2] It was only the first of many graduate schools willing to admit Elizabethtown alumni.

The successful endowment campaign and its very human result was a grand way to welcome the 1920s, a period of growth for the College in many ways. It would also see more changes in the presidency of the College than in any other equivalent period. From 1918 to 1929, five different men held the office.

Two and a half years after taking the helm from D. C. Reber in 1918, H. K. Ober requested a leave of absence to earn his A. M. degree from Columbia University. Several months before, Vice President Ralph Schlosser had requested a similar leave to do graduate work, also at Columbia. At the same time he was also deeply involved in running the endowment campaign.

The Board of Trustees had already elected J. G. Meyer as Second Vice President when Ober had gone to the World Sunday School Convention in Japan. Meyer, the teacher who had stressed the importance of a new science building several years earlier, had effectively acted as chairman of the College faculty during both Ober and Schlosser's absence. Upon Ober's decision to attend Columbia, the board asked Meyer if he would serve as President. He accepted, and occupied the office for three years, until Ober's return.

It was under Meyer's presidency that the school became fully accredited. Meyer also stressed the importance of revising the courses available to more closely reflect the added honor and burden of standardization. If Elizabethtown College was going to grant degrees, then students were to receive the kind of education expected from such a program.

During Meyer's first year as president in 1921, the College community witnessed several other important events beside accreditation. Fairview Hall, a new apartment building, was dedicated on June 7. The first floor contained living quarters for professors and their families, while the upper floors held dormitories. At the same time, The Maples, a double brick building, was built on College Avenue, along with two double cottages to house faculty members.

Another less tangible but just as lasting edifice created in 1921 was the College's Alma Mater. Both music and lyrics were written by Jennie Via, head of the music department, and the song was first performed by a male quartet, of which A. C. Baugher was a member. It was sung often during campus programs and at numerous churches in the districts where the quartet performed. The lyrics are:

We hail thee Alma Mater dear,
As now we sing thy praise.
O let thy walls and storied halls
Resound with endless lays.

(Chorus)
We love thy sons so noble.
Thy daughters fair and true;
We love thee ever, oh E. C.,
And thy colors Gray and Blue.

(Verse 2)
The strong and fair alike do share
The labours of thy hand.
Together they proclaim always
Thy glory through the land.

(Verse 3)
As long as breezes 'round thee blow,
And countless ages roll,
May Heaven's blessings on thee rest
While we thy name extol.

The tune is a dramatic anthem, and the climax contains a tight chromatic harmony that is more suitable for a close-harmony quartet than for non-musicians. In recent years there was some movement to replace the song as being "politically incorrect," but any sexism involved in referring to men as noble and strong, and women as fair and true, was counterbalanced by tradition and, perhaps, the fact that the song was penned by a woman.

With an alma mater and a successful fund raising campaign behind it, the College continued to grow. At a meeting on November 6, 1922, the board of trustees voted to increase the productive endowment fund to $500,000[3] and the building fund to $250,000, as a continuation of the previous campaign. An alumni committee recommended that the College buy twenty-two acres "and 25 perches[4]" of land that bordered the campus on the east, using money from the Alumni Fund, to which the Board concurred.

This area had a stream of running water, and both alumni and students were anxious that a lake be formed for skating, boating, and other activities. Construction was quickly started on a long wall across a ravine that would contain the new lake, but nearly two years after the land purchase, the project was not yet finished. A 1924 editorial in *Our College Times* pleaded:

> *What about the lake?*
> *Is the lake going to be finished in time for skating?*
> *Is it in the embryonic stage? If it is let us hope to*
> *see metamorphosis before cold weather sets in. It is an*
> *eye-sore the way it is at present.*[5]

A month later, the paper carried an article reporting that the alumni decided to pay to have a retaining wall constructed, and the students offered to dig the trench for the 450-foot back wall. After two weeks of work, the concrete wall along the front of the lake was finished. It was 400 feet in length, an average of eight feet high, and had a solid concrete spillway. The students, along with digging the trench, had helped to mix and haul the concrete.

The waters finally overflowed the spillway the following year, 1925, and a contest was held to find the best name for the new campus addition. Eli Engle '27 won the prize for suggesting Lake

Placida, and the name continues to this day to be suitable, not only for the peaceful site, but for the concern for peace that still pervades the campus.

The religious emphasis of the College was still very strong in the 1920s, and most students came from Brethren families. The 1923 college census gives the following list of religious denominations, followed by the number of students belonging to each:

Church of the Brethren: 140
Lutheran: 9
Mennonite: 8
Reformed : 8
Methodist: 5
United Brethren: 3
Presbyterian: 3
Evangelical: 3
Catholic: 2
Undenominational: 18[6]

Eighteen students, some of whom may have been "unchurched," may seem like a large number for what was essentially still a church school, but for those living in the vicinity with no church and possibly no belief system, Elizabethtown College provided an opportunity to receive a college education. The original charter stressed that the College was open to every student, regardless of faith, and this was apparently taken quite seriously.

Student expectations can also be seen in the list entitled "Future," signifying what careers students planned:

Teaching 83
Business 30
Missions 12
Ministry 6
Music 7
Engineering 5
Medicine 1
Undecided 57[7]

That the majority should be interested in teaching, business, missions, and the ministry comes as no surprise. The fact that over a quarter of the students did not yet know what they wanted to do with their lives, however, merely indicates that little has changed among college students. Just as it is today, college was an experience of growth and self-discovery.

For a few years in the 1920s, that experience was not limited to those of college age. With accreditation, all the courses taught were truly on a college level, but such had not been the case before. Many Elizabethtown students had attended in order to receive a fourth year of high school level work, or to take some of the short commercial courses. Now that the College was accredited, however, many felt that it should not continue to offer high school level courses.

By 1923, the "preparatory" department of the College, was known as the Elizabethtown Academy, and was headed by Alvin P. Wenger as Principal. But the Academy was short-lived. At a meeting of the board on October 20, 1925, it was decided to have only college level students and courses on the campus, and the Academy ceased to function after the 1925–26 school year. From that point on, Elizabethtown College would be a college not only in name.

◆━◆

Henry Ober had made good use of his temporary separation from Elizabethtown College. He received his M. A. from Columbia in 1922 and then attended the University of Pennsylvania from 1922 to 1924, where he completed his Ph.D. residency requirements.

The timing for his return to the presidency of Elizabethtown College seemed fortuitous, for by the end of 1923, Jacob G. Meyer, the current President, had decided to continue his own studies and earn his Ph.D. He presented his resignation to the Board, which requested that he stay on until his successor could be appointed.

The Board of Trustees wanted Henry Ober to return to the presidency, and on January 26, 1924, elected him to the office. He attended the next Board meeting, where, surprisingly, he declined the offer. Three of the board members met with him privately and learned that he had several conditions under which he would accept. The College had to hire a "field man" to recruit students, accounts should be audited by a CPA, an annual budget of expenses should be made, there should be a plan to relieve dissatisfied pledge signers, and "an effort be made immediately to clean up the present indebtedness [of $3700]."[8] Finally, at the March 28th board meeting, Ober once again accepted the presidency.

Jacob G. Meyer went off to New York University on a fellowship, and earned his Ph.D in 1926. He never returned in a professional capacity to Elizabethtown. From 1925 to 1939, he served as Dean of the School of Education at Manchester College, a Brethren college in North Manchester, Indiana. During the 1938–39 school year, Meyer was visiting professor at both the University of Chicago and Northwestern University. In 1940, he became President of Milton College, a post he held until his retirement in 1944. He died on March 6, 1951.

Henry Ober's second term began, as it would end, in sadness for the College family. On May 19, 1924, less than two months after Ober's acceptance of the presidency, Elizabeth Myer died. She was the only member of the original faculty of the College still teaching there, and her death at the age of sixty was a great loss for students, alumni, and her colleagues.

Our College Times of June first ran an obituary, extracts of the sermon preached at her funeral, a report on the memorial services held in the College chapel, and resolutions of sympathy. The obituary stated:

> *While her scrupulous insistence upon a high standard of living and good behavior was sometimes resented by those under her charge, no one could doubt her devotion to the right, her love for the cause of religion, and her sincere desire to influence the young people about her for good... She was also sympathetic and kind, and had a warm place in the heart of many a student, who will bless her memory. Her very eccentricities endeared her to us.*[9]

She was buried in her family cemetery near Bareville. Though she neither married nor had children, she had served as a loving surrogate mother to hundreds of students. In 1961 Myer Hall was named in her honor.

⋘⋙—⋘⋙

The alumni over whom Elizabeth Myer had sternly yet tenderly watched were making their own ways in the world. In early 1925, John Miller, secretary-treasurer of the Evy Shoe Company and president of the Lititz Gas Company, was the first of many alumni to serve as a trustee of the College.

Besides being primarily responsible for the land purchases that nearly doubled the size of the campus, alumni were active in other aspects of campus growth during the 1920s. In 1925, the Alumni Board of Directors began to plan for a new gymnasium building that would move the campus athletic facilities from the cramped confines of Rider Hall's basement. The plan was supported overwhelmingly by the student body. An editorial in *Our College Times* predicted that "a $40,000 gymnasium will return $80,000 indirectly to the College in ten years. It will be the greatest asset to the College in attracting new students, it will keep those who are here."[10]

The $40,000 figure stated was a bit of student spin, considerably less than the $60,000 amount the Alumni Board wished to allocate to the project, seen as an auditorium with an 80 by 100 foot playing area. A joint venture between the College and the alumni was set up to raise $70,000. A man named Bayard Heydrick was employed to raise the funds, but by October 18, 1926, only $20,000 had been raised.

President Ober, who had been official manager of the Auditorium-Gymnasium Campaign, asked to be relieved of his duties. The request was but a foreshadowing of the stress that would eventually cause him to resign the presidency. A crushing emotional weight had fallen on him several months before when, on April 12, 1926, his son Stanley had died.

Henry Ober, like so many of his generation, had lost infant children. He and his wife had had a ten-month-old son, Henry, die many years before. But their son Stanley was an adult, full of talent and promise. He had graduated from Elizabethtown College's pedagogical course in 1922, the same year that he was ordained a minister in the Church of the Brethren. Stanley took his senior year at Juniata College, from which he was graduated in 1924, and began postgraduate work in the summer of 1924 at Columbia, the same school from which his father had received his master's degree. He was principal of Salisbury High School when he was stricken with appendicitis.

The attack proved fatal. It was a great shock, not only to his family, but to the entire campus. Fifteen hundred friends and relatives attended the funeral, including the student bodies of Salisbury High School and the College, where classes were cancelled for the day.

Those who knew Henry Ober felt that his son's death, in the words of a church history, was "a blow so shattering that he never fully became his former self, and hence that date marks the beginning of his declining health and vigor."[11] He and his wife Cora were very close: "...for all the years of his life [she] was his beloved. He rarely referred to her as simply his wife; she was his girl friend, his queen, or whatever endearing name his fertile mind could create appropriate to the occasion."[12] Still, their love could not prevent the decline in Ober's health that began with Stanley's untimely death.

The plans for the gymnasium had to be scaled back when it became apparent that the $70,000 goal would not be met. The Board of Trustees voted to erect a smaller building in 1927, and a Lancaster architect submitted plans for a building that would cost $37,000, but even that proved too costly.

As plans for the gymnasium foundered, those for another building were proceeding more smoothly, thanks in large part to the Gibble family, and more specifically to Jacob Gibble Meyer, who had once served as president of the College. Meyer, whose mother was a Gibble, had begun soliciting funds for a science building from the Gibbles years before. During the 1919–1921 College campaign, all Gibble pledges and cash were placed in the Gibble Science Building Fund.

By 1925, *Our College Times* reported: "At a recent reunion of the Gibble family, that clan, which has long had this project in its care, and which has already massed a considerable sum of money in pledges and cash, took definite steps to attain their goal. A number of solicitors were appointed to solicit the members of their family in the various communities, for financial aid."[13] Although it seems that most of the Gibbles would have been contacted by that time, the family ranged widely, and solicitations were made to Gibbles living as far as Illinois.

At the end of 1926 the trustees authorized President Ober, Treasurer J. Z. Herr, and a committee of the Gibble family to develop final plans for a science building. Bids were opened the following May, and a year later, on May 26, 1928, the Gibble Science Hall was finished and dedicated. It completed a vision that had begun twelve years earlier, when science professor J. G. Meyer had presented his first tentative plans for a science building to the trustees. The new facility was a visible symbol of the College's dedication to modern education and the value of the sciences.

While the path to the Gibble Science Hall was slow but steady, the road to the gymnasium was filled with jagged peaks and deep valleys. When $37,000 proved to be too much to raise, the trustees downsized once again. However, this was not a project for which money could be raised over a long period of time; the need was too great, and the demand from students too pressing.

The desire for the new gym may easily be gauged from the response of the students to the rough drawings of the building, which they were shown in January 1927, after chapel exercises: "President Ober showed the plans to the student body amid rounds of applause that surely could have been heard over the entire town."[14]

The students were obviously ready for a gymnasium of any size, and the trustees finally gave it to them. The structure, on which construction would begin August first, would now be 60 by 70 feet with a projected cost of $22,000. It would be only one of several changes that would affect the campus that year. The editors of *Our College Times* looked forward to them with a prophetic editorial in April 1927, describing student excitement for the 1927–28 school year, not only because of the new gym and science buildings, but also because the number of tennis courts would increase from six to twelve, several thousand pine trees planted beyond the lake would be starting to grow, and the new athletic field would be covered with grass.

This athletic field was another gift from the alumni, and during that April much work was being done on it. A new baseball diamond had been staked off and rolled flat, and a new, oval-shaped, quarter-mile track had been surveyed and laid out, and was currently being surfaced and rolled. On the playing fields and in the class-rooms, there was much about which to be enthusiastic.

One of the few areas to come under fire, however, was the library. Lewis D. Rose, a 1911 graduate of the College and an ordained minister of the Church of the Brethren, had been the librarian of the College from 1907 to 1911, and had taken on the responsibility again in 1921. His labors in his *sanctum sanctorum*, where he spent many more hours than were expected of him, were not always appreciated by the student body. A 1928 *Our College Times* editorial complains: "Library accommodations, as found at present, fail to meet the wholesome approval and satisfaction of the students. Who is to blame?"[15]

The insinuation was thinly veiled. Among the specific complaints raised was frustration at the lack of sufficient reference works; on occasion twelve students would be searching for one book, which had already been checked out by another student for two weeks. "Library management...is absolutely undesirable and in no wise should such injustice be tolerated by a democratic institution."[16]

The complaint is noteworthy, not because Rose was neglectful in his duties nor because the students were justified in making such accusations, but because the complaint was made at all, and especially in such a public forum. The editorial was a blatant attack on the way a facility of the College was managed, and the library and its management were depicted as not only unsatisfactory, but unwholesome and even undemocratic. One finds it difficult to imagine such an attack on a pillar of the school in earlier days.

This attack is indicative of the greater freedom of expression that the College administration was allowing students. Instead of ignoring the young whippersnappers, or perhaps even privately chastising those who dared to criticize the institution, the College representative under attack responded. Lewis Rose answered his critics with a lengthy article in the next *Our College Times,* titled "Library Renders Service." The subhead ran, "Equals Other College Libraries. Appreciation Lacking." Rose's text partly reads:

> *The mad, killing pace of running the library in*
> *high gear day and night, that was in vogue during the*

*last five years, is gone. Because a man is interested in
his work is no good reason to make all kinds of
demands. Only with the utmost care has a complete
nervous, physical wreck been avoided.... It may be
possible that the librarian has attempted to do too
much during the last five years, and as a result professors and students may be "spoiled."*[17]

Rose suggests a simple solution to the students' problems: at
the beginning of each semester professors should submit a bibliogra-
phy with the books needed for course work, to be put on the reserve
or non-circulating shelves. The librarian then turns the attack, putting an unexpected onus on the students: "During the last decade
unusual demands have been made on the library and yet, during
this period, not one senior class has presented a memorial to
the library."[18]

Apparently the students were not guilt-ridden enough to cease
their complaints, and Rose followed up his article with a chapel talk
in April. *Our College Times* gave it a mixed review: "While the general tone of the talk may have savored of caustic reproof," the article
stated, "some constructive information was also diffused."[19] *Our
College Times* then resurrects the ogre of anti-democracy: "If the
spirit of democracy should flourish anywhere it should be [in the
library]. However, in regard to a certain change within these hal-
lowed walls, the librarian spoke thus: 'Should you ask me why, I
would hardly be able to supply a reason, but that it is a question of
administration, and as such is not open to discussion.'"[20]

Further complaints against the administration, this time even
more direct, appeared in a 1929 editorial about the lack of cleanli-
ness on the campus:

*Not only is the campus somewhat out of shape, but
the buildings are in the same condition. The basement at
the east end of Alpha Hall is in a filthy condition...some
of the classrooms need a general cleaning out...*

*While the students may be blamed for some of
the uncleanliness, the root of the matter lies in the
administration.*[21]

The question naturally arises as to what created an atmosphere in which the administration of the College could be openly criticized in the official student publication. Actually, a certain amount of openness had always been a part of Elizabethtown College. The administration and faculty had never made a secret of the many difficulties the College faced over the years. That honesty was one of the qualities that had created a sense of family in the school.

Another change was that students were playing a more active role in campus affairs. During the 1923–24 school year, student government was reorganized into a Ladies' and a Gentlemen's Student Council, each having seven members. These students demanded new constitutions and bylaws of the Welfare Associations, to a certain extent adopting the rules and regulations that determined their own behavior. It meant a greater sense of self-government and greater responsibility.

Nevertheless, administration and faculty still ultimately ruled, as could be seen with the new demerit system. If a student received twenty-five demerits, his or her parents were notified by the president; fifty demerits meant suspension for two weeks; seventy-five meant expulsion. The harshness of the system can be seen in the fact that any unexcused absence from church, Sunday school, prayer meeting, chapel, or any class work was two demerits.

This demerit system received its share of student criticism. In 1925 an editorial ran in *Our College Times*, stating that the practice of giving demerits to male students who did not have their lights out by 10:30 P.M. was "not only absurd, but...it cheapens the disciplinary value and significance of the demerit system."[22] The following year a similar editorial on chaperonage said that the female students "regard their rooms as prison cells under present...undesirable conditions."[23]

Another reason for the overall questioning of authority may be found in the times themselves. The "roaring twenties" were in full throat, and youth was in rebellion all over the country. Perhaps it was felt by faculty and administration that a bit of administration-bashing was preferable to parties with bathtub gin, that if the students were not permitted to blow off steam in a literary sense, they might do so in a far more self-destructive manner.

The students had their small victories. In 1925, an editorial entitled "Caps and Gowns" told of the students' desire to adopt this garb at graduation exercises, on the grounds that it would end "uneven appearance," and would ease the financial burden of new graduation clothes. The writer apparently expected administrative opposition, saying that, "Every individual is on most unfamiliar terms with the word innovation, and at its mere mention is apt to shrink back in misgiving and apprehension."[24] The trustees, however, were open to this kind of innovation, and approved the use of caps and gowns in January 1926.

≈§—§≈

At least Henry Ober was spared having to deal directly with the demands of the vocally rebellious students in 1928. On October 27, 1927, he had requested to be relieved of the presidency. The Board was reluctant to acquiesce. S. H. Hertzler, the board president, stated that the resignation:

> *...was accepted only after hearing the one com-pelling reason, the physical condition of President Ober. Next to the members of the faculty probably no one knows better than the trustees what a nerve strain it must be to administer the affairs of a college. To bear up under the daily grind of the routine work in addi-tion to the financial embarrassment due to a constant-ly threatening deficit in the current expenses as well as an assured deficit due to needed repairs and improve-ments, many of which demand prompt solution, besides harmonizing the divergent views of the State Standards and the constituency, to say nothing of the students' appeals for their needs, many of which he would gladly have granted had it been in his power to do so, requires not only rare skill but also a good strong healthy body and practically unlimited energy.[25]*

Hertzler's statement, clearly expressing the financial and philo-sophical problems of running a college, is a further indication of the honesty with which the administration of the College treated its students. What he did not include, however, is the impact of the death of Ober's son Stanley on his decision to resign.

Henry Ober had only a little more than a decade to live, dying in 1939 at sixty-one. He remained active in church conference work, and became pastor of the Elizabethtown Church of the Brethren in 1928. He returned to the College as secretary of the Board of Trustees from 1930 to 1936, when he became chairman, an office he held until his death. Ober was widely known, loved, and respected. Over two thousand people attended his funeral services.

The 1915–1965 *History of the Church of the Brethren* talks about the qualities that endeared him to students:

> *How he loved young people! He loved to be in their lively meetings.... His expression of surprise was a lusty, "Denksht du?", and after an illustration of a grave subject he would exclaim, "Yammer nock amohl." ...He urged the young men to show appreciation and love for their wives. Often he would end his injunction by saying, "If you love her, tell her so, out loud." ...He knew that to identify with people, particularly young people, required that he become one of them.*[26]

One of the young people with whom Henry Ober certainly "identified" was Ralph Schlosser. Ober was teaching at Elizabethtown College when nineteen-year-old Schlosser became a student in the English Scientific and Pedagogical courses in 1905.

Ralph Wiest Schlosser had a typical Elizabethtown College student upbringing. His parents were farmers, who gave him early religious training and encouraged his education. He taught in a rural school before he entered Elizabethtown, and in his second year of study he became a student instructor, teaching preparatory subjects. In 1911 he received a bachelor's degree from Elizabethtown and Ursinus, and a master's degree from Ursinus in 1912. He became a professor of English and languages at Elizabethtown in 1911, Vice President in 1918, and dean in 1922, the same year he received an M. A. from Columbia.

Besides his other contributions, Schlosser had successfully run the first endowment campaign in 1919–1920, without which the College could not have become accredited. Therefore it was only natural that the Board of Trustees should first come to him upon the resignation of Henry Ober. On November 29, 1927, they unanimously elected Ralph Schlosser as President, with the same condition that had been put in place with Ober's second election: a separate field man would be supplied for recruitment.

Schlosser was extremely active in the Brethren church, and had been elected to the ministry in 1911. He often spent his vacations conducting evangelistic services. His religious feeling ran deep, and his editorials for *Our College Times* were always written from a strong Christian perspective. On occasion they could be, as in the case of the screed against athleticism quoted earlier, mildly self-righteous, but their sincerity was never questioned.

Schlosser was considered an excellent teacher and an energetic administrator. The trustees directed that his employment as president would be from the remainder of the 1927–28 to the 1929–1930 school years.

Yet, after only a little more than a year, the College had to seek another President. On January 1, 1929, Schlosser requested a leave of absence to work on his doctorate of literature at Columbia University, which had apparently become a rite of passage for Elizabethtown College presidents. The board readily granted the request for one year, and began to search for someone to fill the temporary gap.

Their choice was Harry Hess Nye, the secretary of the College and professor of history and social science. Harry Nye, born in 1887, was a humorous man whose first entry into Elizabethtown College was by the kitchen door, through which he delivered milk from his parents' farm, which was adjacent to the campus. Due to the urging of the maternal Elizabeth Myer, young Nye enrolled in the pedagogical course. He eventually received his degree in 1915, completing his senior year at Franklin & Marshall.

"Henner" or "Noggy" Nye (for so the senior issue of *Our College Times* proclaims him, along with the fact that his favorite pastime was reading the works of the now forgotten Orison

Swettgarden) completed the work for his M. A. at the University of Pennsylvania in 1916, and married Elizabeth Heagy the week after commencement. Like all his predecessors as president, he too was elected to the Brethren ministry in 1916.

Harry Nye's term as President only lasted one year, until Ralph Schlosser's return. In the fall of 1930, Nye accepted a position teaching history and political science at another Brethren school, Juniata College, where he remained for twenty-three years. He retired in 1953, and died the following year.

On February 14, 1930, the trustees, as had been planned, elected Schlosser once again as President. Ralph Schlosser would remain as President of the College until 1941, the longest term of any president up to that time.

It would also be the most difficult term, one fraught with frightful financial difficulties due to the Great Depression. But for Elizabethtown College, the twenties, if they did not specifically roar, at least hummed.

The activities of student life increased in variety and number. There were enough events to warrant publishing *Our College Times* every other week rather than monthly. Another publication, introduced in 1926, was a student handbook for incoming freshman, and in 1922 the "Senior Number" of the magazine became a full-fledged yearbook called *The Etonian*.

The class of '22 numbered thirty-seven, including those who completed their college work at Elizabethtown in previous years, but were receiving their A. B. degree that year. A. C. Baugher was among them. Their yearbook was 142 pages long, filled with photographs, cartoons, and twenty pages of advertisements, including those from Missimer and Yoder's "Headquarters for Plain Clothes," and established Elizabethtown businesses like Hornafius' Restaurant, Bishop's Photographs, Leo Kob's Heating and Plumbing, and the Klein Chocolate Company.

In its pages were music for the College song, and many photographs of the campus, with the trees planted twenty years earlier growing tall. One photo shows students sitting in a small grove of trees, and another pictures several, the women in their head coverings, studying in the library. At the beginning of the faculty section, a cartoon shows recognizable caricatures of Elizabeth Myer, A. C. Baugher, and J. G. Meyer, who is holding a student's nose to a rather painful looking grindstone.

There are portraits of the faculty, along with quotations they selected, most of which support their subject matter. Historian Nye's is "The proper study of mankind is man,/The glory, jest, and riddle of the world." Laban Leiter, biology, suggests, "Study nature, not books," while Anna Gertrude Royer, piano and organ teacher, prefers: "It's the song ye sing, and the smile ye wear,/That's amakin' the sunshine everywhere."

Portraits of the seniors follow, complete with nicknames like "Floss," "Eph," "Eck," "Falky," and "Shrimp," as well as fairly lengthy essays about each class member.

The yearbook also has several pages of jokes, a brief history of the College, and a calendar of the preceding year, with such entries as "October 7 — Dr. Kill M. Quick with his nurse Ura Fool performed a successful operation on Mr. Coff E. Bean before the assembly of Homerians."

There is also a map showing the "Future Elizabethtown College." It features a separate auditorium and gymnasium, a library, and a dining hall behind Alpha Hall, flanked by men's and women's dormitories.

The largest section of the yearbook, however, is dedicated to student activities, which had a renaissance during the 1920s. Among the first student groups at the College's beginning were the literary societies. At the start of the twenties, the two societies (Keystone and Homerian) were scarcely enough for all the students who wished to become members, so, in 1920, a mildly complicated reorganization took place.

The Homerian Society was open only to students in the College course, including juniors and seniors in the Pedagogical Course. All other students were divided by lot between the two separate but equal societies that the Keystone Society became: the Franklin-Keystone Literary Society and the Penn-Keystone Literary Society.

This state of affairs remained until 1923, when the two Keystone societies were dissolved, and the former Keystone Literary Society was reorganized, only to vanish forever in 1926 when the

Elizabethtown Academy, which supplied most of its members, was ended. The Homerian Society lasted only a few years longer. In October of 1928 it was disbanded in favor of starting more specific clubs in the areas of dramatics, science, music, and current literature.

For many years, these societies provided the bright spots in extracurricular life by filling weekends with oratorical contests, debates and musical programs. They were intended by students and faculty alike to bring high culture onto the campus.

The decline of the Homerian and Keystone Societies was probably due in part to the competition from the Welfare Associations, which came into being in the early twenties. The Young Men's Welfare Association was organized in February 1920, and the Young Women's Welfare Association a year later. According to the 1922 *Etonian*, these associations "came into existence out of a need for more and broader social education and a desire to develop the social with the physical, mental, and spiritual phases of our manhood and womanhood."[27]

In practical terms, that translated into weekly meetings on Friday nights, with character-building lectures, talks, and readings, vocal and instrumental numbers, and dialogues and debates. The meetings were primarily social in nature, a way for students to unwind after a busy week, and think about something other than classes.

The first president of the Y.W.W.A. was a student named Vera Hackman. A photograph in a 1921 issue of *Our College Times* shows her as a handsome young woman, dark hair pulled back and parted in the middle. She is dressed in black and wears a head covering. Her eyes are clear, and filled with purpose and determination. Her chosen quotation is, "There is no genius like the genius of energy and industry."[28] Of her, some classmate has written, "She is a unique personality and we feel that she was needed to complete the list of various types and personalities represented in our class."[29] Her "Likes" are philosophy; her "Dislikes" are "Boys?" and her matrimonial prospects "Hard to tell." She would graduate from Elizabethtown College in 1925 and return in 1944 to teach and serve as Dean of Women for nearly a quarter century, becoming a campus legend.

Although the Welfare Associations did their share of debating, that discipline still retained its popularity as a separate entity. Debating achieved a breakthrough in 1924, when the Board of Trustees for the first time in the College's history permitted an intercollegiate competition to occur. Although two intercollegiate teams had been organized in 1922, and had debated against other college's teams, these earlier debates seem to have been exercises rather than competitions.

The first true debate against another college was held on February 21, 1924, when Elizabethtown's affirmative team argued against Ursinus College in favor of the World Court. They not only won their maiden bout, but on March 14 they beat Juniata College, which had been so far undefeated. "Any team will fairly quiver and quake when our debaters have the floor," *Our College Times* boasted.[30]

A women's intercollegiate debating association was formed in 1926. Their accomplishments equaled the men's, and *Our College Times* praised them in an editorial, "Feminine Forensics," by saying that, "The fair sex are able to hold their own in this as in other fields."[31]

Many students saw the success of debating as a way to open the door to other intercollegiate activities. A 1926 *Our College Times* editorial stated:

> *This first venture into the fields of inter-collegiate activities has proved so profitable in the forming of new relations with other institutions, in bringing about contacts with new and stimulating ideas from the students of those institutions, and in developing a much-needed school spirit at Elizabethtown, that we are justified in believing that other forms of inter-collegiate competition would also be of similar benefit... there is no reason to believe that Elizabethtown cannot develop a basketball team that would add almost as much to the prestige and popularity of the College as has the debating venture.[32]*

Only a year later, however, an editorial on the same subject seemed more cautious, making some of the same arguments put forth by Ralph Schlosser years before. The school should be judged not by what happens on the gridiron, but by what its alumni do with their lives. There was also a danger that sports would overshadow debating. Still, intercollegiate athletics "will be a fine thing if it is not carried to extremes."[33]

But "extremes" were in the immediate future. Football was rearing its seductive head. At the beginning of the 1927–28 school year, there was a meeting of the College Athletic Association, a student group which had been established in 1926, with the purpose of improving the quality and acceptance of sports at the College.

At this particular meeting, William Sweitzer, the association's new president, spoke out strongly for the sport of football. President Ober assured the students that he would present the matter to the trustees and do everything he could to have them approve football.

The response was not long in coming. The following month, the trustees denied their consent that football be played under the auspices of the College. The reasons were the expected ones: the fear of crippling injuries or even death, diversion of student interest from the primary purpose of the College, and the charge that the game "is fundamentally wrong because it is brutal, to say the least, [and] can not be cleaned up."[34]

Another reason, perhaps even more damning than the rest, was that "an urgent request comes from an alumnus just out of school that the *brutal* and *unchristian* game be forbidden. Other alumni are protesting as well as a large percentage of our constituency."[35]

And that was that. Still, if there was to be no football on College Hill, at least there could be other intercollegiate sports. Daniel E. Myers, the athletics administrator, re-entered the fray with an article in *Our College Times*, "Physical Education," in which he stated:

> *There is no definite unifying force on the Hill. ...Elizabethtown College is unique in that it is the only college in Pennsylvania that does not have intercollegiate athletics. Will the College be able to compete with the numerous other schools without this activity*

*is one of the questions that confronts Elizabethtown
College at present....*[36]

There were several good reasons to introduce intercollegiate
games to the College, the primary one being the feared loss of students if such games were not played. One of the most popular
images of college life during the 1920s was the Saturday afternoon
football game, with the resultant growth of school spirit as the students cheered on their classmates. Though football was no longer
an option, baseball and basketball were.

The trustees of Elizabethtown College were at heart practical
men, recognizing the plain fact that fewer students would ultimately
mean the end of the College. By 1929 they had put their qualms
behind them, and in February decided to grant the faculty and students official permission to hold intercollegiate contests, even
though intercollegiate basketball games had already been played in
the winter of 1928, and the summer school baseball team had
played other local college teams as well. Still, the formal imprimatur
had now been granted. There was no going back.

The timing was certainly fortuitous, for Elizabethtown athletics
had recently acquired a true treasure, one who was introduced to
the student body in the November 19, 1928 *Our College Times,* in an
article about the new gymnasium-auditorium:

> *The destinies of the College basketball team will
> be in the hands of a capable leader, one who has a
> thorough knowledge of basketball fundamentals and
> one who possesses a fine personality and who can
> instill a fighting spirit into his men. Permit the writer
> to introduce Mr. Ira Herr, who has been secured to
> coach the College basketball team. Mr. Herr will be
> remembered for developing the 1925 basketball edition
> of Elizabethtown High School. That team won 27 of 35
> games and was the most powerful in the history of
> the school.*[37]

Ira Herr, who will be forever known as the "Grand Old Man" of
Elizabethtown College athletics, was a grand *young* man of 34 when

he came to the College to coach at President Schlosser's request. Herr had attended the Academy at Elizabethtown, and had graduated from Franklin & Marshall in 1916. His athletic career up to that time had consisted of coaching and teaching at several high schools, including Elizabethtown, and in 1928 he was running two W. A. W. Shoe Stores in Elizabethtown and Lancaster.[38] He had been involved in nearly all forms of athletics since his youth, and was a perfect choice for the burgeoning program at the College.

The proof was first seen on December 8, 1928, when the Elizabethtown team played its first intercollegiate basketball game under Coach Herr's direction. The same President Schlosser who had railed against athleticism years before tossed up the first ball at center court, and by the game's end Elizabethtown had defeated Millersville State Teachers College 27–22.

The winning streak continued, with a 35–24 victory over Thompson Business College on December 13, and a 31–24 triumph over Williamson Trade of Philadelphia two days later. Despite the hot start, by season's end Elizabethtown had won five games and lost twelve. Still, it was an auspicious beginning for the new coach, who would soon be coaching a number of intercollegiate sports.

That same autumn saw the first — and last — football season at Elizabethtown College. Although the College had officially forbidden football, that didn't prevent a team from being formed in what President Schlosser years later referred to as a "semi-clandestine manner."[39]

The team scheduled four games with regional colleges and one with Lebanon High School, and lost them all. Home games were played at Klein's Field in Elizabethtown, since they could not be played on campus. *Our College Times* reported the games, so they were no secret, though in retrospect perhaps they should have been.

Elizabethtown scored a total of only 13 points in all five games, and lost to Lebanon High 12–7. In the 18–0 loss to Millersville, the three touchdowns were scored on two interceptions and a fumble. "The Blue and Gray machine played their poorest brand of football of the season," *Our College Times* reported, "but they put up a game fight to the final whistle."[40]

Though many other students enjoyed the games and supported the team, known as "The Brutal Thirteen," football would not survive another season. Powerful critics and lack of money spelled its end. The following April, one team member accepted the inevitable, with an "Open Forum" piece entitled, "Football in the Past." He first thanked the enthusiastic players and spectators, and went on:

> *A spark of enthusiasm was kindled among the public which if left to burst into flame would have aided in increasing the student body two fold. But this spark was smothered by those worthy trustees who came to the conclusion that football is a brutal game, and would thus attract a class of undesirable students to Elizabethtown College....*
>
> *We regret to state that all football schedules which were arranged for next year have been cancelled. At least twelve hundred dollars in guarantees shot into the air and the glory of those games tramped under foot. It thus seems that this was the beginning and is also the end of football at Elizabethtown College....*
>
> *The money earned by the football squad will be used in purchasing blue sweaters for the thirteen men playing the greatest number of quarters, including the manager. They will all be of one color. Thus you will be able to identify any member of the "brutal thirteen" and make your departure before anything brutal happens.*[41]

Football was deeply mourned the following fall, when an editorial bewailed, "A college without football is like a waffle without holes, the taste may be the same and they may be as good, but they are not all that people expect them to be, and are not as attractive as the others."[42]

Still, there were other campus activities to take football's place. By 1927, one could always hang out in the Y.M.C.A. room. This was a large attic room in Fairview which had been turned into a social room, eventually acquiring furniture and, in 1928, an RCA Radiola 17 radio, at a cost of $216.50. The College men, wanting the women to see in what luxury they were lounging, invited the ladies to the room one evening, providing instant furnishings by dragging chairs, settees, plants, pictures, and carpets from their dormitory rooms. The women came out in force (chaperoned by the Dean of Women, naturally).

When boredom set in, there was always the activity of shooting at future college presidents. One Saturday night in late November, A. C. Baugher and student John Bechtel were returning from York where they had bought several chickens to add to the College's "hennery." At around 11:15 p.m., they were putting the chickens into the hen house, and the birds, after their fashion, set up a ruckus. Some other male students, hearing the commotion from their dormitory rooms, assumed that chicken thieves were after the College's prize poultry. Student Ammon King Ziegler grabbed his 12-gauge shotgun and ran outside.

Ziegler fired one blast into the air, and a second wad of buckshot over the heads of the imagined culprits before they identified themselves, probably in no uncertain terms. It marks the first and only time that an Elizabethtown College student ever took a shot at a professor, and was duly commemorated by having one of the spent shells placed on display in a glass case "in Room 304, Fairview Apartments, where it may be viewed by those interested upon payment of the admission fee of one pin."[43] It is a sign of the times that Ziegler suffered no censure other than to be declared, by a very tongue-in-cheek *Our College Times*, a hero for defending the campus.

For those with less ballistic tastes, dramatics finally appeared on the campus in the twenties, after having been long forbidden by the trustees. But attitudes had changed since the College's salad days, and the cry for plays was answered by the board granting the 1927 senior class permission to stage Shakespeare's *Macbeth*. The play was directed by President Schlosser, and performed on April 29, 1927. *Our College Times* followed every step of the rehearsal process as avidly as a Hollywood fan magazine.

The Taming of the Shrew and *The Faith Healer* were staged in the following years, both directed by Schlosser. When he took a leave for the 1929–30 school year, Rebekah S. Shaeffer not only filled the gap, but started what is recalled as a golden age of Elizabethtown College drama.

Shaeffer received her B.Pd. in 1913 from Elizabethtown and higher degrees from Ursinus and Columbia. She had been a high school principal in New Jersey for seven years before returning to Elizabethtown as Dean of Women and professor of English. She also became Director of Dramatics. Her first play, *Prunella,* was staged on April 30, 1930, and her final production, *Little Women,* appeared eleven years later, giving students many opportunities to both see and participate in plays on campus.

Many students became involved in musical performance. The College orchestra was first organized by Charles D. Nissley in 1928, and received official sanction by the trustees the following year. Many other students enjoyed singing in choruses or glee clubs. The Elizabethtown College Chorus had sung cantatas ever since 1905, and one was performed almost every year during the 1920s, under the direction of Ephraim G. Meyer, head of the music department.

The 20s were also the heyday of the College vocal quartets, and Elizabethtown boasted the College Quartet, the Lyric Quartet, the Gleemen, the Aeolian Quartet, the Girls' Quartette, and the Faculty Male Quartet, a highlight of whose repertoire was "Mother Grinding Coffee by the Old Kitchen Stove." The Homerian Quartet was one of the best known, singing in rallies and services in Lebanon, Lititz, Palmyra, and other towns. They had "a splendid repertoire of religious songs, patriotic and secular music, negro spiritual, and sentimental songs."[44]

For a college in the midst of the jazz age, Elizabethtown was nearly devoid of that hot style of music. The only reference to jazz is found in a report of a Homerian Society musical program, where, amid a history of Beethoven, a performance of "To a Wild Rose," and hearing an Edison recording of Schubert's "Serenade," Lou Etta Hershey gave a talk on the "Difference between Jazz and Classical Music." One might suspect that classical music won out in the comparison.

The students were exposed to other kinds of music, not only in their classes and activities, but as part of the Lecture Course (later known as the Lyceum Course) of visiting celebrities, who not only lectured, but also gave musical and dramatic performances. During the twenties, students could pay $1.00 to $1.50 to see such speakers and performers as the wildly popular poet Edgar Guest (a friend of H. K. Ober), the Russian Cathedral Sextette, the Jackson Plantation Singers ("one of the foremost groups of negro singers on the road"[45]), the Filipino Collegians, Anne Campbell ("Poet of the Home"), the Novelty Entertainers ("three young ladies presenting an unusual program of music and cartooning"[46]), and humorist Jess Pugh, internationally famous for his "Snuff-Stricken Reader" routine.

Amusements such as this were few and far between, if a 1924 editorial in Our College Times can be believed: "People ask why so many students leave the 'Hill' over the week-ends. The answer is, because there is nothing to do or going on at college."[47]

An option, "What the Library Has In Store for You This Month," was offered in the next issue, though probably was not what the editorial writer had in mind:

> *Say fellows, have you seen the new "Scientific American"? There's a good article in there on the power resources of the world. The "American" is full of good articles this month. Be sure to read "Interesting People" and "The most important thing in my Life" as well as trying out the mental tests on yourself. The National Geographic is waiting to take you on a real trip to Porto Rico and Siberia. Don't miss this opportunity!*[48]

If a vicarious voyage to "Porto Rico" and Siberia (not to mention Cornwall, which was also in the December issue), did not set young hearts throbbing, there were other, more dangerous amusements. Some were dealt with the following month in a talk by Elder J. M. Moore who admitted that students needed diversions, but that "there is a big danger in harmful amusements...they degrade the mind, weaken the body, and destroy the soul by leading it away from God.... Card-playing was invented to satisfy the whims of an idiotic king...we must have cards out of our list of amusements." He concluded by saying that, "Pool-halls, picture shows, and the dance floors are no place for the Christian."[49]

One wonders how Elder Moore would have reacted to an advertisement that appeared a few years later in the College newspaper for "MOOSE TEMPLE/Center of Amusements/Talking and Singing

Pictures, Home Talent Plays, Basket Ball, Bowling and Dancing."[50] The elder most likely would not have been amused.

❧—☙

Throughout the twenties, the students were very much aware of what was happening in the world outside of College Hill. Labor difficulties and the question of union involvement seemed to split the campus into two factions. Two poems appeared in the same 1922 issue of *Our College Times*. "Organized Labor" by "E. G." proclaimed that:

> *Organized labor spells Industrial Success,*
> *Where the open shops in time will breathe its*
> distress.
> *Our country's saviour has answered the call*
> *When he exclaimed, "United we stand, divided*
> we fall."*[51]

This scansion-challenged effort was answered by S. G. F.'s "The Open Shop," in which he tells a labor agitator:

> *Your methods tend to cause a strike*
> *To cripple industry you'd like;*
> *You do not care how we might live*
> *Just so to you our cash we give.*
>
> *And then you'd leave us to our fate*
> *And go to some far distant state,*
> *That there your poison you might spread*
> *Until its men would cry for bread.*
>
> *When union men are led to see*
> *That unions give less liberty,*
> *They'll throw their nonsense in the air*
> *And work for bosses that are fair.*[52]

This conservative attitude seemed to lie at the heart of most of the political commentary published under the College's auspices, even from alumni. A letter from alumnus Kathryn Ziegler in the mission fields of India shows little sympathy for Mahatma Gandhi's crusade for Indian Home Rule: "The leader at the head of this [Gandhi] says if Home Rule is not gained by the end of this month, he will either go crazy or die. He is already crazy enough, so his days may be few, for the Hindus see that it is not possible to gain self government."[53]

While at least one alumnus may have been sympathetic toward British imperialism, intervention in China prompted a different point of view. In 1927, the paper ran a letter from the Nationalist Chinese government, stating that America had been misled by England into following a course of action in China "mistakenly assumed to be in protection of American rights but which is actually in violation of all those principles which Americans revere and hold sacred."[54] An editorial followed in the next issue, urging readers to carefully evaluate both sides of the China question before deciding to support American intervention.

Collegians became activists in 1928, when they called for President Coolidge to make an amnesty proclamation restoring full citizenship rights to those pacifists who ten years earlier expressed their opinions about the World War. The ACLU estimated that there were 1500 people "still suffering the penalty for their war-time opinions in the deprivations of their rights of citizenship."[55]

Coolidge was not the only president to hear from the College. In 1930 the student body and faculty sent a pair of resolutions to Herbert Hoover. The first approved "the law enforcement program of the president, particularly in relation to the eighteenth amendment [prohibition]," while the second had pacifistic aims, urging the abolition of the battleship and an approval of general disarmament.

The College had overwhelmingly supported Hoover in the 1928 presidential race. The student paper supported him editorially, and a mock election gave Hoover a 90 percent victory over Democrat Al Smith. Lancaster County was then, and remains, a Republican stronghold, but Hoover probably gained further support on College Hill because of his Quaker upbringing and his activities during and after the war as the Director of European Relief. Unknown or disregarded were his salty language, his smoking, his drinking, and his habit of fishing on Sundays.[56]

Unfortunately, Hoover's finely honed skills of management and negotiation seemed to desert him when, less than a year after his swearing-in, the United States entered the deepest financial depression in its history. The 1929 stock market crash and the resulting financial abyss into which the country plunged had the expected result upon a small college that had, since its inception, struggled to stay afloat. The need for funds was a constant, and one of which the students were well aware. In 1927, *Our College Times* ran a story on page one describing how the lack of funds kept many prospective students from entering Elizabethtown College. On the next page was an editorial asking alumni and parents to help to establish more scholarships for those students.

There was the occasional windfall, such as the bequest of $45,000 from the estate of Joseph C. Johnson in 1929, "given on condition that a similar amount be raised in new subscriptions by the Board of Trustees." Johnson was self-educated, "dwelt apart and took an interest in learning but not in persons...he wrote considerable poetry but later destroyed it all. He became a close student of science, evolution, and psychology."[57]

But such unexpected and generous sources of income were the exception rather than the rule; they could not be counted on to sustain the kind of college that Elizabethtown was, and, more importantly, the kind that it was trying to become. One potential source of funds was the Eastern and Southern Pennsylvania Brethren churches, the true owners and managers of the College.

So on August 28, 1928, the trustees asked those churches for a contribution of one dollar per member, specifically to avoid a deficit in Elizabethtown College's Department of Instruction. Some churches cooperated, but others were opposed, and in 1930 a query was sent to the District Meeting, asking that the practice of giving a set amount per member be discontinued. A committee was formed, and its report advised that "church finances be raised on the principle of voluntary, free will offerings."[58] The report was adopted. Though it stated, "*church* finances," the meaning in regard to the College was all too clear, and, for the time being, the *per capita* offerings ceased.

Free will offerings continued to be taken in sympathetic churches. While the district churches had contributed nothing to the College in the mid-twenties, in the 1930–31 year the contributions of the Eastern District were $1,242, and those of the Southern District $293, for a total of $1,535.

With the Great Depression gnawing at the vitals of America and its institutions, such an amount was only a poultice, not a remedy, for the dreadful financial sickness to come.

1 Official Endorsement of Pennsylvania State Council of Education, December 23, 1921
2 Letter from Herman V. Ames to J. G. Meyer, December 1923.
3 Such an endowment would have accumulated to $54,628,026 by the year 2000.
4 A perch is an antiquated land measurement most often equating to 1/160 of an acre.
5 *Our College Times*, October 1, 1924, p. 2
6 *Our College Times*, April 21, 1923, p. 1
7 *Our College Times*, April 21, 1923, p. 1
8 Minutes, Elizabethtown College Board of Trustees Meeting, March 28, 1924
9 *Our College Times*, June 1, 1924, p. 1
10 *Our College Times*, March 1, 1926, p. 2
11 *History of the Church of the Brethren: Eastern Pennsylvania: 1915–1965*, p. 222
12 Ibid.
13 *Our College Times*, October 15, 1925, p. 1
14 *Our College Times*, February 1, 1927, p. 4
15 *Our College Times*, March 1, 1928, p. 2
16 Ibid.
17 *Our College Times*, March 15, 1928, p. 1
18 Ibid.
19 *Our College Times*, May 1, 1928, p. 1
20 Ibid.
21 *Our College Times*, March 18, 1929, p. 2
22 *Our College Times*, November 1, 1925, p. 2
23 *Our College Times*, December 15, 1926, p. 2
24 *Our College Times*, October 15, 1925, p. 2
25 *Our College Times*, November 17, 1927, p. 1
26 *History of the Church of the Brethren: Eastern Pennsylvania: 1915–1965*, p. 226
27 *The Etonian: 1922* p. 62
28 *Our College Times*, Senior Number, 1921, p. 24
29 Ibid.
30 *Our College Times*, March 1, 1924, p. 1
31 *Our College Times*, May 1, 1926, p. 2
32 *Our College Times*, March 15, 1926, p. 2
33 *Our College Times*, March 1, 1927, p. 2
34 Minutes, Elizabethtown College Board of Trustees, October 27, 1927
35 Ibid.
36 *Our College Times*, December 1, 1927, p. 1
37 *Our College Times*, November 19, 1928, p. 1
38 Kathryn R. Herr interview, May 27, 1999
39 *History of Elizabethtown College, 1899–1970*, p. 147

40 *Our College Times*, October 17, 1928, p. 3
41 *Our College Times*, April 25, 1929, p. 2
42 *Our College Times*, September 23, 1929, p. 2
43 *Our College Times*, December 16, 1922, p. 3
44 *Our College Times*, December 16, 1922, p. 1
45 *Our College Times*, December 12, 1926, p. 1
46 *Our College Times*, September 23, 1929, p. 1
47 *Our College Times*, December 1, 1924, p. 2
48 *Our College Times*, December 15, 1924, p. 1
49 *Our College Times*, January 30, 1925, p. 1
50 *Our College Times*, November 24, 1930, p. 4
51 *Our College Times*, February 1922, p. 6–7
52 op. cit. p. 15
53 *Our College Times*, March 1922, p. 16
54 *Our College Times*, May 2, 1927, p. 2
55 *Our College Times*, December 12, 1928, p. 2
56 *The Reader's Companion to American History*, p. 514
57 *Our College Times*, July 18, 1929, p. 1
58 *History of Elizabethtown College, 1899–1970*, p. 168

Chapter 6
1930–1940

"We did not start this College with a view to quitting..."

The Great Depression hit many small Pennsylvania colleges hard. Messiah College found itself $20,000 in debt; faced with a declining enrollment the administration froze faculty salaries and required teaching without pay for one month during the 1932–33 school year. Lebanon Valley College raised student fees and decreased faculty salaries to remain solvent. At Dickinson College, salaries were reduced and based on each teacher's absolute need. Even Franklin & Marshall saw enrollment drop significantly.

College Hill was hit harder than most. During the late twenties, Elizabethtown College had shown a steady increase in the number of full-time students, from 131 in the 1927–28 school year to 159 in 1928–29 and 179 in 1929–30. The College would not reach that heady number again until the 1937–38 school year. Enrollment had dropped to 165 in 1930–31 and reached 122 by 1932–33.

Summer and Normal school sessions, in which teachers met the requirements for a State Standard Certificate, were affected even more, plummeting from a high of 371 students in 1928–29 to a low of 112 by 1933–34. It was not a good decade for small, liberal arts colleges.

Still, the College put up a brave front. In 1931 *Our College Times* announced, "Enrollment Unaffected by Depression,"[1] noting that the College had enrolled 141 students for the 1931–32 school year, calling it only a slight decrease from the previous year. In truth, it was a decrease of 24 students, and a total decrease of 38 from the last pre-Depression year. Of those 141, nearly half were day students, living at home in order to save money on room and board.

Some students' tuitions were paid for in the form of loans made to them by the College, and the minutes of the trustees' financial committee through the thirties are filled with reports of delinquent loan repayments. Starting in 1933, some students could receive loans from the Alumni Student Loan Fund. Others obtained their education through the barter system, such as Robert Trimble, whose contractor father had his services credited toward his son's tuition.

Still others earned tuition dollars by working part-time for the College. By 1938, under the direction of the National Youth Administration, forty-two students were working. Of these, seventeen performed clerical work, seven helped care for buildings and the campus, ten assisted professors in laboratories and the library, four aided in intramural athletics, two were proctors, and two more waited on tables in the dining hall. The students earned an average of fifty dollars a year, which went directly toward paying their expenses.

Outwardly, the attitude seemed to be to ignore the Depression. Only one editorial ever appeared in *Our College Times* on the subject, and its thrust was that the financial Depression did not necessarily mean emotional depression, since life was wonderful and nature gracious. That philosophy was all well and good, but the belt-tightening that the Board of Trustees faced in private sometimes surfaced publicly.

In November 1932, a month after the "Depression?" editorial, the announcement was made that no yearbook would be published that year: "Due to the size of our school, those in authority have thought it advisable that we publish an *Etonian* once every two years."[2] A more truthful sentence might have started, *Due to the current economic state...*

There were other hints as well. A brief article on a meeting of the trustees remarked that "matters of insurance, investments, and the collection of unpaid bills" were discussed.[3] The following month featured a story on President Schlosser's tour of area high schools. He visited four to five schools a day over a six to eight week period in February and March, for the purposes of recruiting high school seniors to attend the College. While such recruitment trips had been a part of the president's duties, they were taking on new significance. Unless new students could be persuaded to enter the College in spite of the Depression and current financial difficulties, there might simply *be* no Elizabethtown College.

Alumni contributed more than simply whatever financial support they could manage in these rough times: they contributed their children, wanting them to receive the kind of education they had received. In the 1933–34 school year, nineteen of the students who enrolled were sons and daughters of Elizabethtown College graduates, and six were from families in which both parents were alumni.

Nevertheless, such alumni devotion had its limits. Costs had to be cut, and less money was allocated to campus activities. In 1935 for example, $200 had been allotted to the men's debating team, but by 1936, although an extra team had been added, that amount shrank to $130.

Although students were aware of these difficulties from the pages of *Our College Times* (which changed its name to *The Etownian* in the fall of 1934, as distinct from the yearbook's title of *The Etonian*), they were mercifully unaware of the heroic efforts behind the scenes by the Board of Trustees to keep Elizabethtown College afloat. The minutes of the board in the first half of the 1930s reveal continuous and near desperate strategies to keep the College's financial head above water.

The attempts began at the November 13, 1931 meeting. When the finance committee presented the budget, it was voted that the executive committee "be requested to take up the matter of receiving donations from the faculty members toward reducing the possible deficit for the year 1931–32."[4]

Two months later, the budget was adopted, with the provision that President Schlosser organize an "Elizabethtown College Loyalty Fund to raise the deficit." Schlosser must have realized that a voluntary fund would not solve the problem, for he "discussed the prospect of reducing the number of teachers during the coming year."[5]

By April, the Board voted to reduce faculty salaries by 10 percent for the next school year, with an additional 5 percent reduction should it be necessary for the school to remain solvent. The faculty accepted, when it was faced with this option or the prospect of having no college in which to teach. The results of the Loyalty Fund were minimal, with only $400 having been raised by July.

At the July 29 meeting, the Board took a drastic step by voting to take $7,000 from the endowment fund for "the general purposes of the institution,"[6] which consisted primarily of paying bills. At that same meeting, a group was formed to attempt the difficult task of balancing the budget.

It was time to turn to the churches, which were most often reluctant to donate any money to the struggling college. The trustees voted to ask the churches of the Southern and Eastern Districts of the Church of the Brethren to make a contribution of twenty-five cents per member, so that the College could at least repay the money it had taken from the endowment fund. The response was less than enthusiastic. Although the districts voted to allow the College to make the request, very few churches contributed. Nearly every member was feeling the crunch of the Depression. By the 1935–36 school year, support from the two districts was less than $2000 a year.

At the January 4, 1933 meeting, it was reported that nearly all the faculty, along with their reduction in pay, were willing to additionally contribute in service the equivalent of one course in the spring or the summer term. Teaching an extra course for no additional payment was a noble gesture, but the wolves in the form of two Elizabethtown banks to which the College owed money were closing in nonetheless.

In August, the trustees decided that Samuel Hertzler, their president, should approach the "annuitants," and plead with them to lower the interest rates they were charging the College on its loans, as well as seeking other possible savings and sources of income. At a meeting of the finance committee on August 24, "Uncle Sam" Hertzler reported that the banks had refused to reduce the interest. It was a predictable reaction; many Lancaster County banks had been forced to close as a result of the Depression, and those that survived would not do so by being lenient with their debtors.

A month later, the full Board had no choice but to dip once more into their principal, and voted to sell off enough low-rate bonds from the endowment fund to pay $10,000 owed to the two Elizabethtown banks. When the trustees made the payment, they asked once again for a lower interest rate. Once again they were refused.

The process was bound to be discouraging, and it reached the point, states Schlosser in his 1971 history of the College, when:

> ...*several members spoke in favor of closing the institution but S. H. Hertzler, Chairman of the Board, saved the day. After hearing several pessimistic speeches he rose and in his inimitable style presented a hopeful picture and concluded by saying:*
>
> *Brethren, we did not start this College with a view to quitting.*
>
> *Others were in accord with his views and finally the Board voted to go forward with the institution.*[7]

Such discussions were not recorded in the minutes of the Board, and Schlosser gives no date nor any source other than his own memory for this incident. An examination of the minutes of the Board from 1930 to 1936, the year of Hertzler's death, suggests the board meeting of June 5, 1933, as a possible date for this stand. In those minutes, a phrase has been struck with a single line, but is still mostly readable. It says:

> *Voted that the following clause shall be implemented [?] (or should there not be funds to pay the monthly payment within thirty days after it is due)*[8]

It is quite possible that the above vote may have referred to a procedure to follow should the College find itself so far in debt that it could not get out. Whether this proposed procedure would have been a declaration of bankruptcy, which would have ended the existence of the College, will never be known. The following page has been removed from the book of minutes, including whatever "following clause" may have been referred to in the above (and excised) vote.

No one except those board members, all now long deceased, shall ever know what that clause contained. Perhaps it was never even written, if this was the point at which S. H. Hertzler dug in his heels. If there was a vote "to go forward," as Schlosser states, it was not recorded, and may have been more of an informal agreement to see the College through, whatever it took.

⇜⧸—⧹⇝

More than likely, the trustees found little hope in the new President Roosevelt's "New Deal," which was at first looked on dubiously in this stronghold of Republicanism. A 1933 *Our College Times* editorial stated, "This adjustment to the changing order has been cited as an ample proof of the optimism and broadmindedness of the American citizen. Of this, however, we cannot be too sure. The docility of a sheep at the slaughter is no indication of its endorsement of the idea."[9]

The following fall, however, the College had embraced the New Deal to the point where a hundred students and a dozen faculty members went to Lancaster to join in a National Recovery Act demonstration and parade. The College, like Lancaster County and the rest of the country, would recover from the pocket-emptying symptoms of the Great Depression, and although the hard times would continue for years, college life would go on.

Much of the credit for the College's financial survival goes to J. Z. Herr, Treasurer and Business Manager through the entire Depression. The son of John Herr, moderator of the first district meeting that led to the founding of Elizabethtown College, Jacob Z. Herr graduated from the College in 1905. He became principal of the commercial department for three years, left the College to work as a bookkeeper for two years, re-joined the College for three more years, and then left the College again to work for seven years as an accountant and office manager.

At last he rejoined the College faculty and remained, teaching commercial courses and serving as the school's treasurer and business manager from 1916 to 1945. Besides holding the purse strings during the Depression, he is credited by President Schlosser with being the person who most often persuaded the trustees to buy tracts of land adjacent to the College when they became available. His foresightedness allowed the College to achieve its present physical size.

The thirties, however, was not a decade of physical growth. Finances would not allow it. Instead it was a time of maturation, and of moving away from one identity and establishing another.

The academic reputation of the College continued to grow. During the thirties, the College faculty boasted fifteen professors with earned doctorate degrees, two with honorary doctorates, and fifteen with master's degrees. These degree holders had a salutory influence on the other faculty members, who either took leaves of absences or balanced teaching with learning, earning their own advanced degrees. Some, like Bible teacher Martha Martin, who had received an A. B. degree from Elizabethtown in 1926, took an extension course from the University of Pennsylvania in the mid-thirties, adding further luster to a twenty-five year college teaching career that would officially last until 1949.[10]

Many faculty members felt that there should be more opportunities for them to get together socially, and on January 3, 1931, the first meeting of the newly organized Faculty Club was held at drama teacher Rebekah Sheaffer's home in Bareville, with the purpose of "mental and social stimulation and diversional recreation." After a talk on "Cultivation of a Literary Taste" by President Schlosser, "...Dainty refreshments were served by the hostess who remembered that it is sometimes necessary to feast upon something other than the classics."[11]

The educational feast that the College was presenting by the 1930s was heady fare indeed. A look at the catalogue shows an impressive listing of courses offered for the 1931–32 school year.

For example, besides the General Chemistry course, Dean A. C. Baugher taught both Qualitative and Quantitative Analysis, Organic Chemistry, Physical Chemistry, and Industrial Chemistry. The English Department offered Rhetoric and Composition, History of English Literature, Children's Literature, Romantic Movement, American Poetry, Development of the English Novel, and Shakespeare. Students of French could enroll in courses in Seventeenth Century French Literature, French Lyrics, or History of French Literature. In every department and every course of study, there were more and more offerings to enrich students' learning.

With a continually improving faculty and an ever-growing course of study, it was only natural that the College seek further recognition and acceptance by other institutions and organizations. As early as 1932, *Our College Times* reported that representatives of the College had attended a meeting of the Middle States Association, and that, "Elizabethtown College expects to be able to comply with the standards for colleges set by this association and to be accepted into full membership this year."[12]

Four years later, President Schlosser wrote a column for *Our College Times* entitled, "Whither Bound Elizabethtown College," in which he stated, "Steps are now being taken to secure membership in the Middle States Association of Colleges and Preparatory Schools, which association is an accrediting agency, and it is hoped that within the near future another piece of good news may reach our College."[13]

Both the 1932 prediction and the 1936 hope were premature. The College would not achieve the necessary status to become a member of Middle States, the premier accrediting association in the region, until 1948. In the meantime, it would have to settle for being admitted to the Association of American Colleges in 1936. Dr. Robert L. Kelly was Executive Secretary of the organization, as well as Executive Secretary of the Council of Church Boards of Education. Only four years earlier, he had been appointed by the General Education Board of the Church of the Brethren to inspect and survey the country's nine Brethren colleges. His job was to make suggestions to the board of ways in which the colleges could be improved.

Elizabethtown College applied for membership on May 2, 1935, and was accepted the following January. This victory was somewhat hollow, since the association, founded in 1915 by several presidents of liberal arts colleges, was not an accrediting or standardizing agency, though its standards of admission were similar to those of the Middle States Association. Also, as Kelly himself put it, "membership is inclusive, not exclusive."[14]

In that same year, 1936, Elizabethtown College received at least some recognition at a meeting of the Colleges of the Middle States Association. It was admitted to the Association of Collegiate Registrars and to the Association of College Deans and Advisors of Men.

From this point on, Middle States membership was a constant goal toward which the College strove. Until it was achieved, much of what Presidents Schlosser and Baugher did would be done with accreditation in mind. A 1936 story in *The Etownian* about the physics department acquiring a new radio, telephone, and television set was couched in the following terms: "Schlosser has revealed extensive plans for the modernization of the physics equipment and the expansion of the endowment funds of the College, with a view toward entering the Middle States Association."[15]

Another part of that goal was to improve library conditions. At the April 17, 1935 board meeting, the trustees appointed a committee of board members H. K. Ober, Rufus Royer, and R. P. Bucher to consider the feasibility of erecting a new library building. An architect was consulted, but it quickly become clear that the funds for such a project could not be raised. A library would have to wait until the 1940s.

There were a few modest additions to the campus during the thirties, however. During the 1933–34 school year, a "microtechnical lab" was built on the north end of the campus. Biology professor George Shortess and his students hoped to finance the lab by selling schools biological materials from the lake and spring.

Other small improvements took place. In 1934 the trustees voted to macadamize the drive from College Avenue to Alpha Hall, and to have the Bible and education departments' rooms in Alpha Hall turned into a large social room. A month later, the campus paper reported on the plans for this "great project of the year." The wall between the two rooms was to be torn down, and a forty-two-inch fireplace installed. A hardwood floor would be put down, doors would be replaced by French doors, and the walls would be graced with "stip-il-art," described as "a rough, shaded plaster that will give the room a rich effect." Half the cost was to come from donations. The sophomore and freshman classes each contributed $25, and the Forensic Arts Club pledged $200. There were also donations from the Sock and Buskin Club, a dramatics organization, and from individuals. "No longer," the article concludes, "need we be ashamed to have our friends visit us at school."[16]

The Social Room (now Alpha Lounge) was opened the following March, and regulations were quickly established. The room would be open between 12:30 and 1 P.M. and after 4 P.M. on all school days. Saturday and Sunday hours were afternoons and evenings, except between one and three on Sunday. Students who had off-campus visitors were permitted to use the room for visits at all hours of the day. A host and hostess were present every evening.

Despite their presence, or perhaps during times when they were not in eagle-eyed attendance, the Social Room could get a little *too* sociable for some students, including the writer of one editorial who complained, "Instead of good conversation we have continuous silly remarks: instead of good music we hear loud and violent banging on the piano."[17] Such "silly remarks" and pianistic banging would seem to indicate that the students thoroughly enjoyed the new gathering place.

Other improvements, such as the new electric scoreboard placed in the gym in 1938, were donated by the alumni, for there was still no room in the College budget for such fripperies. That same year, free tuition scholarships were discontinued, and student aid "will be reserved for worthy students who are in real need of aid."[18] Partial scholarships for top high school seniors would still be available, as would aid to Brethren ministers and missionaries and their children, and to the children of trustees.

The College was taking the debts owed to it as seriously as those it owed to others. There is a story, possibly apocryphal, of Treasurer J. Z. Herr chasing a student from Alpha Hall through the campus because he was overdue on his tuition payments to the College. What *is* true is that debtors were dealt with nearly as harshly, according to the writer of this May 29, 1940 editorial:

> *We are wondering if it wouldn't have been courteous for the office to extend ninety days' credit at six percent to those few individuals who were not able to pay their college bills on time. If this had been done, the College would have benefited from the interest instead of the banks. Furthermore, it was hardly fair to the students to let them pursue their courses, and then suddenly tell them they may not take their exams, even humiliating them by taking them out of class. Christian charity is never amiss.*[19]

For Elizabethtown College, the Depression was a hard time that called for hard measures.

It was also a decade of loss in more than financial ways. Samuel H. Hertzler, beloved old "Uncle Sam," died in 1936 at the age of eighty-three. He had been the second chairman of the board of trustees, serving from 1918 until his death when he was succeeded by H. K. Ober, the past president of the College.

Ober was chairman for only three years, until he passed away on March 12, 1939, sixty-one years old, and greatly loved by the thousands who had known him. Rufus P. Bucher then became chairman, and would remain in that office until 1954.

Bucher was one of the "Faithful Six," the first group of students at Elizabethtown College. His father, George Bucher, was one of the College's founders and served on the early Board of Trustees. A Brethren preacher, evangelist and farmer, Rufus Bucher had become a trustee in 1913. Although he never graduated from college, his was always a strong voice in the church in support of education and of Elizabethtown College, which grew in both size and academic reputation during his tenure.

Most of his children attended the College, and his granddaughter, Christina A. Bucher, is currently chair of the department of religious studies. In 1989, the Rufus P. Bucher Meetinghouse was built and named in his honor.

Rufus Bucher was the last chairman of the Board to wear plain dress. Meanwhile, the College continuied to move away slowly from the more conservative strictures of the Church of the Brethren, despite the administration's concern for the opinions of what they called the College's "constituency."

Indeed, President Schlosser's Brethren-style beard had disappeared by the early 1930s. While in graduate school at Columbia, Schlosser had written a letter to Frank Carper, accepting Carper's invitation to preach in his Palmyra church, in which he said:

> *I now belong to the "beardless" eldership, but I suppose that will not interfere with my coming. I felt there was nothing to be gained here by wearing it, and besides it would have made me the target of much unnecessary jesting and unpleasantness as it did the other time I was here. And I believe that there are many more at home even who will give me credit for it than will criticize me for it.*[20]

Both Schlosser and A. C. Baugher became sartorial chameleons during the thirties, their garb switching from plain to fancy depending upon the company in which they found themselves. Nevin H. Zuck, a pastor of the Elizabethtown Church of the Brethren and a former Elizabethtown College student, stated, "They would start out at Elizabethtown not wearing a [plain] vest and stop along the road and put it on. That's the story...and I think it was probably true."[21]

Another Brethren minister and former Elizabethtown student, Harold Z. Bomberger, remembered a time during the thirties when A. C. Baugher visited the Brethren congregation at Annville to ask for donations to the College: "Oh, he was plain as midnight, you know, plain garb and all that. The next day I saw him with a tie. And everybody knew..."[22]

Of the eleven trustees in a photograph for the 1930 *Etownian*, only one is not wearing plain garb. Yet, of the nine male faculty members, only two were photographed wearing such garb. President Schlosser and Dean Baugher, the College's official images to the world and the church, are, of course, wearing the traditional closed collars without ties.

In the 1933–34 yearbook, Baugher, along with three more trustees, is finally pictured in a tie, and of the faculty only Librarian Lewis D. Rose is clothed "plain." By the following year, President Schlosser's official photograph showed him wearing a necktie as well.

For students, the choice seemed to be far easier, and the pressure less great. By 1930, only two male students wore plain clothing, and by 1934, every one was pictured in a necktie.

There were other signs that the *Weltanschauung* of the College was becoming less in accordance with that of the church. In 1931, the College orchestra appeared for the first time on the chapel platform. It was at an educational program rather than chapel services, but still a large step for a school that had formerly banned musical instruments within its precincts. It appears to have been a triumph of the desire to promote culture over the need to mollify the shrinking conservative sector of the "constituency." *Our College Times* reports that, "President Schlosser expressed the fact that the realizations of the orchestra was a realization of another of his dreams for a greater Elizabethtown."[23]

The College remained anti-alcohol, but was no longer as vocal about it. One of the few mentions of it in the College paper was a 1933 editorial disapproving the constitutionality of allowing 3.2 percent beer to be sold.

Tobacco, that other evil, had proven to be a popular vice with many students. "Today, while smoking is prohibited on campus," reported a 1933 editorial, "some of our finest students are addicted to the habit."[24] Smoking off-campus was treated so cavalierly that *The Etownian*'s gossip column, "Here & There," reported: "Pipeman makes good: It took a piece of silver paper from a pack of Camels to get Miss Shaeffer's car to Maple Grove Friday night. Gallant Jake was the donor."[25] That a student should feel comfortable enough to take out a pack of Camels in front of Professor Rebekah Shaeffer speaks worlds about its tacit acceptance.

Another initially condemned practice that managed to achieve some acceptance was hazing. Although social fraternities remained outlawed, the students introduced hazing into such organizations as *Der Deutsche Verein*, a German club begun in the 1931–32 school year, and the Candles, an honorary social club established in 1926, whose motto was, "To have a friend be one."

According to the campus paper, these new friends were inducted by being "forced to go through many obnoxious operations including the taking of some cod liver oil by means of a straw and the rolling of a peanut the entire length of the gym with their noses."[26]

This was child's play compared to the Prussian discipline required to join *Der Deutsche Verein*, among whose perils were walking a plank blindfolded, drinking half a teaspoon of castor oil and eating a marshmallow filled with alum. Only six out of ten aspirants chose to undergo the ordeal, which also included a "fake cutting of the artery in the wrist."[27]

By 1935, however, the paper reported, "Rough-House Initiations On Decline," and stated, "…in previous years, the first mention of initiation brought to the nervous aspirants visions of raw eggs, eels, dead cats, electric shocks, hot sugar water, and the paddles…"[28] Today, the story goes on, initiations are more solemn and meaningful. One has to wonder if the reason might have been the reactions of the "constituency" to such headlines as "German Club Requires Aspirants to Eat Alum and Drink Castor Oil."[29]

The conservative segment of the constituency still made its voice heard, despite the slow liberalization of the campus. The minutes of the January 2, 1932, meeting of the Board of Trustees record a protest from the elders of the Midway Church in Lebanon against students at the College performing plays "like *Othello*." Since the protest did not state that the Midway Church was against Shakespeare in general, one might safely assume that they were uncomfortable about plays that presented miscegenation. *Othello* had not been performed at the College, so this seems to have been a preemptive strike. The president was requested to speak to dramatics coach Rebekah Shaeffer about it, and *Othello* was never performed during her tenure there.

There were other taboos that survived through the decade. Profanity was prohibited, and "The [student] council will take immediate definite action with anyone caught cursing."[30] Card-playing and social dancing were still frowned on strongly enough for Editor Elwood P. Lentz to warrant their inclusion as "negative" social programs that "cannot be reconciled with the idealistic traditions of Elizabethtown."[31]

Dancing was possibly the most resented prohibition by students during the mid-thirties, because of its impact on May Day celebrations. Students had long wanted a May Day program, but every request had been denied because of the trustee ban on dancing. Searching for loopholes, an *Etownian* reporter wrote in 1937:

> *Investigating the situation farther, your reporter tried to find out how, last year, under the 'no-dancing' ban the Student Association was able to 'put on' a colorful and highly pleasing (and harmless) minuet dance at the annual Valentine party. It is revealed that numerous complaints were received from the constituency of the College for having the minuet in a down-town appearance.*[32]

An editorial on the following page, written by Editor Donald M. Royer, who had replaced the anti-dance Editor Lentz, pleaded that "...the folk dance, or minuet is a thoroughly wholesome, healthful, and enjoyable form of recreation...The objections to minuets and rustic folk dances on our campus are surely but traditional prejudices against any thing that bears the name of dancing...and brand us with a sense of narrowness."[33]

The plea fell on deaf ears. The next year the same request was made, the same denial given. "Why can't we plan a May Day program which deletes dancing entirely?"[34] an *Etownian* writer suggested, but to no avail. Elizabethtown College would have to wait for World War II to change attitudes toward dancing, and until 1947 for its first May Day.

The relationship between church and college was often uneasy, and that unease was skillfully defined by A. C. Baugher in a speech he made before the Board of Christian Education of the Church of the Brethren in Washington, D. C., where he said:

> *There has been a weakening of the bond of cooperative effort in higher education between the Colleges and the related churches. The primary reason for this*

definite change is found in the problem of financial support of the Colleges. It is almost a truism, that financial support carries with it the right to control; and stated conversely, the right to control implies the responsibility to support.[35]

When the College desperately needed financial support from the churches, it received only a fraction of what was required. Still, many church members wanted to exercise their control over the College, a control that, according to Baugher, they had not earned with contributions. In a variation of the revolutionary war cry, Baugher seemed to be saying, "No representation without taxation."

It was a difficult time for both church and college, and the financial woes and changing attitudes of students and staff created an uncomfortable gap between the two. Before too long, however, they would become united again, with the specter of war on the horizon.

⟨⟩

For the students, however, the 1930s at Elizabethtown College were a time of tightening one's belt and finding pleasure where one could. Theatre became a more prominent activity, and the Sock and Buskin Club, launched by Rebekah Sheaffer and a band of ambitious young thespians, proved to be one of the most popular groups in the school.

Along with the regular plays in 1931, President Schlosser staged the court scene from Shakespeare's *The Merchant of Venice*, translated by him into Pennsylvania Dutch, and featuring such lines as, "Well is der Antonio do?" The scene was performed not only on campus, but also for the Pennsylvania German Society in Pennsburg in 1932, as well as on WGAL radio.

That same year the senior class presented an outdoor pageant depicting the history of the College. The two-hour production consisted of ten tableaux, among which were the first public meeting at Reading in 1898, Alpha Hall groundbreaking, opening of the College and arrival of the first student, meeting of the trustees, solicitors collecting pledges, student life in 1900 and in 1932, seniors in class, and a visual prediction of what college life might be like in 1942, ten years hence.

Although the quality of theatrical performances steadily improved through the decade, the criticism grew more severe. Though most reviews of student productions were very positive, William Willoughby dissected the 1938 senior play, Sheridan's *The Rivals*, in no uncertain terms: "...the presentation...although exceptional for a college this size, could not do justice to the play for two reasons: first, the actors were not of the calibre to present such a play, and second, the audience was not capable of appreciating it."[36] Oscar Wilde himself might have applauded the succinctness of Willoughby's description of a no-win situation.

Debating, though past its heyday, was still an ongoing campus activity. In 1934 a Forensics Arts Club was established to encourage skills in debate, oratory, extemporaneous speaking, and interpretive reading.

Other campus clubs included The Commerciantes, a business club; Sigma Zeta, which replaced the Science Club; Ministerium, made up of prospective ministers; Zeta Sigma Pi, a social science fraternity; *Der Deutsche Verein*; and the old standbys, the Y.M.C.A and Y.W.C.A, the Volunteers, the Candles, and Student Government, which in 1934 had voted to combine the Men's and Women's Student Associations into one.

Many students were active in the music organizations. Vocal quartets still flourished, and the A Cappella Choir remained active, performing a cantata every year. Instrumentalists could join either the orchestra or the College band.

As for athletics, the 1930s were years in which the College knew the agony of defeat more often than the thrill of victory. The bright side was Ira Herr's arrival as full-time Coach of Athletics in 1932, overseeing the men's basketball team as well as the newly formed women's team, which would ultimately prove to be the College's most successful sport. The downside was the high caliber of competitive players that Coach Herr's teams had to face when they played such powerhouses as Saint Joseph's, Haverford, Bucknell, Millersville, and Dickinson. Both Coach Herr and the students remained optimistic. "Basketball Team Looks Promising," blazoned a headline in the November 16, 1932 *Our College Times*. "Let's all be around for the first game," the writer burbles, "and see what the team can offer under the direction of the new coach, Ira Herr."[37]

Alas, it was not much. Nor had things improved the following year, when the paper published a headline that could have appeared every fall during the 1930s: "Coach Herr Optimistic Despite Dearth of Material." Herr was honest in saying, "Hope for a good boy's team lies in the type of players that can be produced from the new students. After all, the success of the team will depend upon the spirit and enthusiasm of the girls and fellows who play."[38]

A few months later, *Our College Times* ran several front-page stories on the sports crisis, the banner reading, "Common Sense Overcomes Blind Optimism As Athletic Situation Shows No Sign of Improvement." Subheads ran, "A Coach Is No Magician" and "First Class Material Is Seen As Crying Need." Another story was headlined, "Little Hope Remaining/School Spirit Does Not Score Many Field Goals." The story goes on to say:

> For a period of four years the local college club has failed to annex a major engagement and the last successful season we had was in 1928 when our present coach Ira Herr had such stars as Clyde Wenger, "Red" Angstadt, and Harry Bower around whom to build a team...Most of the players from Elizabethtown College are recruited from B and C class high schools while the majority of colleges today have men available that have been stars on first class high school and prep teams.[39]

An adjoining article looks beyond basketball: "Not alone basketball, but tennis and baseball have fallen into a category where not even the best friends of the men on the teams can wish them luck without a half smile."[40]

Headlines from the sports pages in following issues are uniformly discouraging: "Millersville Club Slaughters Boys," "Doctors Nose Out Varsity," "Maryland Trips Varsity," and the report of a game against Gallaudet College in Washington, D.C.: "Deaf Mutes Handle Boys Rough to Get 36–16 Win."[41]

Thanks to Coach Herr's positive attitude and fine coaching, as well as determined young athletes, the thirties saw a few athletic highlights. In May of 1936, the baseball team had its best average ever, winning seven out of eight starts, and ended the season with a 9–2 record.

Still, Elizabethtown's teams generally experienced more defeats than victories, since they often faced opponents whose rosters were made up of students on athletic scholarships. Once, before a baseball game, Coach Herr and a spectator were watching the opposing team, made up of "subsidized" student-athletes, take batting practice. As the balls whizzed far into the outfield, the spectator remarked that it must be a coach's dream to be able to have such brilliant players to work with on the first day of practice. Herr's reply was, "Probably so, but the supreme thrill to me is seeing a diamond in the rough report as a freshman and develop into a first stringer."[42] Coach Herr would work such alchemy, transmuting leaden beginners into golden athletes, for many years to come.

In 1937, a college athletic landmark was established with the first games of soccer on campus. Coach Herr first thought of the sport as a way for his basketball players to work out. There was intramural play, as well as games with local high schools, and scores were seldom kept. An intercollegiate team was formed in 1938, but with little success, winning only one game in its first year and two in its second. The glory years of soccer at Elizabethtown would have to wait.

⋘—⋙

There were headier issues confronting Elizabethtown's students during the thirties. International affairs, racial justice, the crusade for peace, and the looming prospect of war filled many columns of the student paper, and the thoughts of many of the students.

The first African-American student was C. F. Jenkins, who is shown as a junior in the 1930 yearbook. He was a commuting student, living with his wife in Harrisburg. "Mr. Jenkins is an ideal student," his entry reads, "a thinker, always making distinct contributions in our class discussions... His congeniality, his courtesy, his dignity, his intellect, his culture, his sincerity, blend admirably in bestowing to him a personality which well fits him for his chosen work, the ministry."[43]

In May 1931, *Our College Times* reports that the Reverend C. F. Jenkins, "in charge of the largest Baptist church for colored people in Harrisburg, assumed on Thursday, May 14, the pastorate of a leading Baptist church in the city of Pittsburgh."[44] The Harrisburg Civic Club held a banquet in Jenkins's honor, which Professor and Mrs. A. C. Baugher and two other college faculty couples attended.

In early 1935, the campus Y.M.C.A. further aided the cause of tolerance by sponsoring a series of race relationship programs as chapel talks. Africans, rabbis, and others spoke on such topics as "How Large Is Your World," "The Filipino and the Indian Problem," "The Jewish Problem," "The Negro Problem," and "The Far East." The proposed lessons were learned at least by some, if an *Etownian* editorial appearing the following October is any indication. After quoting Mussolini calling Ethiopia "a barbarian country unworthy of ranking among civilized nations," the writer recalls how early settlers stole the country from the American Indians using the same rationalization.[45]

Anti-Semitism took a hit in "We Are Anti-Anti-Semitic," a 1938 editorial. "Acknowledged that every one of us has his own particular prejudices," the writer stated, "it seems nevertheless foolish for one people to set themselves up as a 'superior' race, among whom an industrious, law-abiding, though unfortunate 'inferior' people, may not associate."[46]

Still, throughout the 1930s, racial stereotyping was a natural and accepted way to look at minorities. When in 1931 lecturer Anne Frierson gave a presentation on the Gullah of South Carolina and the Sea Islands, *Our College Times* said, "There is...something about the happy-go-lucky attitude of the negro that could well be absorbed by us practical, energetic Pennsylvanians."[47]

Native Americans fared little better. A 1934 Y.M.C.A. Thanksgiving program presented four tableaux. The first was a Pilgrim carrying his gun and Bible while "Faith of Our Fathers" was played. The second showed an Indian peering into the distance to the tune of "Indian Serenade." The third was of Priscilla Alden posing to "Believe Me If All Those Endearing Young Charms." And the fourth? As reported, "'The End of a Perfect Day' closed the tableaux as the three people posed together with the Indian slain at the feet of the girl and the man."[48]

Still, there was no apparent sense of meanness in this perpetuation of stereotypes, but rather an acceptance of the status quo of the 1930s. In spite of the ban on *Othello,* the College was consistently far more progressive in terms of racial and religious tolerance than was the surrounding community. When the Southernaires, an African-American vocal quartet, performed at the College in the 1930s, they were unable to find lodging at any of the hotels in Elizabethtown. Indeed, when members of minorities came to perform or to speak at the College, they would lodge with members of the administration, since the local hotels were closed to them. Like so many small towns in Depression-era America, Elizabethtown was a xenophobic community, suspicious of the "outsider" in their midst.

As a result, the College itself was looked upon with suspicion by some townspeople, an attitude that would grow stronger in following decades, due in large part to the College's traditional views on peace and social justice, philosophies which were less than universal in the community at large.

The emphasis on peaceful resolution of conflicts had long been a part of the Church of the Brethren, and it was reflected in the activities and opinions of the students throughout the thirties. In 1931, Elizabethtown students signed petitions asking the U. S. Senate to approve World Court treaties. That same year two students, Leroy Rosenberger and Ray A. Kurtz, spent their summer touring southeastern Pennsylvania, speaking on radio and at business clubs in the interest of world peace and disarmament. Their audiences ranged from six to six hundred, and they distributed petitions and held forums in the face of antagonism and ridicule, though there were always some who lauded their work.

By 1934, a real threat to peace loomed. Adolf Hitler was Chancellor of Germany, and his strategies and goals were all too clearly obvious for those who cared to look. The first brief mention of Hitler in *Our College Times* appears in the February 13, 1934 issue, in which an editorial observes that in Europe, "there is intense Nationalism and Anti-Semitism as stirred up by Hitler in a country which hasn't freedom of press."[49]

The following October H. R. Dunathan, President of Findlay College, spoke at Elizabethtown about trends toward religion in Germany. He sounded a warning by relating how, after the Nazis won the national elections, a Nazi leader suggested that the Old Testament be removed from Bibles, that all references to Christ as a pacifist be removed, as well as all teaching by "Jewish propagandists," such as Paul, which would have considerably shortened the New Testament as well.

In January 1935, the Reverend H. L. Harstough closed the annual Bible Institute with a charge to renounce warfare, a charge that inspired the editorial, "A War Against War," urging students to work for peace, and conduct a student "peace poll."

Of those who participated, the results were as follows:

Can we stay out of war? Yes, 25; No, 16.

Do you favor defensive warfare? Yes, 19; No, 21.

Do you favor offensive warfare? Yes, 1; No, 39.

Do you advocate government control of munitions? Yes, 34; No, 6.

Do you advocate universal conscription of all resources of capital and labor? Yes, 32; No, 5.

Should the U. S. enter the League of Nations? Yes, 20; No, 21.

Do you favor compulsory military training? Yes, 8; No, 31.[50]

The students showed a united front against offensive warfare, but were almost evenly divided on defensive warfare. While a large majority seemed to prefer government control of munitions, capital, and labor, most were against compulsory military training. It was still very much a peace school.

From April 20–24, 1936, the College sponsored a Peace Institute in conjunction with the Peace Action Program of the Brethren Church. On each of the five days, students listened to varied approaches and philosophies of peace, hearing from speakers from Franklin & Marshall College, Manchester College, and a Rabbi

Bookstaber, among others. Several weeks later, a number of students joined those from other colleges at the First Methodist Church in Lancaster for a Peace Day rally.

Anti-war sentiment seemed permanently entrenched at Elizabethtown; editorials calling for world peace became commonplace. A campus election for president showed Franklin Roosevelt with only 34 student votes to Republican Alf Landon's 130, but how much of Landon's campus victory was due to habitual Lancaster County Republicanism and how much to distrust of Roosevelt as commander of the Armed Forces is not known.

Though students and faculty were coming to realize that a great tyranny was arising in Europe, Hitler still had his defenders, the oddest of them being mild-mannered L. D. Rose, the College librarian. Rose, a teacher of German whose love for Germany, its culture, and its people was no secret, had first leapt to the country's defense in 1932, with an article entitled "German Culture." Amid the praise of Goethe and Schiller, one found this passage:

> *During this college year the statement was made on this rostrum that the German soldiers entered Belgium to rape and ruin. The rape charge is disproved by the testimony of the Allies' own generals who now admit that the worst thing the German soldiers did in Belgium was to ask women for freshly baked cookies and pies.*[51]

Rose's love for Germany ill-served him when he wrote an article that appeared in the "Through Alpha Windows" section of *The Etownian* on October 23, 1936. By this time it was common knowledge that Hitler was driving the Jews out of Germany, yet Rose attempted to answer his apparently self-composed question, "From your observations in Germany during pre-Hitler days, do you consider Hitler a blessing or a curse to the German people?" He began by saying that the answer was difficult, partly because of "the deliberate attempts put forth by Germany's former enemies in the World War to discredit Adolf Hitler, his aims, policies, and regime. Adolf Hitler is both a blessing and a curse; it all depends on your viewpoint." Rose saw postwar Germany as being humiliated by:

> *...a forced contract of hate, that...outdid a*
> *Pharaoh or even an ancient Assyrian despot, robbed*
> *the German people of all sense of honor, deprived*
> *them of land that had been German for centuries,*
> *despoiled them of their colonies, robbed them of their*
> *sovereignty, and above all else tried to rob them of*
> *their soul...Adolf Hitler has dispelled this defeatist*
> *spirit. His constant message has been, "Germany,*
> *wake up, there is a bright future." Adolf Hitler has*
> *revitalized the German people; he has given them*
> *renewed hope; for his accomplishment, he deserves an*
> *endowing place in history.*[52]

Clearly Rose's admiration for Hitler is evident; however, if he had any further fascist sympathies, he never espoused them in his teaching.[53] Like Hans Sachs at the end of Richard Wagner's *Die Meistersinger von Nurnberg*, what matters most is the survival of *"die heil'ge deutsche Kunst"* or holy German art, regardless of the methods used to preserve it.

Rose could prove to be surprisingly dictatorial, and in one instance his actions started still another war between the library and a portion of the student body. Sometime during the early thirties it had been decided to exclude newspapers from the College library. There were enough complaints that Rose felt it necessary to provide an explanation in *The Etownian*.

He said nothing about the expense involved, surely a consideration in those trying times, but rather defended the exclusion of newspapers because he considered them useless for term papers. "Page after page," he stated, "is devoted solely to murders, kidnappings, divorce proceedings, and crime in general."[54] He retained only the subscription to *The New York Times*, since it was bound and indexed.

Student frustration must have increased in 1936, when the *Times* was dropped from the library and radios were practically outlawed in the dormitories. Still, Elizabethtown students were slow to anger. The roaring twenties had become the gloomy thirties, and times were hard for students and their parents. Battles had to be chosen carefully and fought wisely. There were threats far greater than the banishment of newspapers, such as the Army's plan for a universal draft.

When Elizabethtown students did finally decide to act, they did so deferentially. The March 6, 1937 *Etownian* had two contrasting stories, one about students affiliated with the American Youth Congress at a demonstration in Washington where several arrests were made, and another about Elizabethtown College students visiting members of congress in Washington to discuss neutrality legislation currently on the floor of the House of Representatives.

By 1939, however, the absence of newspapers provoked student wrath. With the political and military situation in Europe changing every day, students were hungry for news, and finding it difficult to readily obtain. An editorial complained once again about the lack of a daily paper by writing of the impression it presented to the public and to potential students:

> *Another one on hearing of this deplorable condition replied, "Well, that's what you might expect at Elizabethtown." Couldn't it be that a comparatively little thing like this does more harm to the school than the fact that it is not fully accredited?*
>
> *If any puritan minded person should object that the students might contaminate their virgin-pure minds by reading the comics, let them not forget that the "New York Times," which would be an almost ideal paper, does not contain any such scrofulous influences.*[55]

A month later, a letter was published by sophomore William Willoughby, a grandson of G. N. Falkenstein. It identified the absence of a daily paper as not just an isolated omission, but as a symptom of a greater problem:

> *...you [the editor] have not taken the pains to investigate the problem, of which the lack of newspapers is but a minor indication. As long as the choice of periodicals reflects a partisan attitude, which few*

will deny, Elizabethtown College is not conducive to good citizenship, the primary requisite of which is a thorough knowledge of the issues of the day, and the ability to evaluate that knowledge. So far as I can ascertain, there are no magazines in the library which are in sympathy with the present administration... Another fundamental weakness of the library is the lack of many worthwhile books...The NEA gives in its journal for January a list of 100 books which everyone should read, chosen by prominent Americans. Of the books listed, only fifty-eight are in our library.[56]

It was a serious and eloquently worded accusation. In a recent interview, Willoughby recalled that there were no magazines that presented a liberal view, such as *The Nation* or *The New Republic*, and that the sole newspaper subscribed to was that bastion of capitalism, *The Wall Street Journal.*[57]

L. D. Rose did not publicly reply to Willoughby's accusations. If they were true and if Rose, by the careful selection of certain publications and the specific exclusion of others, was attempting to color the opinions of those who frequented the library, he did not do so much longer. Though listed as librarian in the 1939–40 catalogue, by 1940 a young woman named Florence Becker occupied the position. Rose, in his mid-fifties at the time, would remain as director of the College's Brethren Historical Library until 1956, and as alumni secretary until 1947. He died in 1962.

It must have been a nightmare to him to see what became of his beloved Germany. By 1939, the world was rushing headlong toward war. An October editorial, "War Bells Ring," bemoaned:

We have not yet been drafted, taken out of school, and put in an army camp, nor have we been humiliated, beaten, and put in solitary, but we have been the objects of a well-directed bombardment of propaganda and a forceful barrage of public pressure endeavoring to prepare us to die willingly for the fatherland.[58]

The front page of the following issue of *The Etownian* ran the results of yet another poll on student attitudes toward war. By a two-to-one majority they held Hitler responsible for the present war in Europe. Thirty percent of the students indicated that they would be willing to support the United States in a war against Germany, should England and France appear to be losing. Possibly the same 30 percent said that they would be willing to support their country in any foreign war it declared.

Fifty-six percent believed that the teachings of Christ did not condone war.

Twenty-nine percent believed that war was inevitable.[59]

---

1 *Our College Times*, October 15, 1931, p. 1

2 *Our College Times*, November 16, 1932, p. 1

3 *Our College Times*, January 9, 1934, p. 1

4 Minutes, Elizabethtown College Board of Trustees, November 13, 1931

5 Minutes, Elizabethtown College Board of Trustees, January 2, 1932

6 Minutes, Elizabethtown College Board of Trustees, July 29, 1932

7 *History of Elizabethtown College 1899–1970*, p. 124

8 Minutes, Elizabethtown College Board of Trustees, June 5, 1933

9 *Our College Times*, March 16, 1933, p. 2

10 Martin continued teaching part-time into the late 1950s.

11 *Our College Times*, January 15, 1931, p. 1

12 *Our College Times*, December 15, 1932, p. 1

13 *The Etownian*, January 30, 1936, p. 2

14 *The Etownian*, January 16, 1936, p. 1

15 *The Etownian*, October 9, 1936, p. 1

16 *The Etownian*, November 28, 1934, p. 1

17 *The Etownian*, November 7, 1935, p. 2

18 *The Etownian*, February 18, 1938, p. 1

19 *The Etownian*, May 29, 1940, p. 2

20 Letter dated October 1, 1929, quoted in *Moving Toward the Mainstream*, pp. 130–131

21 Quoted in *Moving Toward the Mainstream*, p. 133

22 Quoted in *Moving Toward the Mainstream*, p. 133

23 *Our College Times*, November 19, 1931, p. 3

24 *Our College Times*, December 14, 1933, p. 2

25 *The Etownian*, October 9, 1935, p. 2

26 *Our College Times*, December 14, 1933, p. 1

27 *Our College Times*, November 29, 1933, p. 1

28 *The Etownian*, February 13, 1935, p. 1

29 *Our College Times*, November 29, 1933, p. 1

30 *The Etownian*, January 16, 1935, p. 4

31 *The Etownian*, February 13, 1935, p. 2

32 *The Etownian*, April 13, 1937, p. 1

33 *The Etownian*, April 13, 1937, p. 2

34 *The Etownian*, May 3, 1938, p. 1

35 *The Etownian*, January 14, 1937, p. 1
36 *The Etownian*, November 5, 1938, p. 2
37 *Our College Times*, November 16, 1932, p. 3
38 *Our College Times*, October 13, 1933, p. 3
39 *Our College Times*, January 23, 1934, p. 1
40 Ibid.
41 *Our College Times*, February 28, 1934, p. 3
42 *History of Elizabethtown College 1899–1970*, p. 150
43 *The Etonian* 1930, p. 52
44 *Our College Times*, May 19, 1931, p. 1
45 *The Etownian*, October 9, 1935, p. 2
46 *The Etownian*, December 8, 1938, p. 2
47 *Our College Times*, January 22, 1931, p. 1
48 *The Etownian*, November 28, 1934, p. 4
49 *Our College Times*, February 13, 1934, p. 2
50 *The Etownian*, February 27, 1935, p. 1
51 *Our College Times*, May 3, 1932, p. 2
52 *The Etownian*, October 23, 1936, p. 2
53 Interview with William Willoughby, Summer 2000. Also, in Rose's defense, it must be stressed that Lancaster County continues to have a large German-American population who are proud of their heritage, and preserve it still in such organizations as *Liederkranz*. The College itself had both a German Club and the social club, *Der Deutsche Verein*, during the thirties.
54 *The Etownian*, October 17, 1934, p. 4
55 *The Etownian*, February 21, 1939, p. 2
56 *The Etownian*, March 8, 1939, p. 2
57 Interview with William Willoughby, Summer 2000.
58 *The Etownian*, October 3, 1939, p. 2
59 *The Etownian*, October 19, 1939, p. 1

Chapter 7
1940–1950

"War has just sprung into our lives..."

The history of the first half of the 1940s at Elizabethtown College is, of necessity, the history of the Second World War. The College, like every other American institution of that time, was deeply affected by the war, in matters of both life and death. In some cases, former pacifists turned into young warriors, while others remained non-combatants, but demonstrated great bravery under fire. Some gave their lives, but no one remained untouched.

In the years before America entered the war pacifism continued to be the watchword of Elizabethtown students. In the fall of 1940, students William Willoughby and Ernst Lefever, the editor and assistant editor of *The Etownian*, left the school for a semester to tend small children at a migrant labor camp at Moxee, Washington. They hitchhiked both ways across the country, waging a free-lance peace campaign in the process, and were given a hearty bon voyage by the campus paper. In the same issue *The Etownian* reported Roosevelt's signing of the Burke-Wadsworth Conscription Bill as an example of how the United States had "slipped into the dictatorial tempo, shoulder to shoulder with the European combatants."[1]

On October 16, twenty-five Elizabethtown College students were among the sixteen million young Americans who dutifully participated in the first selective service registration in the country's history. As if this disruption wasn't enough for the students, the situation was further complicated by a change in the presidency that had been in the hands of Ralph Schlosser for the past ten years.

At the January 1, 1941 meeting of the Board, the trustees accepted Ralph Schlosser's resignation of the presidency to take effect on July 1. Part of the Board's vote stated, "Due to the valuable services President Schlosser has rendered to the College for many years we recommend that he be appointed as teacher of English for next year."[2] The Board also recommended that Schlosser be relieved of the task of student solicitation during the summer, and be permitted to teach two summer courses instead.

According to Schlosser's own *History*, the trustees had been experiencing "a period of deliberation on the election of a President for the next year," but whether due to Schlosser's continuing request that he be allowed to devote time to teaching, or for other reasons is not clear. Whatever the motivation for his resignation, it did not take the trustees long to choose a successor.

A. C. Baugher had been the dean of instruction since 1928, and had been a part of the College for a quarter of a century. He was universally respected as both a teacher and an administrator. He had earned his B. S. in chemistry from Franklin & Marshall College, his Master's degree in chemistry from the University of Pennsylvania, and his Ph.D. from New York University in 1937. His church credentials were nearly as extensive as his educational ones.

The offer of the presidency was made on February 15, and Baugher accepted the office on several conditions. From now on, the faculty would be selected by a committee made up of the president, the treasurer, and one or two members of the Board of Trustees. Along with this new hiring procedure, there would also be a two or three year faculty program mapped out.

Baugher also felt that the president of a college should not devote the majority of his time searching for prospective students;

rather, this task was so important to the future of the College that it should be headed by a full-time student solicitor. The trustees agreed, and graduate Galen C. Kilhefner was appointed "Field Representative" for the 1941–42 school year.

During the 1940s, President Baugher put most of his energies into two areas, the first of which was the academic growth of the College. The second, heavily dependent upon the first, was the accreditation of the College by the Middle States Association. Baugher realized that a college was only as strong as its teachers, and continued his predecessors' practice of enhancing the academic excellence of the faculty.

In the years between 1941 and 1951, the total faculty grew from twenty-one to thirty members, and, while the number of doctorates remained the same, the number of professors with master's degrees increased from five to thirteen. By the end of Baugher's tenure, the College boasted a faculty of 58, 35 with master's degrees and 13 with doctorates.

But all that was in the future. For the present, along with Baugher's long term goals, the College had to survive the tenuous financial problems that beset it. One of the new President's most difficult jobs was to release one of the most beloved teachers on campus, a decision dictated solely by financial necessity. The terms of ex-President Schlosser's resignation returned him to the teaching staff, and since the budget had room for only one English professor, Rebekah Shaeffer, the dean of women who had done wonders with the College's dramatic programs, had to be dismissed. Dr. Baugher carried out the Board's directive, a hard introduction to the difficult tasks that he would face during his twenty years as president.[3]

The College's financial state remained precarious for some time. In 1941 a deficit for the previous school year drove the trustees to vote to go to the church districts once again and ask for donations to the College on Education Day. The districts made the request to the churches, but the response, as in years earlier, was less than hoped for.

In desperation the Board voted to make up the deficit by deducting the amount from the faculty salaries, but eventually were able to find and use the money in a nearly forgotten reserve fund.

This seems to have been the last time, hat in hand, that the trustees were forced to go begging to the church districts.

After the war, the influx of veterans into colleges brought higher education within reach of more people than ever before. As a result, college education became less exotic and a greater part of the mainstream, so that the churches of the supporting districts gave far more generously than before. The 1940–41 school year showed only $1434 in donations from both districts, while only five years later the amount had increased to $9983, and contributions for 1950–51 swelled to $14,718.[4]

That generosity, however, had not yet begun, so the Baugher administration and the trustees were obliged to wage a financial battle while a far greater battle developed, one for which the Church of the Brethren was already preparing. The advent of conscription had been a harbinger of what might be expected for the country. On February 22, 1941, 850 Brethren delegates met in the College gymnasium to discuss how to support the Brethren Public Service Camps program, which had been created to assist the many conscientious objectors that the church expected from their ranks.

War clouds continued to form until, finally, Japan attacked the American naval forces at Pearl Harbor in the Hawaiian Islands on December 7, 1941. President Roosevelt and congress promptly declared that the country was at war. Only five days after the attack, James R. Young, author of *Behind the Rising Sun*, spoke about Japan at the College. The same issue of *The Etownian* that reports on Young's upcoming speech contains an editorial, "Christmas in Time of War," in which there is no mention of the Japanese attack, no cry for revenge, no beating of battle drums. Instead, the editor states, "Although war has just sprung into our lives let us not replace that most desirable spirit of Christmas cheer, carols, holly, and all the pleasures of the Yuletide with war songs and feelings of hatred."[5]

Lancaster County swung into wartime mode. Young men poured into recruiting offices to enlist, and many factories, such as Armstrong Cork and Hamilton Watch, changed over to war production. The county and the country mobilized for war.

Elizabethtown College would prove to be no exception. From this point on, the College paper, as well as the minds of nearly everyone on campus, was filled with the presence of war. From the time of the entry of the United States into the war, the general feeling was that this war was different — it was being fought to preserve freedom and the American way of life. Instead of defending pacifism, the students, at least, seemed to veer in the opposite direction.

In a 1942 *Etownian* front page article, "Elizabethtown College's Part In Defense," the writer states, "The accusation has come to our ears that the College is not doing its part in defense. That they are only supporting pacifist activity. This is a false accusation as the following list will attest."[6] The list consists of the names of 25 former students now in the service.

On the next page in a column called "Random Thoughts," Henry Glade '42 writes, "What we are witnessing is nothing more nor less than a decisive struggle over the spiritual destiny of the planet. The ferocious assault of totalitarian barbarism...is directed against culture itself and the ultimate aim of totalitarianism is the de-humanization of man.... Everything is uncertain, our future is veiled, the horizons darkened."[7] For Glade the enemy is identified and the battle worth fighting, though he does not state in what form.

Whether or not to fight was a question still confronting many in the Church of the Brethren. One session of the annual Bible Institute was devoted to the role of the Church in the current crisis. Four options for young men were discussed: the first was to refuse to comply with the draft registration laws and go to prison; the second was to register as a conscientious objector and go to a Civilian Public Service (CPS) Camp; the third was to take non-combatant duty in the army; and the fourth was to go straight into army duty. A number of related questions came up, including whether or not the Church could "purchase war bonds which are used to build more instruments of death."[8]

The leadership of the Church of the Brethren had spent much of their time since the first World War ensuring that there would be a place for their young men to practice pacifism in any future conflict. They had pressed for provisions in the Selective Service Act that would enable Brethren to serve as noncombatants or perform other service under civilian direction, and planned to financially support special CPS camps for conscientious objectors.

Still, with the CPS program well established, only 10 percent of Brethren youth chose this option, while another 10 percent selected noncombatant military service. Approximately 80 percent chose full, combatant military duty when the time came.[9] Most of the Brethren churches were supportive of their men in uniform from the start of the war, a striking contrast to earlier wars in which the combatants would have been either severely disciplined or ejected from the church.

Over the years, the church had become more active in not merely avoiding evil, but facing it head on. The Axis was an evil that had to be dealt with, and acceptance of a harsh reality replaced what many were starting to believe was an impractical idealism. In most Brethren congregations it was already acceptable to be a soldier.

While the war caused moral dilemmas for the Church, it caused both moral and financial ones for Elizabethtown College. In April of 1942 the problems had come to a head, and the College paper reported:

> *For the first time in the history of the College the faculty of Elizabethtown College and Alumni Council will meet with the trustees for a two-hour session in the morning. The subject for discussion for this joint session will be "Elizabethtown College and the War Emergency."*
>
> *The Church Related College as well as practically all our institutions are in the grip of circumstances over which they have little or no control. Income from investments are shrinking while living costs are advancing. Enrollments in the Colleges are decreasing as the call of the army increases. Faculty members are being called away from the classroom to the military service of the nation. The Federal Government may offer financial aid to colleges which participate directly in a military training program.*
>
> *How shall the program of the Elizabethtown College be adjusted to meet these war emergencies?*[10]

An example of one of the problems mentioned above occurred a few months later, when Herman G. Enterline, professor of business education, was granted a leave of absence to attend the United States Naval Training School at Indiana University in Bloomington. The same issue of the paper that reported this leave published a list of former Elizabethtown students in the service. It included Ensign Stanley Disney, piloting a Patrol Bomber in southern waters, Second Lieutenant Roy Rudisill, who was instructing in ordnance training school, Captain H. M. Leister, pilot of a B-26, and Second Lieutenant W. W. Raffensberger, pilot of a B-17-F, the "Flying Fortress."[11] These were hardly non-combatant positions.

Even those who remained on campus were affected by the war. Along with the effects of rationing, the students experienced numerous air raid drills and all-night blackouts. Plans were made to completely black out the library and the social room so that students could continue studying and fraternizing.

Though the College did not participate with the government to the extent of allowing military training on campus, they did grant a request from the United States Procurement Board to make an official visit to campus to discuss reserve corps enlistment with students. In November of 1942 U.S. Naval officers came to the College to interview students interested in enlisting in the Naval Reserve.

Many former students who were now servicemen wrote letters to Dr. Baugher, some of which were printed in *The Etownian*, and all of which were answered. Support of these student and alumni servicemen was strong. A plan was organized to write letters to them, and in January of 1943 *The Etownian* began to print a list of "Men in the Service" in every issue.

That same issue carried a statement from the trustees concerning drafted students. Since many men were being called up mid-semester, a college policy was required that would give them enough benefits to sign up for the coming semester rather than simply wait to be drafted. Under the new policy, draftees would receive academic credit for the work they had so far completed, and would receive a *pro rata* refund of their tuition fees. "Students are therefore encouraged," the statement read, "to register for the second semester and take advantage of all the time possible before they are called."[12]

Many *were* called. The following issue reports the departure of six students into the service, and Navy representatives showed up in April to administer the V-12 Qualifying Test, which drew more men from the student body. The Navy Department even tried to persuade female students to enlist, by contributing an article on the WAVES and SPARS to the campus newspaper. By March 1944, the newspaper's back page was filled with another article about the WAVES, including an official Navy photo of a WAVE operating an aircraft machine gun.

Other changes were occurring on campus. At a meeting on April 17, 1943, the trustees optimistically voted full salaries for the faculty for the current and the following year. They also decided to increase their own number from twelve to twenty-four, three of whom would be nominated to the board by the Alumni Association. It was a vivid contrast to the days when the trustees and administration dictated whether or not food could be served at alumni functions.

Now, however, alumni were a strong source of educational, administrative and financial support, as they had been for decades. It may have been due to the presence of those alumni in the General Conference of the Church of the Brethren, as well as the obvious drain on College finances caused by the war, that led to an unexpected windfall for the College.

For the first time the General Conference voted to provide annual financial support to church colleges. Elizabethtown College received a check for $5000 from the Church's General Education Board, and was promised the same amount every year for the duration of the war.

The local churches of the Eastern and Southern Districts were also joining in, with many individual congregations writing the College into their budget. It was estimated that these local churches would give another $5000 to the College, bringing the yearly total to more than $10,000. In addition, it was further estimated that "the productive endowment of the College has been increased by more than $200,000 during the last two years."[13]

But while the circumstances of the war brought some unexpected gains to the College, it also brought losses. The same issue of the newspaper reporting the financial contributions also stated that,

"Due to the very acute drop in male students for the coming term, the athletic outlook for the year is indeed very doubtful. Soccer has definitely been dropped and the question of a men's basketball team is still hanging fire."[14] While the 1942 yearbook showed men's baseball, tennis, and basketball teams, the 1944 Etonian shows only a basketball squad, and of the eight men pictured, only one, Guy Buch, had any previous varsity experience.

There were far greater losses, however, than sports teams. Reports were received of the death of John Espenshade, followed by that of Lt. Stanley Disney who was killed in a plane crash at Norfolk, Virginia. A year later, Louise Baugher, President Baugher's daughter, started writing a column for *The Etownian* entitled "With Our Men And Women In The Service," in which she reported that, "Seven men and women from Elizabethtown College have already given their lives in the service of their country: Stanley Disney, John Espenshade, Luke Sauder, Mary Albright, Richard Albright, Edmund Duckworth, and Henry L. Metzler."[15]

They would not be the last. Pfc. Ralph E. Shank, who had attended the College from 1940 to 1943, was killed in action in Holland; Richard M. Palmer was killed on D-Day; and First Lieutenant Raymond E. Sheckard, Jr. was missing over Germany, after thirty-seven missions as navigator for a squadron of Flying Fortresses. John D. Giter and Adda Jane Patterson also died in the service of their country.

Others were more fortunate, surviving their wounds. Lieutenant Paul A. Hoffman '38 was wounded in France, while Edwin Boll was wounded on three different occasions. Nearly two hundred Elizabethtown College students served during the war. Many distinguished themselves, like Pharmacist's Mate Oscar Wise, a Naval hospital corpsman who constantly exposed himself to enemy artillery fire to treat his wounded comrades.

There were also acts of quiet heroism performed closer to home. Dr. Guy R. Saylor, professor of modern languages at the College, volunteered four nights a week to teach English to German prisoners of war who were being held at the military base at nearby Indiantown Gap.

Though campus support for the war effort was overwhelming, support for the Roosevelt administration was not. In November of 1944, with the war drawing toward an inevitable victory for the Allied forces, a mock national election held on campus gave Republican Thomas E. Dewey sixty-eight votes, while Roosevelt garnered only nineteen, just two more than Socialist candidate Norman Thomas. Republicanism held strong.

Still, the voice of the College as expressed in *The Etownian* proved socially liberal when it came to matters of injustice. An article entitled, "Armed Forces Enforce Jim Crow Regulations" by Don Lefever attacked racial segregation in the armed services, concluding, "Is this what we are fighting for, when we say we are fighting for the freedom and equality of all men? Is it any wonder that some British soldiers recently said that the German brand of supermanism or Nazism could not be much worse than some Americans?"[16]

That same issue contains "The Broader View," an editorial suggesting that the countries freed from the Nazis may not all choose democracy, but may instead model their post-war societies after Soviet Russia:

> It is our duty as students to unbind our minds from the common prejudices and biases and look at the problem subjectively. Too many of us when we hear the word Russia still think in terms of "blood and liquidation." We see "Red." But, their system has made them a great people.
>
> Then, if that system can be won without the shedding of a great sea of blood and a people seem suited to it, let us not close our eyes and say the world is going to ruin because the people are not realizing democracy.[17]

That is exactly what many people would be saying only a few years later, during the height of the McCarthy era. For the present the Russians were our allies who helped to bring about victory in Europe. On May 7, 1945, a V-E service was held in the chapel, at which Dr. Ralph Schlosser proclaimed, "This morning our hearts are filled with emotions of joy and sorrow — of joy because of the news flash that organized resistance has ceased in Europe and of sorrow because of loved ones who shall not return to their homes."[18]

Many, however, who did return to their homes were anxious to take advantage of the Servicemen's Readjustment Act of 1944, known as the G. I. Bill. Besides establishing veterans' hospitals and offering vocational rehabilitation and low-interest mortgages to veterans of the war, the act granted stipends covering tuition and expenses for veterans who attended college or trade school. Between 1944 and 1956, the education and training provisions gave benefits to almost ten million veterans.

The G. I. Bill proved a blessing to Elizabethtown College, and could not have come along at a more opportune time. In the summer of 1944, the trustees and the alumni council had voted to start a three-year building and endowment campaign with President Baugher as its director. His administrative duties would be performed by members of the administration and faculty while he concentrated on raising $300,000. The breakdown of goals included $35,000 from the trustees, $10,000 from alumni council, $80,000 from alumni and former students, $75,000 in special gifts from individuals, and $100,000 from corporations and organizations.

For the next few months, college publications emphasized the campaign and stressed the importance of giving; by October the fund had reached $42,500 and continued to grow. In early 1945, the Reverend John C. Zug donated $20,000 to be used for a room in the new library as a memorial for his father, founder Samuel R. Zug.

The combination of a successful campaign and the influx of money from the G. I. Bill put the College on its best financial footing ever. Fifty freshmen enrolled in the fall of 1945 with five returning veterans among the student body that semester. At the start of the next semester, thirty ex-servicemen entered the College.

The presence of these ex-GI's caused some changes on campus, nearly all of them positive. Dean Henry Bucher noted, "The administration is considerably heartened by the prompt and excellent adjustment that the ex-GI's have made. They have fit in very nicely and enthusiasm has grown out of the enrollment of these men."[19] Of these students twenty were enrolled in business administration, ten were preparing to teach, four were in liberal arts, and three in science. Those in pre-professional courses included six in medicine, five in dentistry, four in engineering, and two in chiropody. One planned to become a veterinarian, while another was going into agriculture.

Most of the other students were delighted with their new companions. An *Etownian* editorial reveals why:

> *The whole atmosphere on the hill has changed. Classes are quite different this semester with the ex-GI's enlivening class discussions by drawing from their wide experience. Basketball games played by a super team, bolstered by ex-GI's, have taken on a new excitement. Social functions are enhanced by the rousing school spirit brought by these men. The whole campus looks the way a campus should look again!*
>
> *Men with little gold buttons on their lapels are seen strolling around the campus wearing initiation placards. Welcome to our clubs, fellows!*[20]

Those initiation placards and all that went with them proved to be a sticking point for the returning veterans. It was not likely that men in their twenties who had undergone military training and experienced enemy fire were going to become meek freshmen docilely accepting the dictates of fresh-faced, eighteen-year-old upperclassmen. A letter from a female student to *The Etownian* criticized the attitudes of these freshmen during initiation night, when some disobeyed assignments and refused to carry out direct orders from the head of the student government.

It was quickly understood, however, that what had worked for freshmen in the past would not be suitable for the post-war crop. Senior John Dunham's opinion was that the veterans deserved such latitude:

> *Veterans are not attending college to indulge in childish performances that some students might include under the heading of "school spirit." Many laws that the Senate ordinarily would have passed or enforced concerning freshman conduct, etc., have been completely revised. The GI has had the training and*

> *discipline necessary to teach him respect for the group*
> *as a whole, an attitude which many freshmen in other*
> *times may have lacked.*[21]

There were other aspects of college life that some of the veterans found difficult to accept. Paul Reed expressed one problem clearly in a guest editorial:

> *Is it necessary for the ex-servicemen to go to chapel*
> *every morning and continuously hear a speaker relate*
> *to us the horrors of war, and how he objects to war and*
> *compulsory military training?... Are we going to chapel*
> *for a summary of the war, or for spiritual guidance?*
> *Every person that was a member of the armed*
> *forces objected to war and never have I heard any of*
> *them say that they wished the war would continue...If*
> *everyone would have objected to fighting, what would*
> *have happened to our democracy?*
> *It is very disappointing to enter chapel, thinking*
> *that you will hear a speech that will help you; instead*
> *we hear a speech that only incites anger within us, and*
> *promising ourselves never to attend another chapel serv-*
> *ice. Of course, we are good-natured and always return*
> *for more. We have compulsory chapel services, so why*
> *not forget the war, and use our energy and will-power*
> *in building a peace-loving world, a world in which our*
> *children will never witness the horrors of war.*[22]

World War II veterans adapted well to peaceful civilian life, and the other students and the faculty did whatever they could to make the transition smooth. Half a dozen students tutored fifty of the ex-GI's in special refresher classes and in other special subjects. Dr. Schlosser and Professor Horace Kaufman, along with their Elizabethtown College duties, taught at the GI Area College, which was established at West Penn High School in Harrisburg, with an enrollment of 361 students.

One particular prize from the large crop of ex-servicemen was freshman Edgar Bitting, who had played both flute and saxophone in various Navy bands, and served as first flautist of the Harrisburg Symphony during his college years. His professional future was not in music, however. Bitting graduated from the College in 1950, went on to earn his doctorate, and in 1955 joined the Elizabethtown faculty as professor of accounting. His wife Doris was also on the faculty of the College.

Bitting served as chairman of the business department from 1959 through 1976, and in that capacity increased enrollment in the department more than threefold. He retired in 1984, but continued to teach part-time until 1987, when he received an honorary doctoral degree from the College. He died in 1994.

≈§—§≈

The College gained other post-war benefits besides Edgar Bitting. The start of the 1946–47 school year saw over 300 students enrolled, 145 of them veterans. Additional dormitory space was essential, and the government came through with two former WAVE quarters that would serve as dormitories for sixty men.

The erection of these two government-issued buildings delayed the start of classes until October 1. By then, the new buildings, North and South Hall, stood at the right of the entrance to the gymnasium. Each building had ten single rooms, ten doubles, shower and bath facilities, and a living room.

The following spring the government donated another building measuring 4070 square feet. Originally planned as a library, it actually became a business education building with five classrooms and two offices.

This physical growth, along with the increasing student population, a more secure financial standing, and the academic improvement of the faculty, fit in perfectly with A. C. Baugher's vision for accreditation for the College. Preparation had initially begun in November 1944, when Dr. Baugher attended the annual meeting of the Middle States Association, and conferred with the Secretary of the Association, Dr. Karl Miller of the University of Pennsylvania. When Miller learned to what extent the College's financial position and the academic caliber of the faculty had been strengthened, he suggested that Baugher file an application for accreditation.

After several months of work, Baugher submitted a 150-page report in June 1945 to the Commission on Institutions of Higher Education. When Dr. Roy DeFerrari of Catholic University visited the campus and found a number of weak areas in the program, the commission tabled Elizabethtown's application.

At the 1946 meeting of the association, new accreditation rules were put in place that tabled Elizabethtown for a full year. During that time, the College administration worked diligently on strengthening the areas of weakness, which still included the faculty and the school's finances, as well as greater selectivity of the student body. President Levering Tyson of Muhlenberg College was appointed by the association to serve as an advisor and visited the campus, where he made a number of suggestions.

At last in March 1948, a five-person committee headed by Dr. M. E. Gladfelter, Provost of Temple University, inspected the College and presented their findings to the Middle States Association. On May 7, Dr. Baugher announced in chapel that Elizabethtown College was now fully accredited by the Middle States Association. It had been a long time coming, and the announcement was greeted with thunderous applause. It meant that Elizabethtown College was accorded full academic standing among the leading colleges of the United States.

Two months later, the College became a full member of the American Council of Education, and in March 1949 was approved by the New York State Department of Education.

❧—☙

Among the new faculty members whose credentials helped to boost Elizabethtown's academic reputation were several who would become mainstays of the College. Vera R. Hackman had started her collegiate career as a student at Elizabethtown, graduating in 1925, and earned her master's degree from Columbia in 1936. She taught in Pennsylvania public schools and, for two years, in a settlement school in Harlan County, Kentucky. She came to Elizabethtown College as a professor of history and the dean of women in 1944, and immediately made her presence known by serving as the advisor of Sock and Buskin, *The Etownian*, *The Etonian*, and the

Women's Honor Society. Her journalism skills led her to teach the first journalism course at the College.

She was known as strict but fair, and many women students who were first frightened by her stern qualities soon grew to know her as a warm and understanding friend. In 1968, she retired as dean of women after serving for twenty-four years, but remained at the College as a professor in the English department for another five years.

In 1947 another alumnus was appointed to the faculty. Mark Ebersole graduated from the College in 1943 after a sterling stint as an undergraduate. His yearbook entry reads, in part, "Our amiable, genial Reverend, with sparkling wit, a driving enthusiasm, a dynamic, disarming, magnetic personality, has revealed unfaltering and inspiring leadership in sundry activities...from staid scholarly and theological pursuits to athletics..."[23]

In the few short years between his graduation and return to Elizabethtown as instructor in Bible and philosophy and director of religious activities, Ebersole had received his B.D. from Crozer Seminary and was doing graduate work at the University of Pennsylvania. In addition, he had held pastorates at Mt. Olivet, Newport (Pa.), and was associate pastor of Tioga Baptist Church in Philadelphia, where he counseled students at both Penn and at Drexel. Most recently he had been doing post-war relief work in Italy, and had also served as a director of youth camps and as a member of the National Youth Cabinet of the Church of the Brethren.

The comment in the yearbook about "unfaltering and inspiring leadership" would prove prophetic when Mark Ebersole, '43, became the President of Elizabethtown College in 1977.

Two other faculty appointments that proved of immense value to the College were those of Charles S. and Bessie D. Apgar. Dr. Charles Apgar joined the teaching staff in September, 1945 as an associate professor of biology, and his wife, Dr. Bessie Apgar, became an instructor in the same department a year later.

From the start, the Apgars proved to be a fascinating and, at times, a delightfully eccentric pair. They owned a massive Rolls-Royce, which Bessie would often drive while Charles sat in the back like a chauffeured millionaire.[24] He also proved to be great material for *Etownian* interviews, presenting a mixture of utopian optimism and scientific prophecy. A few months after he came to Elizabethtown, he was quoted as saying, "The prevention of future wars is a certainty if we share our ideas with other nations, for ideas are the things men fight for. Also, all the young men in the world must be kept busy and satisfied, for young men make the schemes of older tyrant-dictators possible...I predict that not very far in the future, electrical waves may be used to imprint knowledge on the student's brain."[25]

At one point, Apgar's office was above a large room in which the College band rehearsed, a situation with which he was far from happy. One day he entered the dean's office unannounced with a tape recorder, opened it, plugged it in, turned it on, and sat down.

From the tape recorder came his voice, saying:

"This is Charles Apgar. I am in my office. The time is 4:15 P.M. It is Friday. Listen."

The sound of band music was clearly heard. Dr. Apgar switched the machine off and turned to the dean. "Well," Apgar said, "what are you going to do about it?"

"Not a thing," said the dean.

"That's what I thought," said Apgar. He packed his equipment and left without another word.[26]

Several years later, Charles described the Apgars' home life in the foothills of the Blue Mountains, where they had, "a cabin, kennel house, pigpen, chicken house, and garage." Besides growing all their own vegetables, Charles said, "I like to camp, hike, canoe, watch sunrises, sunsets, storms, and paint! I love trees and abhor the destruction of any of them. I am an avid hunter but have recently given it up for photography of wild and ocean life."[27]

Somewhere in the midst of this frenzy of activity, the Apgars also found time to guide the curriculum development of the College's biology department. By the time of their joint retirement in 1967, Elizabethtown College had been recognized by medical schools and graduate schools nationwide for the high caliber of biology students it produced.

Charles Apgar never stopped learning. After the death of his wife, he remarried, taking the name of his second wife to become

Charles Farver-Apgar, and traveled throughout the world, even in his nineties. As he stated when he was interviewed for the College's centennial video, he lived his life as he studied science, as "an unending pursuit of the truth, on and on and on."[28] He died in 2001 at the age of 98.

What the Apgars were to biology, Oscar F. Stambaugh was to chemistry. In 1946, Stambaugh came to Elizabethtown after eight years of teaching at Penn State, a year at Juniata, and three years working as a chemist for Gulf Oil, experiences that gave him both an academic and industrial background. He began at Elizabethtown as an associate professor, and was made a full professor two years later. In his years as head of the chemistry department, the chemistry curriculum, facilities and teaching staff all showed remarkable development. In 1965, he was appointed to the newly created position of Director of Curriculum Development.

K. Ezra Bucher was another strong force in guiding Elizabethtown College through the 1940s and 1950s. A 1932 graduate of the College, he became an alumni trustee in 1942, and treasurer of the College in 1945, as well as a business professor. Bucher had been instrumental in acquiring the two surplus government buildings to ease the campus housing shortage in 1946, as well as the structure that became the Business Education Building.

Many alumni may recall Bucher as an active member of the All College Players, a group of faculty and students who regularly staged plays on the campus. Bucher used his skills as business manager of the group, but also directed and starred in several of the productions.

Under the keen eye of Bucher, President Baugher, and the trustees, the College made the most of the postwar boom, solidifying their financial base and using the opportunity to initiate both building programs and other overdue changes. At the end of 1946 the trustees at last established a retirement plan for full-time teachers and administrators. (The participants were required to contribute 5 percent of their monthly payment, a move that was widely welcomed.)

In 1948, the board approved plans for a new $100,000 library and an enlarged gymnasium. The gymnasium project, however, entered a financial black hole. Money raised for it was funneled into other projects that demanded greater urgency; it was not until 1970 that a new field house would appear on campus.

The plans for the library, however, proceeded more smoothly, though it was fortunate that the College did not have to depend on a book auction held to raise money for the library. It brought in a paltry $32.85. The Zug Memorial Library was dedicated on October 20, 1950. The total cost was $160,000. The library had room in its three-tiered stacks for 50,000 volumes, which seemed more than sufficient for growth, since in 1950 the College owned only 16,500 books. The building would serve the College as its library for the next forty years.

⊸§—§⊷

The postwar period also ushered in a renaissance in sports at Elizabethtown College. The war years, with their shortage of male athletes, saw much of the school's attention focused on women's sports, but the influx of veterans provided a needed source of players for men's teams.

Much of the athletic excitement of the postwar years, however, centered around one young man from the little town of Cornwall, Pennsylvania. To Coach Ira Herr, Freshman Frank Keath must have seemed like the answer to his prayers. The basketball team had just lost Guy Buch, who had graduated in 1944, and had led the nation in scoring that year.

In his first year Keith scored 371 points in 20 games, for an average of 18.6 points per game, which placed him as the second highest scorer per game in the state. Keath depended on skill rather than height, since at 5'10" he was the third shortest member on the team. He proved to be an all-around athlete, playing first base on the baseball team and goalie when soccer began to be played again in 1947.

But it was basketball in which Keath excelled. During his sophomore year, he scored 433 points in 21 games, finishing the year with a 20.6 points per game average, the highest in Pennsylvania. As a junior, he established a new state record in total points scored in a season, with 564 points in 23 games, for a 24.5 points per game average, again the highest in the state. He also set a record for the most points in a single game, with 43 against Bridgewater.

Keath ended his college career with 504 points in 1949, giving him a total of 1872 points for a career average of 21.2 points per game, which placed him fourth among the all-time point scorers in collegiate basketball. As *The Etownian* accurately observed, "It must be taken into consideration that he was a marked player and opposing coaches continually assigned two men the task of trying to hold the scoring wizard down,"[29] which made his feats all the more amazing. He and fellow hoopster Richard Hivner were presented with varsity sweaters at the end of the 1948–49 season, a tradition which would continue for all seniors who had won two varsity letters in basketball. As a further honor, Keath's number (25) was retired. His uniform is still on display in Thompson Gym.

The success of the College tennis team also culminated at the end of the decade. The 1948–49 team was the first in the school's history to have an undefeated season. It was led by Captain Frank Zink, "who has yet to taste defeat during his collegiate career," according to the College paper.[30]

The 1940s ended on another sterling note for Elizabethtown athletics, with the school's election to full membership in the Middle Atlantic States Collegiate Athletic Conference on November 15, 1949. It was a goal toward which Coach Herr had been aiming for several years.

As if in celebration, the following spring witnessed the birth of the Bluejay. Until 1945, Elizabethtown teams were often referred to as the Gray Ghosts or the Phantoms. During the 1945–46 school year, students submitted suggestions for a new mascot, and when those suggestions were voted on, the Blue Jay was the winner.

It was not, however, until 1950 that C. Frederick Horbach created the Blue Jay with a capital *B*. "With its blue body and gray and white breast," *The Etownian* boasted, "the bluejay wears the colors of the school, and with its well known fighting spirit characterizes the efforts shown by our team in competition."[31]

As always, the 40s saw other extracurricular activities on campus besides athletics. While many of the old clubs and organizations had fallen by the wayside due to lack of interest, others took their place. Among the newer entries were the International Relations Club, the Lutheran Student Association, the Peace Team, the Student

Christian Movement, and the Future Teachers of America. The Debating Team remained active, and during the 1949–50 school year, under the direction of history professor Mahlon Hellerich and manager Gerald Fosbenner, set the best debating record ever at Elizabethtown College, winning 34 of their 38 debates.

In 1949, popular films, which had been vilified years before, were finally coming to campus. *The Etownian*, which had been running film reviews for several years, conducted a poll asking students if they would be willing to pay fifteen cents to attend a film shown on campus each month, and the result was overwhelmingly positive. Among the movies screened on campus were such non-controversial classics as *Little Men*, *Little Lord Fauntleroy*, *Swiss Family Robinson*, and *Tom Brown's School Days*, as well as more worldly entries, like *A Star Is Born*, the caveman epic *One Million B.C.*, and Alfred Hitchcock's *Foreign Correspondent* and *Jamaica Inn*.

The activity that may have given Etown students the greatest cause for rejoicing, however, was the first May Day at the College on May 14, 1947, with Arlene Kettering serving as the first May Queen. The establishment of this celebration was certainly due in part to the general easing of restrictions that had come with the advent of veterans to the campus.

The end of the war brought something else to the campus as well, an even greater sense of the College as part of the world around it. Military service had been a great melting pot, and one of the many lessons that veterans brought home with them was that national heritage, religion, and skin color didn't matter when there was a job to be done. World War II had been fought against racial hatred and prejudice as much as it had been fought against aggression. From the end of the war to the early 50s, *The Etownian* reflects these liberal social sentiments in many ways.

An editorial that appeared in the fall of 1945, "Time for Housecleaning," objected to the Daughters of the American Revolution denying the African-American pianist, Hazel Scott, access to Constitution Hall for a concert appearance:

> *Biologically, all races are equal; everyone agrees to that. But our prejudices, ungrounded though they may be, set up barriers that make equality impossible.*

> *This post-war era, in which some other glaring*
> *evils are being remedied, would be a good time to do*
> *away with race discrimination.*[32]

A year later, another editorial welcomed those who were different to the campus: "We welcome the different religious, racial, and cultural additions and the enriching contributions they bring to Elizabethtown College. Jewish, Catholic, and Negro students are represented in small numbers."[33]

Beginning in 1947, the paper ran a political cartoon nearly every week whose message was against intolerance, targeting specific hate groups like the Ku Klux Klan. A typical cartoon showed, in the first panel, a John Q. Public type labeled "Average American," saying "Did you know that I'm intolerant, too?" to a weasel of a man, who is grinning evilly and is labeled "The Intolerant." The bigot replies, "Swell! Of what?" The second panel has John Q. saying, "Of the likes of you — *that's what!*" and drop kicking the bigot a good six feet into the air.

Altogether, it was an admirable point of view for the College to be promoting as it readied itself to begin its second half-century. The golden anniversary of the school's founding was fast approaching, and the College decided to honor the man who had done the most to ensure that the fledgling Elizabethtown College would survive.

On November 20, 1948, at the closing session of the forty-ninth annual Bible Institute, President A. C. Baugher conferred the honorary degree of Doctor of Divinity upon 90-year-old George N. Falkenstein, "In recognition of his pioneer work in education and in the pastoral work of the church and in appreciation of his untiring services in founding Elizabethtown College, in recognition of his achievements in writing and preaching, he is indeed a most worthy recipient of the degree."[34]

There could not have been a better way to approach the fiftieth anniversary than honoring G. N. Falkenstein. He, more than any other person, had been responsible for both the birth of the College and its survival through those earliest and most difficult years. Falkenstein passed away less than a year later, on August 17, 1949. It was due to him and those like him that A. C. Baugher, who had himself been a part of the College since 1914, was able to look back in a 1950 *Etownian* editorial and see how far Elizabethtown College had come.

From one building on one acre, the school now had nine buildings on fifty acres. The student body had grown from six to over 800, the faculty from three to thirty-three. Nearly 200 courses were now offered.

In its fifty years of existence, the College had seen over 11,000 students and 194 teachers on its faculty. Half of the students and well over a third of the faculty had been women. From operating on a shoestring, the current budget was in excess of a quarter million dollars.

Elizabethtown College was entering its second half century fully accredited, well respected, and stronger than it had ever been before.

1 *The Etownian*, October 7, 1940, p. 2
2 Minutes of the Board of Trustees, Elizabethtown College, January 1, 1941.
3 Interview with Louise Baugher Black, May 28, 1999
4 *History of the Church of the Brethren Eastern Pennsylvania*, p. 199.
5 *The Etownian*, December 10, 1941, p. 2
6 *The Etownian*, February 10, 1942, p. 1
7 op. cit., p. 2
8 op. cit., p. 4
9 *Moving Toward the Mainstream*, p. 204
10 *The Etownian*, April 13, 1942, p. 3
11 *The Etownian*, August 20, 1942, p. 1
12 *The Etownian*, January 28, 1943, p. 1
13 *The Etownian*, September 1, 1943, p. 1
14 Ibid. p. 1
15 *The Etownian*, November 1, 1944, p. 3
16 *The Etownian*, May 1, 1945, p. 1
17 op. cit., p. 2
18 *The Etownian*, June 1, 1945, p. 1
19 *The Etownian*, February 25, 1946, p. 1
20 op. cit., p. 2
21 *The Etownian*, November 22, 1946, p. 2
22 *The Etownian*, April 16, 1946, p. 2
23 *The Etonian 1942–1943*, p. 27
24 Interview with Jerald L. Garland, May 25, 1999
25 *The Etownian*, January 28, 1946, p. 1
26 Recollection of Dr. Jobie E. Riley, February 23, 1999
27 *The Etownian*, May 16, 1950, p. 3
28 Interview with Charles Farver-Apgar, 1999.
29 *The Etownian*, April 15, 1949, p. 4
30 *The Etownian*, June 14, 1949, p. 4
31 *The Etownian*, April 18, 1950, p. 2
32 *The Etownian*, October 26, 1945, p. 2
33 *The Etownian*, September 27, 1946, p. 2
34 *The Etownian*, November 15, 1948, p. 1

"Heisey Hall," the site of the College's first classes on the corner of Bainbridge and South Market streets in Elizabethtown. It is believed that this photograph shows one of the three trips required in "moving the College" from the Heisey building to Rider House while Alpha Hall was still under construction.

Rufus P. Bucher, one of the "Faithful Six" first students enrolled at the College and later chairman of the College's Board of Trustees.

Jay G. Francis, the young Church of the Brethren minister whose idea for a Brethren college in central Pennsylvania resulted in the founding of Elizabethtown College.

George N. Falkenstein, right, who is credited with the survival of the College in its early years. He is pictured here on the Henry Hess farm near Aberdeen with Daniel Miller, left, and Samuel R. Zug.

The Class of 1904, first to graduate from Elizabethtown. Standing (l-r): John Henry, Walter Gish, H.K. Garman, and Irvin Shoop. Seated (l-r): Samuel Kieffer, Mary Stayer, and Harry Lehman.

Rider Hall, left, and Alpha Hall. Physical landmarks of the College until Rider was razed in the early 1900's.

Elizabethtown College's first baseball team, circa 1905.

Faculty and students gather for a ceremonial tree planting, circa 1912.

Early dorm life in the upper floors of Alpha Hall.

An aerial view of the College and surrounding community in 1929.

An early women's basketball team.
Standing (l-r): Lydia Landis, Ella Steffy, and
Ellen Merkey. Seated (l-r): Frances Musser,
Elizabeth Holsinger, and Mary Strickler.

An early business class.

The College faculty in 1924. Notables include Elizabeth Myer and five presidents: Henry Ober, Ralph Schlosser, A. C. Baugher, J. G. Meyer, and Harry Nye.

Early dining facilities for students in the basement of Alpha Hall.

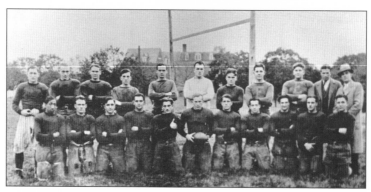

Elizabethtown College's first and only football team. "Undefeated since 1928!"

Lake Placida in its early days was host to memorable tug-of-war contests, as well as the occasional ice-skating session.

Bookend presidencies of the first 50 years: A. C. Baugher, left, and I. N. H. Beahm.

Samuel H. Hertzler, chairman of the Board of Trustees who is credited with keeping the college open during the worst days of the Great Depression.

Commencement in the "old" gymnasium.

Legendary coach and athletic director, Ira R. Herr
(left), and Ethel Wenger, the College's first
woman trustee.

Dean of Women Vera Hackman '25
at her best, teaching.

A May Day celebration in an era gone by.

The late trustee and College benefactor, Carlos R. Leffler. His daughter, Linda Castagna '67, received the Centennial Medal given him posthumously.

The College's 50th anniversary was commemorated during a Halloween parade through Elizabethtown. "Educate for Service" was quite evident 50 years ago.

Bessie and Charles Apgar, seminal figures in the College's science program, with their famous Rolls-Royce.

A freshman ritual in the 1960's, wearing the beanie, or "dink."

Today, the College retains its heritage while building state-of-the-art facilities, like High Library.

The College's Centennial Quilt project, organized by Tana Parrett '69 and art professor Lou Ellen Schellenberg, involved the labor of many volunteers from Church of the Brethren congregations.

Edgar T. Bitting '50, who built the reputation of the College's business program.

The College's Centennial celebrations took on many themes, none more relevant than the Empty Bowls dinner, organized by Jason Bugg '00. This event raised awareness of world hunger and money for the Heifer Project.

On the kick-off day for the College's Centennial celebration, members of the campus community dressed in plain garb to act as tour guides for visitors to the campus. Pictured here are Carroll Kreider '60, professor of business *emerita*, and her husband Ken Kreider '61, professor of history *emeritus*, and their daughter, Brenda Kreider Barlet '81.

College president Ted Long welcomes Nobel laureate Archbishop Desmond Tutu, who spoke movingly about peace and reconciliation to a filled Thompson Gymnasium on March 17, 2000.

Chapter 8
1950–1960

"Great days..."

The 1950s fulfilled the promise that the late 40s had heralded. The combination of accreditation and the unprecedented influx of new students, thanks to the G. I. Bill, had at last put Elizabethtown in a position where not only its existence, but its continued well-being, seemed assured. So it would be, for at least another quarter century.

There would, however, be no resting upon laurels for President Baugher, his administration, or his faculty. The 1950s were a time of major fundraising, construction, and building upon the academic base that had been so greatly strengthened in the previous decade.

In the 1951–52 school year, the College had thirty faculty members. By 1960–61, that number would nearly double to fifty-eight. The number of earned doctorates nearly doubled as well, from seven to twelve, and those with Master's degrees almost tripled, going from thirteen to thirty-five. The academic accomplishments of Elizabethtown's professors were growing, and would continue to do so. The number and variety of courses that these teachers taught also increased, offering students ever greater choices.

With an increase in faculty and students came the need for more facilities. During the first fifty years of its existence, Elizabethtown College had been graced with five major buildings: Alpha Hall, Rider Hall, Fairview Apartments, Gibble Science Hall, and the Student-Alumni Gymnasium. From 1950 through 1960, four more buildings were added, and the decade from 1960 to 1970 would see another seven. It looked as though Elizabethtown College was leaving behind its insecure past and looking into a bright and solid future.

As Elizabethtown entered its second fifty years, it bade farewell to several of the people who had helped to bring it to its present era of confidence. A year after G. N. Falkenstein's death in 1949, I. N. H. Beahm, the College's first principal, died on November 11, 1950. At a still robust 91, death claimed him in a head-on automobile accident. Only a few months later J. G. Meyer, president in the early 1920s, died in Seattle.

Still, most of these founders and early pioneers remained only names and portraits to most Elizabethtown students. The 1950s were starting out well. At the beginning of the 1950–51 school year, the first floor of Memorial Hall had been renovated, the campus had been newly landscaped, and there were many positive reports of graduate placement in the booming job market. The sole negative was summed up in a September *Etownian* headline: "Despite War, 90 Freshmen Enroll."[1]

The Korean conflict began on June 25, 1950, when North Korean troops pushed across the 38th parallel between North and South Korea. By July 7, a U.N. Command had been established, at the instigation of the United States, beginning a war in which 1.8 million Americans would serve, and in which over 54,000 would die.

By October, ten male Elizabethtown students had been inducted into the military due to the war, officially referred to as a "police action." Most were deferred until the end of their current semester, thanks to the Selective Service Act of 1948, which stated that students could have their induction postponed until the end of their academic year.

Student outcry against the Korean War was practically non-existent at the College. The Communists had become the boogeymen of the 1950s, and an *Etownian* editorial entitled "The Bear Is On The Rampage" opined that "The war in Korea...proved that Russia would willingly equip aggressors against democracy with all types of war material...It also indicated that Russia may be planning a gigantic clash between communism and democracy in the very near future."[2]

One of the few disapproving views of the conflict was couched in senior Armon Snowden's attack on the draft and how it destroyed the rights of individuals: "When a nation adopts Universal Military Conscription, it creates...a people who are indirectly controlled by the military."[3]

No matter what one thought of that control, it was having an effect upon the College. The following September, only sixty freshmen enrolled, due in large part to so many potential male students being inducted. Along with transfers and graduations, total enrollment dropped 15 percent.

The loss was keenly felt, and the pressure to replenish the supply of students fell to Eby Espenshade, a 1935 Elizabethtown College graduate who now served as field representative for the school. His job was to visit high schools and persuade worthy students to attend the College. In 1950–51, he had visited 192 high schools in twenty counties, and that number would increase after the administration decided to recruit a minimum of 125 students for the 1952–53 school year.

That year's freshman class numbered only 106, but it signaled a healthy increase over the previous year. With the signing of the armistice in Korea on July 27, 1953, the conflict ended, and young men could once again feel free to enroll in college without a pressing fear of induction.

Unfortunately, one of the College's best and brightest had already graduated when he was inducted. Paul Eugene Greiner '54 was the College's only Korean War casualty. He did not die in combat, but of an illness contracted shortly after his induction in June of 1954, passing away at Walter Reed Army Hospital on September 17 of that year. Greiner had been editor of both *The Etownian* and *The Conestogan*, which the yearbook, formerly *the Etonian*, had been called since 1951. The 1955 *Conestogan* was dedicated to his memory.

⪻—⪼

Growth, both physical and financial, continued as a primary concern of President Baugher, the administration, and the trustees, and it was money that fueled that growth. At the end of 1952, Elizabethtown College joined the newly formed Foundation for Independent Colleges, an affiliation of 38 non-tax supported schools in Pennsylvania. They joined together to mount joint appeals to industries and commercial concerns for gifts to help educate the future employees and leaders of these businesses. The real contributions, however, would come as a result of the College's own fundraising activities, which would greatly expand the College's physical plant.

Nor was the faculty immune to the expansive charms of growth. As early as 1952, science professors Charles Apgar, Oscar Stambaugh, and Carl Heilman collaborated on plans for a new wing to Gibble Science Hall. Both classroom and laboratory space were at a premium in the building, and conditions could only worsen. Their plan would double laboratory space for biology, chemistry, and physics, and add two large classrooms, a lecture hall, and faculty office space.

There was also a pressing need for dormitory space, and in 1954 President Baugher recommended that a new women's dorm be built. These two new projects, along with the long-felt need for a new field house and the conversion of the current gym into a chapel/auditorium, caused the trustees to hire a fund-raising agency to develop a ten-year fund-raising campaign.

The ultimate goal was one million dollars. K. Ezra Bucher, the College treasurer and business manager, was appointed director of the campaign, Wilbur E. Weaver was named business manager in Bucher's place, and Robert S. Young, assistant to the president, was asked to help Bucher.

By the end of the first year, the development fund had reached $328,000. Shortly thereafter, the Gibble family came to the fore again, launching their own campaign to raise $70,000 to add a west wing to the building that bore their name. Construction began in the fall of 1957.

Money continued to be pledged, thanks in large part to Bucher and Young's enthusiastic efforts, and at the end of the first three-year stage totaled $438,000. Bucher resigned in 1958 for a position with Continental Press of Elizabethtown. Earl H. Kurtz '35 replaced Bucher as college treasurer, and J. Albert Seldomridge '52 took over as director of the development program. In August 1958, Seldomridge reported that the amount raised was over $666,000. Seeing only good omens in this "number of the beast," the trustees voted to raise the total amount to $1,500,000.

Then and in the years to come, a good percentage of the gifts to the College would come from alumni. In 1958–59, an Alumni Giving Fund was established, raising nearly $170,000 that year.

A more modest support of college activities came from the Women's Auxiliary, which was organized in 1956 at the Paxtang apartment of Miss Ethel M. B. Wenger. Miss Wenger, a loyal alumnus of the College who had spoken at Elizabeth Myer's memorial service in 1924, was the first woman trustee of Elizabethtown College. Over the years the auxiliary made numerous contributions to the school, the first of which was a silver tea service for Myer Hall. Later, there were monetary gifts as well as other contributions of deeply needed materials.

However, it was not long before the money raised by the development fund was exhuasted. A Federal Housing Agency loan of $582,000 was taken to meet the most immediate need, that of the women's dormitory. Construction began in 1955, but due to delays was not completed until December of 1956; by January the women were moving in. The dormitory, which included a modern kitchen and large dining room, was not named when it was dedicated. The administrative hope seemed to be that a donor would come along who would repay the loan. At that point, the College would offer to name the building in the donor's honor.

Unfortunately, no donor stepped forward. An *Etownian* editorial in January 1959, two years after the dormitory's dedication, bemoans the fact that the building cannot be referred to except generically, and hints about a rumor that $100,000 will name it. "Couldn't the residence be named," it suggests, "in honor of a particular person's service to the College rather than a financial contributor?"[4]

Editorials were still being written about the lack of a name nearly two years later, after a trustees' naming committee had been in place for over a year. It was not until May 1961 that the Board finally announced that the building would be named for a campus legend, Elizabeth Myer, one of the original faculty members — the first woman to teach at the College and one who had taught there until her death in 1924. No one could deny the correctness of the choice.

The west wing of Gibble Science Hall experienced no such naming delays. It was opened for inspection on May Day of 1958, and dedicated on September 24 of that year, during the sixtieth Charter Day Convocation. An honorary degree was conferred upon David E. Brinser, who, along with his wife Sadie, had been the donors of the new lecture hall.

The final building project of the 1950s was a men's dormitory that was deemed an "absolute necessity" by the trustees.[5] Another loan of $675,000 was made from the federal government, and the building, which housed 232 students, was erected in 1959–60 and dedicated on October 15, 1960. It consisted of two adjacent three-story buildings joined by a large lounge area, permitting hundreds of male students living in private homes to move onto the campus. The building had to wait only seven months after its dedication for a name. It became Ober Hall in honor of past President H. K. Ober.

The field house, alas, would have to wait for the next decade before finances permitted its construction, in spite of President Baugher's plea to the trustees that, "It is important that early and definite attention be given to the need for a field house."[6]

❧——❧

Elizabethtown College achieved even further growth during the early fifties by looking outside the campus. In 1951 Elizabethtown and Lebanon Valley College decided to establish the Harrisburg Area College Center, providing college level classes in the afternoons and evenings for adult students in the Harrisburg area. Classes were first held in the Central High School building in Harrisburg, and credits could be applied toward a degree at either Elizabethtown or LVC.

This joint venture was so successful that Temple University, Penn State, and the University of Pennsylvania later joined in the program so that the center was able to offer graduate work as well. Robert A. Byerly, a professor of religion at Elizabethtown, was the center's first director, and A. C. Baugher the first chairman of the board. In 1966 the name was changed to the University Center at Harrisburg, and by the end of the 1960s an average semester had an enrollment of up to 1500 students and a six-acre campus complete with classroom buildings, offices, and a library. It still flourishes as the Dixon University Center, part of the Pennsylvania State System of Higher Education, and Elizabethtown College continues to offer classes there.

The College entered into another collaborative effort with a fellow college in 1954, a joint engineering program with Penn State. A student could take three years of classes at Elizabethtown, and then transfer to Penn State for a two year program in several types of engineering. At the conclusion of studies, the student would receive a B. A. from Elizabethtown and a B. S. from Penn State.

The College attempted further outreach programs, and used the new medium of television, both to reach prospective students and to gain further exposure for the institution and its faculty. WGAL-TV, a Lancaster television station, ran a program called *College of the Air*, a show which reached 760,000 viewers in six counties. On October 13, 1953, A. C. Baugher gave a televised lecture, "From Alchemy to Chemistry," marking the first of many appearances by Elizabethtown faculty, including one in which Dr. Phares H. Hertzog spoke on reptiles. Another WGAL program, *March of Science*, showcased Oscar Stambaugh and Albert L. Gray, Jr. telling "The Story of Steel," and Charles Apgar speaking on "Backgrounds of Biology" and "Nature of Life."

The College also telecast programs on WHUM-TV, Channel 61 in Reading, as part of their "Live and Learn" series. There were musical concerts by Elizabethtown students, presentations of Sock and Buskin plays, and lectures by Carl Heilman on the Pleiades and Ralph Schlosser on Robert Browning. The College also used radio to reach the community. Twice a week, WEZN in Elizabethtown broadcast *From the Elizabethtown College Campus*, a show dealing with current activities on campus as well as subjects related to higher education in general.

Even more people were reached through the community service courses the College offered. These classes were held on campus, and a fee was often charged. Ministers and church workers could enroll in a weekly Bible study course, farmers could take a nine-week course in dealing with federal income tax, and the many grocers in the area could attend "Grocers School," an eleven-week course in modern food store operation. These courses were highly successful and ran year after year.

One of the most highly publicized and successful programs of outreach to the community was "Three Great Days," held in October 1954. The program featured speakers, performances, and assemblies held throughout Elizabethtown, as well as concerts, open houses, and teas, all of which were open to the public.

❧—☙

The decade reflects a large number of other advances: changes in policy brought about by changing times, further reaching out to the wider academic community, and a number of new faces on campus. More foreign students were enrolled at Elizabethtown College. The 1950–51 school year saw Chwan Chang Yang from Chungking, China, and the following year brought Carlotica Chegwin to the campus from Colombia. Next year Carlotica's brother Eduardo, and Korean student Kim Sun Kyung arrived. At least one foreign student a year would attend the College through the fifties.

There were new faculty faces as well, many of whom proved memorable. One of these was Phares H. Hertzog, who was appointed in the fall of 1953 to direct all science laboratory activities at the College, as well as serve as part-time instructor. Hertzog graduated from Bucknell, and received his master's degree from Princeton in 1914. For 39 years he had been the head of the science department at the Peddie School in New Jersey, where he had taught Adlai Stevenson, sportscaster Red Smith, and actor/governor George Murphy.

Hertzog became one of the most loved figures at the College. Over the years he donated a baseball scoreboard, his personal butterfly collection valued at $6,000, and another collection of plant samples. He helped to plant myriad trees and shrubs on campus, and was also active in the Boy Scouts, from whom he received scouting's highest honor, the Silver Beaver. He was well known for knot tying, and gave lengthy presentations on the subject, as well as on herpetology.

After his "second retirement" from the College, he visited dozens of schools in the area, charming and frightening generations of children with his snakes and other reptiles. He remained active until his death in 1988 at the age of 107.

Another new face was that of a young man who became dean of the College in the fall of 1956. Roy E. McAuley, who would become president of the College in 1961, succeeded Dean Henry G. Bucher, who resigned his position to become superintendent of the Manheim schools. McAuley was not an Elizabethtown graduate, but had received his B. S. from another Brethren college, McPherson College in Kansas. There he had majored in biology, with a minor in English.

He had gone on to earn a B.D. from Bethany Seminary with a major in religious education, and a Master's degree from Omaha's Municipal University, where his major was English literature and his minor psychology. He earned his doctorate from the University of Denver in the field of religious education.

Like so many Brethren educators, he was also a minister. During his senior year at McPherson, he had first become pastor of a Church of the Brethren in Wichita, and then of one in Omaha. When he returned to McPherson as a professor of English and education, he took a pastorate at the Monitor Church of the Brethren. He left McPherson to work in public relations and teach general semantics at Northern State Teachers College in Aberdeen, South Dakota, and from there came to Elizabethtown.

His humorous side appears in a tongue-in-cheek article he wrote for *The Etownian* on how to fail your finals: "Sometime after midnight boil up a pot of coffee, put your text and notes in front of you and stare at them between catnaps. By 8 A.M. you should be quite cobwebby and in excellent condition to fail any examination."[7]

An *Etownian* article published when he was dean praises his "broad, extensive education and a keen sense of humor." He gave his philosophy of education: "Any separation of material from moral education is false, because as man evolves scientifically, he must also evolve morally." This, he continues, is the reason that he came to a church-related college, and that, although he is an educator and an administrator, he considers himself first a minister.[8] It was a philosophy that would win him a great many supporters in the College.

One more gentleman who came to the fore during the decade was Wilbur "Bud" Weaver. Weaver, the son of a farming family, worked his way through Elizabethtown College, graduating in 1937, and receiving his M. Ed. from Temple in 1942. He taught high school in Reading for ten years, then returned home and worked at the College bookstore. He was appointed business manager of the College in 1954, and assistant treasurer in 1958. Weaver, a vital participant in the College for many years, was honored in 1998 with the Educate for Service Award for Service to Humanity.

Among the long line of fine women teachers at the College, many will recall Mildred H. Enterline, who, with her husband Clarence, joined the faculty in 1956 as a speech teacher. Her interest in dramatics led her to direct many of the productions on campus. She died unexpectedly in 1964. Though she only spent eight years at the College, her influence was great and her loss deeply felt.

Although Elizabethtown College had long been blessed with excellent female faculty members, there had never been a woman trustee, a situation that the alumni association intended to rectify. In the spring of 1954, ballots were sent out with the names of three female alumni, one of whom would represent the alumni association on the Board. They were Grace C. Blough, Hilda I. Gibbel, and Ethel M. B. Wenger. Miss Wenger was the winner, and served her first three-year term from 1954 through 1957.

Two years after Wenger's election, the Board of Trustees nominated Martha Bucher, who served a three-year term from 1957 to 1960. With the door finally open, women would play a larger role on the Board in years to come.

Another major change occurred on the Board of Trustees when, on July 29, 1954, Rufus P. Bucher, chairman of the board, requested to be relieved of his position. He had served on the Board for forty years, and had been chairman for fifteen of those. His letter of resignation is filled with the humility and kindness for which he was known:

> *Dear Brethren of the Board:*
>
> *Due to my physical condition I am not able to perform my duties as I should as Chairman of the Board.*
> *I would kindly asked to be relieved of that position.*
> *My interest in the College will continue. I am sure you understand.*
>
> *Humbly submitted,*
>
> *Your servant,*
>
> *Rufus P. Bucher*[9]

The request was granted, and the Board voted to designate Bucher Chairman Emeritus. He passed away less than two years later, on April 19, 1956, one of "The Faithful Six" who had remained faithful to the end.

The board elected Joseph W. Kettering, a 1923 graduate of Elizabethtown, as only the fifth chairman of the board. He became a C. P. A. in 1930, and served as treasurer and head of the commercial department of Blue Ridge College in Maryland. Later he joined the accounting firm of Main, Lafrentz, and Co., becoming a resident partner in 1943 and a general partner in 1955, and retiring in 1966. During the 60s and early 70s, he served on the State Board of Law Examiners.

Kettering first became a member of the Board in 1936, served as secretary from 1943 to 1954, and as chairman from 1954 to 1968. In 1958, the College granted him an honorary doctorate of Commercial Science. He died on July 27, 1971.

◄§—§►

There were a number of other changes initiated by Elizabethtown College that brought the school further into the mainstream and even further away from the sheltered cloister of the early 1900s. In 1951, by a vote of 53 to 8, the College's employees had chosen to be covered by Social Security. However, since there were a number of ministers on the faculty and staff, the Bureau of Internal Revenue stated that coverage depended on "whether the College was operated as an integral agency of a religious organization under the authority of a religious body constituting a church or church denomination."[10]

After some negotiations, the agency ruled that ministers on the faculty would indeed be included in Social Security coverage, and that their wages should be included in the "Employer's" federal quarterly tax returns. Social Security was now added to the staff's retirement, group health, and accident plans.

The spirit of change on campus resulted in a further loosening of the reins on students. In the 1951–52 school year, an optional "cuts" system was introduced. Juniors and seniors were permitted to be absent from any class in which they maintained an "A" average without being penalized for cuts.

The following year even greater leniency was permitted. New regulations developed by the faculty permitted each student, regardless of grade average, two cuts per credit in each course during the semester. If students exceeded the number allowed, they were to present an excuse to the professor; if that excuse was deemed "unsatisfactory," they would automatically receive a "D" in the course unless the professor recommended otherwise.

Even the library, known as one of the most strictly run campus facilities under L. D. Rose, experimented with an open stack system in 1953. Until that time, students had had to request books, which would be retrieved for them by library staff.

One area that did not change was mandatory chapel attendance. No matter how the outside world had encroached upon the students and the College, here at least was one institution, born of the College's religious heritage, that would remain sacrosanct despite cries to the contrary. Those cries were coming more frequently, and so loudly that *The Etownian* felt it necessary to remark on the opposition to chapel in a 1958 editorial:

> *Perhaps misunderstanding prevails here because
> the Church of the Brethren is a relatively small denomi-
> nation and because numerous other denominations are*

well represented here. And perhaps some friction exists because Brethren beliefs are a bit more conservative than most others.

For some students the changes here haven't come often enough or in large enough numbers. Unfortunately, these students made the wrong choice in colleges. Fortunately, Elizabethtown doesn't need them should they decide to satisfy their wants more fully.... Religious influence, conservatism, and deliberate progress are all needed. But how much is hard to say.[11]

A month later, a letter from student Richard Sharpless presented another point of view:

The protest of the dissenting student is no less valid than the right of the College [to hold compulsory chapel] ... It has even been hinted that several students have escaped through the gym windows. The penalty for being caught in these acts is usually a two-week suspension.... Certainly, one cannot understand why a student would risk a suspension in order to spend that extra hour drinking coffee downtown. On the other hand, the idea of a college administration acting like grade-school supervisors is absurd.[12]

In 1959, chapel services were moved to the Elizabethtown Church of the Brethren, a larger venue. There would be no change, however, in attendance regulations. "We will continue," said Dean Edward Crill, "to take attendance on the basis of the signed chapel programs turned in after the service."[13]

To many students, signing and turning in programs as proof of their attendance struck them as a combination of enforced morality and punching a time card. Their protests and attacks on the administration would steadily increase, becoming more heated during the sixties. A mild sample of the kind of criticism directed against "the establishment" of the College can be seen in a 1959 editorial, "Is the Brass Acting Polished?" It accuses the administration of taking for granted that the class of 1959 would donate a memorial:

> *...and then it coldly shunned a list of suggestions submitted by the class while handing down an "official" list of possible memorials with restrictions and provisions from which the class could choose.*
>
> *It seems that the administration should allow a bit more leeway when dealing with contributions — and a little more tact.*[14]

Despite the resentment over compulsory chapel, many students and staff alike still seemed to adhere to the motto of the College: "Educate for Service" — the desire to use one's education to help others. The 1950s are filled with examples of such concerns and sacrifices, both major and minor. The Japan International Christian University, whose name is self-explanatory, became one of the College's favorite causes during the early fifties. A. C. Baugher was one of the university's trustees, and Elizabethtown students were asked to consider how they could make a contribution to the Japanese college. In the spring semester of 1952, a Campus Community Chest was formed in which students actively solicited funds for three international aid foundations, one of which was the Japanese university. The other two were the International Rescue Committee and the World Student Service Fund.

It was a time in American history when working in support of international agencies could be viewed with suspicion. For several years, Senator Joseph McCarthy had been waging his notorious campaign to ferret out communism in every nook and cranny of the government and American society, whether it existed there or not. Though McCarthy's motives were self-aggrandizement rather than patriotism, the fever was catching and the fear of being identified as a communist sympathizer was widespread.

A 1951 New York *Times* story reported that two things which college students feared most were a "pink" or communist label, and "the spotlight of investigation by government and private industry for post-graduate employment and service with the armed forces." These concerns made students reluctant to talk about controversial issues outside of the classroom, and even hesitant to discuss "currently unpopular concepts in regular classroom work."[15] These fears made students less likely to join organizations and subscribe to humanitarian causes, since one was more free from suspicion by remaining "unaffiliated."

Nevertheless, Elizabethtown College continued to support worthy international organizations. In 1953 the Campus Community Chest again supported the Japanese ICU and the World Student Service Fund (which aided refugee students and promoted anti-discrimination), but also added to the list Piney Woods Junior College, "making a contribution to the colored race by providing education and culture to young people at a minimum cost."[16] Two Elizabethtown College juniors, Mildred Holloway and Sally Johnson, had graduated from the school.

The practical results of "Educate for Service" was also seen in the constant reports of the College's alumni. A 1953 issue carried two full pages on "Alumni Work on School and Mission Frontiers on Three Continents." Among the stories were those of Emma Ziegler '21, who was teaching in India, Ethel Heisey '43, teaching at a West Rhodesian mission, and Anna Engle '25, Mary Heisey '46, and Earl Musser '49, who were administering a hospital-clinic, three schools, and a farm at Wanezi Mission in Southern Rhodesia.[17]

Moreover, the church still played an active part in many students' lives. Even though there were 28 religious affiliations represented among the students, including Jews, Catholics, and even Russian Orthodox, Dutch Reformed, and African Methodist Episcopal, a large number were still Church of the Brethren. Deputation teams served a number of churches in eastern Pennsylvania, and in 1953, 32 students directed worship services at various churches over a three-week period.

Just as the spiritual sphere was of concern to Elizabethtown College, so too was the political sphere. Students were increasingly aware of the world around them, since thanks to television it intruded into campus life more than ever. By 1954, there were large RCA television sets in both the living room of Alpha Hall and the South Hall social room, along with cracker and coffee dispensers to supply food and beverages to those glued to the set's gray glow.

Television was a solid hit on campus as soon as it became available. A 1952 editorial pitted TV against the movies, with TV coming out on top, thanks to:

> *...the superb clowning of Sid Caesar and Imogene Cocoa* [sic]*, the razzle-dazzle of Super Circus, the daringly different news coverage by Edward R. Murrow, the dramatic works of Studio One. Witness, too, the 12-hour commercials. They are the scourge of the industry, the nasty little brats which must be tolerated and never spanked.*[18]

Besides bringing entertainment onto the campus, television also brought the visual immediacy of news. The 1952 presidential election was the first to have wide television coverage, and Elizabethtown students seemed to agree with the simplistic slogan, "I Like Ike," choosing Eisenhower over Adlai Stevenson in the student election by a ratio of three to one. The new president's brother, Milton Eisenhower, president of Penn State, spoke at the 1953 graduation ceremonies. A cartoon published in the College paper showed a male graduate with a diploma in one hand and induction papers in the other, with the caption, "One from Milt and one from Ike."[19]

The draft would continue to remain a point of contention among students. In March of 1953, the Student Christian Association sponsored a discussion with a student team from Dickinson College about "The War, the Draft, and the College Campus." The head of the R.O.T.C. unit at Dickinson College also spoke.

Editorials in *The Etownian* ranged from bucolic to rabid, depending on the editor and the subject being discussed. Editorials in the 50s had vicious words for Argentina's Juan Peron ("a modern Hitler"[20]), India's Nehru ("a hypocrite"[21]), and such homegrown menaces as the hydrogen bomb, Joe McCarthy, and Arkansas Governor Orval E. Faubus, who had ordered state militia to prevent nine African-American students from entering Central High School in Little Rock. The editorial's title was "The South Will Lose Again."[22]

There was further criticism of the Governor of Georgia for his outburst against the mixing of races when the football teams of Georgia Tech and the University of Pittsburgh played each other. Even though the Georgia Tech students pleaded with the governor to allow a Pitt African-American back to play, he had remained adamant.

Elizabethtown College had always tried to be a bastion of racial equality in a less than integrated area of the state. "Since its inception," read a 1952 Brotherhood Week editorial, "Elizabethtown College has not discriminated against races and religions in the acceptance of students. ...man's respect for man is the core of freedom."[23]

Although there had been a number of African-American students at the College, the first African-American professor was John Jasper Spurling, who began teaching sociology in the 1956 fall semester. He received his A.B. from Talladega College, and his A.M. from New York University. He took further graduate work there and at Columbia, but spent only one year on the Elizabethtown faculty.

≈§—§≈

There was no lack of student and institutional causes. Tirades against careless driving launched in the 40s grew even stronger in the early 50s, when the College paper was filled with gory examples of what might be the result of inattention on the highways. A front page story called "Drips," complete with a grim cartoon, provides one of the most painfully and unintentionally funny pieces of prose in the history of *The Etownian*:

> *Drip...drip.*
>
> *Red, still warm blood drips with little splashy thuds on the grimy highway, then trickles and soaks away.*
>
> *Maybe it's the blood of another motorist, or of your traveling companion, or maybe it's the blood of you.*[24]

For many students, the causes that concerned them most were the battles fought on the basketball courts and the athletic fields. When Director of Athletics was made an official position, Ira Herr, the natural choice, was appointed and Stanley E. "Whitey" Von Nieda was named basketball coach.

January 11, 1951 must have brought a smile to the new coach's face, as it marked the first time that Elizabethtown had ever defeated Albright College. The season ended with a decent 16–11 record, although the Junior Varsity racked up an impressive 16–4 record.

Elizabethtown fans went through periods of support and disinterest over the years, if the frequent editorials bemoaning the lack of school spirit at games is any indication. In the winter of 1951, a song and cheer contest was held, and Junior Allan Whitacre claimed the prizes. His cheer?

> *Rickety, Rackety Russ.*
> *We're not allowed to cuss.*
> *But nevertheless, you must confess*
> *There's no better team than us.*[25]

Fortunately for Whitacre, English professors did not seem to be among the judges.

Von Nieda was soon replaced as basketball coach by Joseph Dodd, dean of men and a physical education instructor. But the big news was the first women's field hockey team. Evelyn Heath, former physical education director at Manor Township schools, coached the team, which was christened the "Bluebirds," as opposed to the male "Jays." Only eight of the nineteen young women had any hockey experience, so their first season record of two ties and four losses (two of them close) was nothing to be ashamed of.

The following year finally saw some victories. Although the team lost their first four games, they won their final three. The soccer team had an impressive year as well, racking up a 5–2–1 record, with three men up for All-American mention.

One of the outstanding single athletes of the decade was Nelson B. "Nels" Chittum, who lettered in basketball for two years. His main talent, however, was pitching, and he was a mainstay of the baseball team in his years at the College. His talent was quickly recognized by the major leagues, and in 1953 he signed with the St. Louis Cardinals, but was taken out of the AAA American Association Minneapolis Millers for a two-year tour of duty in the armed forces.

By 1958, he was pitching for the Cardinals, and by the final day of the season had faced every National League team, pitched 13 games, and lost only to Pittsburgh. The next two years found him at

Boston, where he pitched 27 games in relief, after which his professional playing days were over.

A student-athlete whose success was more local was Bill Pensyl, a 6'3" center on the late 1950s basketball teams. One of the finest players ever at Elizabethtown, he scored a career total of 1372 points, 487 of which came in his final year, giving him an average of 23.2 per game. The National Association of Intercollegiate Athletics listed him as one of the top scorers and rebounders in the nation.

The 50s were a good decade for Coach Ira Herr, who celebrated his twenty-fifth year of coaching baseball in 1956, for which he was recognized by the American Association of Collegiate Baseball. In 1959 he received the Sports Headliner of the Year Award from the association of Lancaster Sportswriters and Broadcasters "for contributions to local sports during his lifetime."

But perhaps Coach Herr's biggest thrill of the decade came a year after he started to coach men's soccer again, after a nine-year absence. His 1959–60 team, undefeated in fifteen games, won the Middle Atlantic Conference Championship by defeating Washington College 6–1. They then traveled to Slippery Rock to vie for the NAIA title. Though they won their first game, beating Howard University 5–2, they lost their second game to Pratt Institute during the second overtime of the game.

Athletic events at the College in 1958 were further sparked by the actual appearance of the Blue Jay mascot in the form of sophomore Hank Osborn, who got the idea from watching the Princeton Tiger and began to show up as the Jay on basketball courts between halves and quarters. *The Etownian* reported:

> The bird is college property because the Student Senate decided to reimburse Osborn for his expense on the project, and the Jay became property of the Pep Band.
>
> Hank credits Pat Williams with a fine job in dying his old pair of discarded long underwear which forms the legs of the Jay. Barbara Marzoff labored hard to sew the feathery thing together.

> *Bill Spaeth and Bruce Tinglof were instrumental in assembling, painting, and adjusting the batch of dyed wool, hardware netting, and felt to fit its bearer.*[26]

As always, there were plenty of activities for non-athletic students as well. Most of the long term campus organizations were still going strong, and new groups during the 50s included the Society for the Advancement of Management, the Political Science Club, Student Education Association of Pennsylvania, Dramatic Workshop, Student Teachers Association, Lutheran Student Association, the Canterbury Club (for Episcopalian students), Eta Gamma Kappa (for future ministers), and even a Chess and Checker Club.

Hundreds of guest artists and lecturers continued to appear. Students were exposed to actor John Carradine performing scenes from literature; Vincent R. Tortora lecturing on "Behind the Iron Curtain"; the Vienna Boy's Choir; former intelligence officer Dan T. Moore speaking on "Spy Warfare Today"; and the Don Cossack Chorus and Dancers (who, the advance press assured readers, were White Russian emigres "who fought communism in Russia as early as 1918–1920").[27]

Students were also able to amuse themselves with television, movies, and music. Student John Dean's column, "Discourse on Disks," reviewed new records, reserving special praise for the new RCA extended-play 45s with two to three songs on a side instead of only one.

Pop music did more than just delight. It enraged, if the attacks of John E. Way, Jr. on rock and roll are any indication. In his *Etownian* article, "American Popular Music on Skids as Rock and Roll Hits New Low," he traced pop music from jazz to rock and roll, and agonized over the fact the public now calls:

> *...for the lowest state that American music has ever reached...nothing more than the sound created by a wailing, screaming moron, backed by a loud drummer and a poor excuse for a hill-billy guitarist.... It is inevitable that the decadent processes of the times will eventually kill Rock 'n Roll, but until this slow process*

*takes place there will be gang wars and unharnessed
immorality among the teenagers of the day.*[28]

In case there's any doubt about the identity of this artist, Way
clarified it in his next article on modern music: "Has this moron
Elvis driven every teenager and college student into a monotonous
repetition of old song craze [sic]?"[29]

George Gerlach and Curtis Reiber's hearse offered proof that
students were still able to amuse themselves without any help from
the media. The two seniors had bought a 1938 hearse, which they
used to carry cheerleaders and the pep band to athletic events. "We
pulled into the parking lot at the Hershey Sports Arena before the
basketball game with Lebanon Valley," one of the seniors related,
"and I thought the parking attendants were so shocked we might
have to haul them away."[30]

The college hearse undoubtedly ceased to be a source of amuse-
ment several months later, when, on August 14, 1958, a KLM airliner
crashed. Among those killed in the crash were Eby Espenshade,
Director of Admissions at the College since 1947, the mother of
sophomore Kenneth Kreider, alumna Audrey Kilhefner, daughter of
trustee Galen Kilhefner, and alumnus John C. Hollinger. All were
returning from the celebration of the 250th anniversary of the
Church of the Brethren in Swarzenau, Germany. The author of this
history, ten years old at the time, vividly remembers the shock and
grief that swept the town. The event was made even more tragic
since Kilhefner and Hollinger, both recent graduates, had fallen in
love and had just begun to plan their life together. The memorial in
the 1959 *Conestogan* includes an excerpt from a letter written by one
of their friends:

> *Audrey and John, so recently graduated from
> College, have now gone on together to a larger life than
> the one they had planned for here. Bound together by
> their love in death as well as in life, they are now expe-
> riencing joys which you and I can only dimly imagine.
> To us, with our earthly eyes and limited vision, it
> seems a tragic ending to hopes and dreams, but for*

*them it is glory unspeakable and the complete fulfill-
ment of all of life.*[31]

⋘—⋙

Another death was soon to follow, one more in keeping with the
expected skein of life. J. G. Francis died in Lebanon, Pennsylvania on
August 27, 1958, at the age of 88. Regardless of his later aversion to
those who ran it, Elizabethtown College would in all likelihood not
have existed without his initial efforts. The trustees wrote in a letter
to his family:

> *His pioneering interest in higher education is
> understandable when we note that he had completed
> four years of college work and the three-year course
> leading to the B.D. degree before Elizabethtown College
> was founded.*
>
> *The history of Elizabethtown College bears witness
> to his interest in Christian higher education. For nearly
> a decade before the founding of the College he labored
> earnestly in advocating the establishing of an institu-
> tion of higher education for this part of Pennsylvania.*[32]

Francis had been the last surviving member of those early pioneers who had been present at the founding of Elizabethtown
College: Falkenstein, Hertzler, Ziegler, Bucher, and Light. Francis had
outlived them all.

And now the second generation, those who had been among
Elizabethtown College's first students and later teachers, were entering their twilight years. A. C. Baugher, who in 1914 had stepped
onto a campus consisting of only two buildings and filled with people in plain garb, saw that the time was coming to lay down some
of his burdens, even though they had filled his life with joy.

Baugher had decided to, if not fully retire, at least pass on the
duties of president to a successor. In a letter to the trustees, he
wrote:

> *After having been affiliated with Elizabethtown
> College for more than forty-five years as student,
> teacher, dean, trustee, and as President, I wish to offi-*

cially inform the Board that I plan to retire from the office of President at the end of the next academic year on June 30, 1961.[33]

Baugher made a number of requests concerning his future employment at the College, all of which were approved by the Board. Upon his retirement he would be designated President Emeritus and work in the area of development and fund raising; he would work only part-time and receive a salary commensurate with the time spent; and he would prepare a manuscript on the history of the College with no commitment from the Board as to its publication.

The resolution from the trustees that followed the announcement of his retirement praised him, specifically for four major areas. First was his effort to gain accreditation for the College. Second was the tremendous improvement in financial support for the school, particularly from the Church of the Brethren. Due to his efforts yearly support from Brethren congregations had increased from $3,555 in 1941 to $43,275 in 1959.

Third was the increased physical facilities. The campus had expanded from fifty to seventy-five acres, with four major buildings constructed. And fourth was the overall broadening of the academic prestige of Elizabethtown College.

Amid all the accolades that whirled around A. C. Baugher during the year of his retirement, there surely was a moment when he stood alone on the steps of Alpha Hall, as he had forty-six years earlier, and looked out over the campus of which he had once hoped to become a part, and whose present he had done so much to create.

As he did, he surely must have smiled as he remembered what he had thought all those years before, the words that appeared underneath his photograph in the Senior Number of *Our College Times* the year he was graduated:

He can who thinks he can.

---

1 *The Etownian*, September 19, 1950, p. 1
2 *The Etownian*, October 17, 1950, p. 2
3 *The Etownian*, April 17, 1951, p. 2
4 *The Etownian*, January 24, 1959, p. 2
5 Minutes of the Elizabethtown College Board of Trustees, September 1, 1957.

6 *The Etownian*, November 19, 1956, p. 1

7 *The Etownian*, January 9, 1960, p. 3

8 *The Etownian*, January 24, 1959, p. 1

9 Rufus P. Bucher: Letter to the Board of Trustees, July 29, 1954.

10 quoted in *History of Elizabethtown College 1899–1970*, p. 218

11 *The Etownian*, November 8, 1958, p.2

12 *The Etownian*, December 6, 1958, p. 2

13 *The Etownian*, December 12, 1959, p. 1

14 *The Etownian*, April 25, 1959, p. 2

15 quoted in *The Etownian*, June 19, 1951, p. 2

16 *The Etownian*, February 24, 1953, p. 1

17 *The Etownian*, March 28, 1953, p. 5–6

18 *The Etownian*, March 18, 1952, p.2

19 *The Etownian*, May 26, 1953, p. 2

20 *The Etownian*, April 7, 1951, p. 2

21 *The Etownian*, March 18, 1957, p. 2

22 *The Etownian*, October 11, 1958, p. 2

23 *The Etownian*, February 19, 1952, p. 2

24 *The Etownian*, December 11, 1951, p. 1

25 Ibid., p. 2

26 *The Etownian*, March 24, 1958, p.4

27 *The Etownian*, February 23, 1954, p. 1

28 *The Etownian*, May 20, 1957, p. 6

29 *The Etownian*, November 25, 1957, p. 3

30 *The Etownian*, May 12, 1958, p. 1

31 *The 1959 Conestogan*, p. 5

32 *The Etownian*, September 15, 1958, p. 3

33 A. C. Baugher: Letter to the Board of Trustees, May 28, 1960

Chapter 9

1960–1970

"It certainly is a trying time..."

The 1950s were a period of steady growth and maturity for the College. Although a few controversies reared their heads, for most students the campus was imbued with a sense of well-being and propriety, an island of academic and social safety, a shelter that would stand strong against most storms.

In the 1960s, however, those storms would start to sweep through the College itself, and that ivy-clad demilitarized zone would become a bloodless battlefield in a cultural and political war. The changes would be due to a number of factors: the war in Vietnam, which made citizens question more than ever the actions of their government; the so-called sexual revolution, which stood old ideas of morality on their heads; and the birth of "flower power," the hippie movement and psychedelia, which offered new ways of looking at the fundamental aspects of reality.

For many, it was what the title of the old song described as the results of the American Revolution, "The World Turned Upside-Down." Elizabethtown College would not be immune to the motion.

The very first *Etownian* editorial of the 1960s responded to the widespread criticism on campuses of the government's actions concerning college students. A year before, the Office of Education had introduced the National Defense Student Loan Program, which provided college loans for students in need. The colleges chose worthy recipients and paid one-ninth of the amount, with the government paying the rest — up to $1,000 a year or $5,000 for a student's entire education. Sixty-one Elizabethtown students were benefiting from these loans, which were to be repaid at a 3 percent interest rate.

One condition of the loans, however, was the signing of a "Loyalty Oath" by the students to the effect that they were not communists and were loyal to the United States. "Discriminatory or not," the *Etownian* editorial read, "why should any loyal American have qualms about taking an oath and swearing his solemn allegiance to his country?"[1]

Young mathematics instructor Bruce H. Tyndall thought there was something very wrong with such a required oath, and in a following issue criticized the editorial approval of what he considered not only an unnecessary intrusion into citizens' personal affairs, but further evidence of government encroachment in many walks of life. It was only the first of a barrage of letters and editorials that would question the motivation and judgment of not only the government, but the administration of the College itself.

The next few years, however, would be similar to the previous decade, a relatively calm period of growth. The transitions between presidents was smooth and predictable, although Dean Roy E. McAuley, the successor to A. C. Baugher, was the first Elizabethtown College president who had not been an alumnus of the school.

The youthful, thirty-nine-year-old McAuley was elected by the board on October 15, 1960, only a few months after John F. Kennedy, another youthful candidate, received the Democratic nomination for President of the United States. Part of McAuley's official statement said, "The college has a fine teaching staff, a select group of students, an interested trustee board, a dedicated group of administrators, and a fine church standing behind it. With God's guidance, there are wonderful days ahead for Elizabethtown College." When

asked informally what his plans for the College would be upon taking office, McAuley answered, "We no longer can be satisfied with
American and European history. We need now to teach Asiatic history and other cultures to meet the needs of today's students in
today's world."[2]

By the end of his term six years later, McAuley probably had
more than enough concentration on Asiatic history. But for the time
being, the future looked as untroubled as McAuley's statement suggested, and between the new president's election and his inauguration, a number of positive occurrences took place.

That summer the College had been accepted for membership in
the American Association of University Women; now all women
holding degrees from the College could join their nearest AAUW
chapter. The 1960–61 school year also saw the College inaugurating
its first foreign exchange program, with student Sylvia Hixon attending the Jugenheim Institute in Germany.

Plans were underway for three honors houses for junior and
senior coeds: "The Brick House" opposite the main entrance to the
College; Cedar Hall, the men's dormitory on Mount Joy Street; and
West Hall, also currently occupied by men. In February of 1961,
plans for a new women's dormitory and a new student union building were announced to the College community.

In May, the same month that Ober Hall was named, an announcement was made that the student union building would be
named for retiring President Baugher, who had just been feted at a
testimonial dinner at the Penn Harris Hotel in Harrisburg.

It was also announced that the College would buy the Cameron
estate, a twenty-five-room mansion on fifteen wooded acres, which
had been part of a William Penn land grant to James Stephenson in
1734. Simon Cameron, Secretary of War under Abraham Lincoln,
had bought the property in 1872. It would be used, the trustees stated, "for educational purposes."[3]

The mansion had been leased to Camphill Schools and con-
verted into a school where thirty-one mentally challenged children
aged nine to fourteen lived and were taught. By 1968 it was being
used as a men's residence, housing fifteen college students.

In the midst of this healthy and bustling environment, Roy McAuley assumed the presidency of the College in July 1961. The College paper reported that under the new president, "the college plans to continue its program as a service institution with obligations to its alumni, the Church of the Brethren, the community, and the general constituency built up over the years." McAuley announced that one of his immediate objectives would be, "a long range plan to guide the programs of the college in terms of personnel, academic approach, and areas of service."[4]

McAuley, his wife, and three children moved into what became known as the College's "White House," the first official home of the president, a ten-room house at 307 College Avenue that had formerly belonged to Paul Grubb.[5]

While the College warmly greeted a new president, it said goodbye to an institution. The previous May, sixty-seven-year-old Coach Ira Herr had announced his retirement at the end of the summer season. He had been at Elizabethtown College since 1928, a total of thirty-three years. His wife Kathryn would remain at the College as an extremely popular teacher of French for many more years.

Coach Herr, however, was not ready for full retirement. The Patton Trade School in Elizabethtown needed a coach, so Herr coached baseball and basketball there, while also teaching physical education and social studies for eleven more years, retiring for a second time in 1972, at the age of seventy-seven. Even then, he continued a full and active life. He was inducted into the Pennsylvania Sports Hall of Fame in 1975, and received honors and awards from the Church of the Brethren, the Elizabethtown Rotary Club, the American Association of Collegiate Baseball, and many other organizations.

In 1966, the College made his name a part of everyday life when it named the new athletic field in his honor. A large boulder with a bronze tablet was placed adjacent to the field bearing the inscription: "This Field is Named for Ira R. Herr, First Director of Athletics at Elizabethtown College."

Ira Herr died in 1986 at the age of 92. Edward E. Brunner '52 said that Coach Herr "took an interest in each kid and really cared. The impact he had on people was incredible. He had rules and values, and expected you to follow them. I just loved the way he led, quietly, by example…He was a legend."[6]

Former head basketball coach Don Smith agreed. "Coach Herr is to Elizabethtown what Coach [Amos Alonzo] Stagg is to Susquehanna. He was the institution."[7]

❧—❧

The following year would see the end of another human institution at Elizabethtown College. In the spring of 1962, A. C. Baugher had made plans to enliven his retirement by returning to the classroom to teach chemistry at Messiah College, the same way that Ira Herr would be teaching and coaching at Patton. Unfortunately, he suffered a heart attack while working in his garden on the morning of November 2, 1962. It was just two weeks after his old German teacher and colleague L. D. Rose passed away at the age of seventy-eight, and four months after another president of the College, D. C. Reber, had died at the age of ninety. Baugher was rushed to the Lancaster General Hospital but died in the intensive care unit. He was sixty-nine years old.

Baugher had enjoyed a full and rewarding life. He had seen the College that he loved grow to fruition, like the plants he was tending on the morning of his death.

Along with his college work, he had been active in the Church of the Brethren, and chaired the committee that would eventually publish *The History of the Church of the Brethren in Eastern Pennsylvania 1915 to 1965*. He had organized the Teachers for West Africa Program and served as its director. He was the moderator of the 1957 Richmond Conference and served many times on the standing committee of the Annual Conference, in which he was reading clerk and a congressional delegate. Baugher was a member of the General Brotherhood Board for twenty-eight years, on the board of trustees of Bethany Theological Seminary for nineteen years, and moderator of the Elizabethtown Church of the Brethren from 1938 until his death.

An *Etownian* editorial remembered him:

> *We knew President Baugher as a man not isolated*
> *in his executive office, but rather as a college leader*

*genuinely interested in and active among the students,
in the welfare of the school, and in the general
advancement of Elizabethtown...the Student Center is
concrete evidence that Dr. Baugher wished, as College
President, to provide for the entire interests of the student body. First envisioned in his mind, the Center
became a reality to Dr. Baugher when he toured the
building one day before his death.*[8]

That student center with A. C. Baugher's name emblazoned on
it was dedicated on Sunday, November 18. It was intended for the
extra-curricular enjoyment of the students. Built around the existing
Student-Alumni Gymnasium at a cost of $1,400,000, the building
included a spacious snack bar, three bowling lanes, a recreation
room, the College bookstore, a publication center, a radio station,
lounges, conference rooms, a post office, and a large swimming
pool, whose construction had been urged by President McAuley.

At the dedication, a portrait of A. C. Baugher was unveiled and
placed in the building's lounge. His countenance would continue to
smile down upon the students who attended the College that he had
made his life's work and his home.

⋟—⋞

Roy McAuley, who had inherited the president's mantle, had
been hard at work ever since he had moved into the corner office of
Alpha Hall. The Board of Trustees had asked him to choose a dean
of the College, and several of the Board's requirements show that
the church still exercised a strong influence on hiring. The new dean
was to be a married man under middle age, and "a churchman
kindly disposed toward the beliefs and practices of the Church of
the Brethren," but who should also have "broad educational sympathies."[9]

Jacob E. Hershman, who had graduated from Elizabethtown
College in 1936, was chosen as dean, in spite of his having had no
college teaching experience, another prerequisite of the position.
With Hershman, Treasurer Earl H. Kurtz, a 1935 Elizabethtown graduate who had assumed his position in 1958, Administrative Assistant
to the President Robert S. Young, and Director of Public Relations

and Development James L. M. Yeingst, President McAuley had his core administrators in place.

McAuley pursued his primary goal of strengthening the academic standing of the College by improving the curriculum and methods of instruction. His concern with the academic training of his faculty can be seen in his hiring of many young, well-trained, and enthusiastic professors. By the time of McAuley's resignation in 1966, the College possessed 16 faculty members with earned doctorates, and many more with master's degrees who were active doctoral candidates.

Adding to the innovations of the early 60s was a new program initiated through a grant from the Hershey Chocolate Corporation. The Teachers for West Africa program would select, prepare, and support American elementary and secondary teachers to teach in Ghana and Nigeria, two countries from which the corporation imported their cocoa beans. The committee to administer the grant was made up of McAuley, John O. Hershey, president of the Milton Hershey School, and President Emeritus Baugher, who directed the program until his death. In 1962, the first teachers went to Africa at starting salaries of $2880 per year. One requirement was that "sixteen percent of the teachers are negroes."[10] The program was an excellent way to place Elizabethtown graduates into true service positions.

Another new program at the College offered advanced high school students the chance to experience college early. In December 1961, the Board announced that qualified students would be permitted to begin their college work at the end of their junior year in high school. The innovation not only attracted more top students to Elizabethtown, but it also brought them in a year early, helping to increase attendance levels.

The College's music program continued to thrive through the 1960s. Starting with the 1963–64 school year, a B. S. in Music Education was offered, and by the end of the decade, the department had taken over much of Rider Hall, had expanded its courses of instruction from eleven to forty-seven, and boasted a concert choir, a college chorale, a stage band, and a concert band.

Physical growth continued on campus. Only a month before the Baugher Student Center had been dedicated, a new women's dormitory housing 150 students had opened. This was the Mary Royer Residence Hall, named after a 1921 graduate of the College who had served as a missionary in India from 1913 to 1947, and died in 1951.

In the fall of 1963, the College purchased another eleven acres of land southeast of the campus from Mr. and Mrs. Charles Simon. Two years later another 12.4 acres were purchased from the Elizabethtown Kiwanis. The plot, the former site of the Elizabethtown Fair, was used as a repair shop, storage area, and garage, and later for parking.

That same year, the amount of land owned by the College nearly doubled, thanks to a gift from Dr. and Mrs. Troy M. Thompson. Dr. Thompson had long been associated with the College as physician for its athletic program, and deeded his 110-acre farm to the school in exchange for an annuity.[11] Another large gift to the school came from the Daniel B. and Ella G. Withers estate in the amount of $175,000.

Further money was raised as the result of a fund-raising effort that President McAuley had recommended to the trustees in 1963. The intention of this "Pathway to Fulfillment," as it was called, was to raise $1,250,000 in three years. Among the projects for which the money would be used was a new classroom building and the long hoped for physical education building.

But the first project to benefit was the enlargement of Zug Memorial Library in 1965. Two large wings were added to either side of the main building, so that the library could accommodate 100,000 volumes and a student body of 1200.

The day after the Zug Library additions were dedicated, the new Brinser Residence Hall for Men, housing 210 students, was opened. It was named for its primary donors, who had also donated the lecture hall in the Gibble Science Building.

New housing continued to pop up on the campus; the following year, 1966, the Schlosser Residence for Women was ready for occupancy by 200 students. It was named in honor of former president Ralph Schlosser, who was still teaching courses at the College.

At the dedication ceremony on October 22, Schlosser stated that his greatest joy in spending sixty years at Elizabethtown College was not in the growth of the campus, the student body, or the number of buildings, "but in having had the privilege of writing my personal philosophy of life into the lives of thousand of students who were in my classes."[12]

The Pathway to Fulfillment proved to be fulfilling indeed when a new classroom building was dedicated on May 13, 1967. Its completion had been greatly aided by a large donation from Elmer L. Esbenshade of Lancaster, who died before its dedication. Named in his memory, Esbenshade Hall was air-conditioned and contained eighteen classrooms, seminar rooms, a large lecture auditorium, and laboratories, as well as thirty-three faculty offices.

While a new gymnasium had long been on the drawing board, it would finally become a reality. In October 1967, a sketch of the proposed million dollar physical education center and an article on the plans for its construction were published in *The Etownian*. Construction began in the spring of 1968. The building was completed by fall of 1969, though the dedication did not occur until the College had entered the 1970s.

Gifts to the College increased greatly during the 1960s. The Annual Giving Fund of the Alumni Association, which had been organized in 1959, grew every year. From 1966 to 1969, the number of contributors increased from 209 to 906, and the amount given from $140,000 to $470,000.

There were impressive individual gifts as well, the greatest being a contribution of $500,000 from Mr. and Mrs. Wayne A. Nicarry. This gift from Nicarry, a Brethren minister and a future chairman of the Board of Trustees, was the largest single gift received by the College up to that time. Nicarry Hall was later named in honor of Mr. and Mrs. Nicarry.

~§—§~

It is undeniable that for Elizabethtown College the 1960s were a decade of great physical growth. Another kind of growth, however, was taking root, a growth in student maturity, awareness, and cynicism toward institutions, one of which was the College, as both concept and concrete reality. There would never be a decade in which all segments of the College — students, administration, and faculty — would be in deeper adversarial relationships with each other than the 1960s.

There was a slight taste of greater freedom and maturity in the early sixties. In the 1960–61 school year, students played a major role in supervising dormitories for the first time, with female upper-classmen in primary charge of five residences, including three honors houses. Dances had been going on for some time, and *The Etownian* frequently printed announcements of record hops.

Films with adult themes were being shown on campus, such as *On the Waterfront, Pal Joey,* and *From Here to Eternity*. Students put on a production of J. B. Priestley's *An Inspector Calls,* of which the review said, "Despite criticism against strong language and sugges-tive themes, the play was probably one of the better attended productions..."[13]

Despite such worldly and sophisticated presentations, the College's connection to the church remained strong enough that chapel attendance was still required for all students. There was a modification, however, starting with the 1961–62 school year. Wednesday and Thursday were assigned as chapel days, and students could choose which day to attend. Two absences were allowed each semester, the same basis as scheduled courses. Students were still required to sign the chapel bulletin and hand it to an usher as they left in order to prove their presence, a policy becoming less popular among students every year.

Junior Frank Zimmerman spoke for many students when he was asked what he thought of compulsory chapel: "I don't think that chapel itself is good, because religion...is not something that should be forced or mandatory — especially on the college level. We should be able to decide for ourselves at our age."[14]

In November, 1964, a letter signed by nineteen students was sent to *The Etownian* accusing it of an act of censorship in not print-ing a column and accompanying cartoon. Editor Betty Derencin responded:

> *The column and cartoon in question were rejected because they degraded satirically a policy (compulsory attendance at chapel) which every student knows he must accept prior to the time he first enrolls here...it*

*was presented with an air of ridicule that, in the opin-
ion of the editor, was in poor taste.*[15]

The debate over chapel would drone on until attendance
became voluntary for seniors in 1967. More serious controversies
loomed on the horizon, however, and from 1965 on, American
involvement in Vietnam would receive the lion's share of concern,
along with the wider subject of human rights.

The majority political opinion on campus during the early sixties
was, for the most part, a holdover from the red scare of the fifties.
The U. S. S. R. was still the villain, intent on world domination.

A 1960 *Etownian* editorial, "A Few Sweet Words to Nikita With
Love," quoted U. S. General Frank Howley's comment, "No pig-
faced bag of wind is going to push us out of Berlin," with the editor
approvingly adding, "Maybe that's the kind of talk [Khrushchev]
understands and appreciates."[16] In the next issue, an editorial criticized Fidel Castro and the so-called "Fair Play for Cuba Committee."
Anti-communist articles appeared frequently, including one headlined, "U.S. Reds Court 'Progressive' Students In Drive to Form
Marxist Campus Groups," a stern warning about the risks of being
"progressive."[17]

Even though the Russians and their bombs remained a constant
threat, there were some who refused to panic. Edith Fellenbaum, an
assistant professor of education, stated that the United States should
not judge everything else in relation to Russia, for our national purpose was greater than simply reacting to what Russia did or did
not do.

Even the General Brotherhood Board of the Church of the
Brethren advised its members not to panic and build fallout shelters,
an activity which reached its peak in the early 60s. "The fallout
shelter program," stated the board, "is but another aspect of war's
impingement upon our total life… We believe it is our witness to
dedicate our efforts to prevent war rather than to the more negative
task of trying to protect ourselves against the eventualities of war."[18]

War, however, became harder and harder to ignore. It was not
the constant threat of nuclear annihilation that would claim the
notice of the nation long into the following decade, but a war in

Vietnam. The United States had supported the French for anti-communist rather than pro-colonialist reasons, and found itself supporting Ngo Dinh Diem, who had become South Vietnam's president after the 1954 partition of the country into North and South Vietnam.

By 1961, the United States had poured over a billion dollars worth of military aid into Diem's coffers, but South Vietnam continued to suffer economically while North Vietnam embraced communism as a social and economic remedy. By 1960, communist cadres were prepared to challenge the autocratic Diem regime. They called themselves the National Liberation Front, and were led by Ho Chi Minh, who had created the Vietminh Front in 1941 as a nationalist movement that first battled the Japanese and then the French colonialists.

United States policy toward communism was contingent at the time upon the domino theory, which held that if one country in a region fell to communism, the others bordering it would also eventually fall. A communist Vietnam therefore meant that all of Indochina would likely follow. During the Kennedy administration, that theory led to increasing American aid threefold, while the number of American "advisors" rose from 6,000 to over 16,000, with still no social or economic improvement by Diem.

Vietnam was already a major area of concern when thirteen students and four professors from Elizabethtown College held a peace seminar on October 12, 1963 at Camp Chester. Dale Aucherman, an outside speaker, expressed his views on why it was necessary for Christians to be pacifists, while Bible and philosophy professor Armon Snowden presented the opposing argument.

What seems to be the first mention of Vietnam in *The Etownian* appeared that same month in a letter from Dr. James Berkebile, a chemistry professor, who explained why he felt that student riots were less likely in America than in Vietnam, where they had recently taken place. In 1960, Berkebile had been in Saigon, where a Vietnamese teacher had told him that in Vietnam, people entered politics to get rich. The Diem family had been poor, but in two years had become the wealthiest in the country. Berkebile quoted the teacher as saying, "Every key productive enterprise was either placed directly or indirectly in their control by themselves." The author concluded by observing: "The implication of this is revealing as to why the students rioted in Vietnam. I am surprised that they did not riot before this."[19] Diem's crimes against his own people were already well known.

Only two weeks after Berkebile's letter appeared, Diem was killed in a military coup with which the U.S. did not interfere. President Kennedy was assassinated only three weeks later.

Kennedy, a liberal Democrat and a Roman Catholic, was admired much more abroad than in Republican and Protestant Elizabethtown College. While the December 6, 1963, *Etownian* printed front page articles about how the martyred president's death had been deeply grieved in France and Germany (reported by student Janet Jones, who was studying in Strasbourg, and Dr. Robert A. Byerly, directing the Brethren Colleges Abroad Program in Marburg, Germany), student reaction was less emotional. Of the students questioned as to whether or not Kennedy should be memorialized by placing his image on money, all seven thought such an act would be "overdoing it."[20]

The comments seemed to lend credence to Professor James L. M. Yeingst's suggestion that Elizabethtown College was overwhelmingly politically conservative, since the vast majority of students came from Lancaster County. On the basis of the last presidential straw poll, Franklin & Marshall College had proven liberal, Millersville neutral, and Elizabethtown conservative.[21]

If one needed further proof of the area's conservative credentials, a front page story in the December 6 issue of *The Etownian* provided it in a far more accusatory manner. The Reverend A. L. Stephans, an NAACP worker, said in his address at the College, "In Elizabethtown and similar communities, a Negro does not work, is not seen buying land, can in fact not live in the town itself."[22] At the time, it was an accusation grounded in a sad reality.

There was a liberal contingent on campus. Richard Hartman, president of the Young Democratic Club, wrote a number of politically oriented columns for the College paper, one of which predicted that the nomination of Barry Goldwater as the Republican presidential candidate would doom the GOP. "The coalition behind Goldwater," Hartman said, "is made up first and foremost of

Southern whites, who want an end of civil rights and most likely an end of the Supreme Court. The leaders of this section of Goldwater's coalition are Governor Johnson of Mississippi, Governor Wallace of Alabama, and the old Dixiecrat Thurmond of South Carolina."[23]

His opinion, however, was not shared by the nine college students pictured on the following page, singing in front of a huge picture of Goldwater at the Elizabethtown Area Republican rally.

In another column Hartman predicted the victory of Lyndon Johnson in the 1964 election, and also predicted that "within 20 years [Johnson] will be among the 10 greatest Presidents in our history."[24] History was not as kind to Johnson as Richard Hartman had predicted.

Johnson, who became president after Kennedy's death and was reelected in 1964, significantly escalated the war in Vietnam by having Congress pass a resolution allowing American military forces to fight there. By 1965, hundreds of thousands of American men were battling in the jungles and rice paddies, involved in a war that very few Americans understood, but about which everyone had an opinion.

Many of those opinions changed over the years as more and more young men went overseas. The tide slowly shifted; more Americans opposed the war, seeing it as a huge morass to which the country was committing more men, money, and resources to little effect. Students in particular mounted protests, most peaceful, some violent.

Many, feeling that their own lives were at stake, burned their Selective Service cards, unwilling to fight in a war they opposed. Some fled to Canada where they could not be prosecuted for evading the draft. Others used real or manufactured physical complaints to avoid induction. Many simply went when they were called. But the protests continued, escalating along with the war itself.

A 1965 *Etownian* editorial by Carol Hamilton cautioned students against joining the March on Washington, suggesting that burning one's draft card was "an immature act which shows the student's compliance to outside influence and his inability to think for himself."[25] The editorial was the first salvo in a minor war that mirrored the conflict being waged in American society.

Editor Hamilton received further support in a letter from Lt. Lawrence J. Kozubal, a 1964 Elizabethtown graduate who was serving in Phu Bai, Vietnam. His feelings clearly expressed those of many of the men serving there, as he spoke of the compassion with which Marines treated the Vietnamese, and criticized "the pusillanimous babblings of these college cut-ups."[26] An opposing viewpoint was published in the same issue from senior Jim Fitz, who said that the mistake the United States made was in supporting any government, no matter how corrupt, as long as it was anti-communist. "It is quite undemocratic, immoral ethically, and stupid politically to try to cover our mistakes by military means, which cause more Vietnamese to hate us and many Americans to die."[27]

One of the College's ugliest incidents involved an angry reaction to young J. Kenneth Kreider, who wanted to expose students to deeper knowledge of what was happening in Vietnam. Kreider had graduated from the College in 1961, after which he served a two-year term in the Brethren Volunteer Service Program, working with Eastern European refugees who settled in West Germany. He then returned to Elizabethtown as a history professor, simultaneously working on his doctoral dissertation.

In the fall of 1965, Kreider participated in a student assembly in which he gave a brief history of Vietnam and, in the words of an *Etownian* reporter, "indicated his opposition to the present U.S. policy in Vietnam, adding that it was destroying the social structure of the country and laying waste to its resources."

Kreider closed by telling the students, "Don't leave saying that Kreider is anti-U.S. This is the greatest country in the world — and I've been in over forty of them. I am anti-U.S. policy of death and destruction; and I'm pro-U.S. policy of help, understanding, and of representing the true meaning of the United States of America."[28]

A poll was taken following the assembly. Students were offered six alternatives, and 710 of them responded as follows: 18 percent felt that current U.S. policy should be more aggressive; 12 percent felt it was the best possible policy at the present; 32 percent said it should be continued but with greater effort toward negotiation; 23 percent said U.S. troops should be replaced by a United Nations peacekeeping force; and only 5 percent felt that U. S. policy was wrong and that American troops should be withdrawn. The remainder said they lacked sufficient information to make a choice. The end of the article reporting the poll results added an official *caveat*: "President Roy E. McAuley indicated that Elizabethtown College has no official position on political questions except in terms of legislation affecting higher education."[29]

Although there was no official stand, the majority of faculty and students in 1965 supported the government. That Christmas, many students contributed letters and Christmas cards to the Christmas Vietnam project, providing enough cards to supply three companies of soldiers. Although another faculty member, Rollin Pepper of the biology department, publicly came out against U. S. involvement, he remained in the minority.

The response to Kreider's stance was highly antagonistic. During the next few weeks he was verbally and nearly physically attacked by several of his colleagues on the faculty, some of whom circulated and signed a petition urging the administration to dismiss him, a tack also taken by some of the students' parents, who urged President McAuley to fire the young professor. Kreider also received angry letters, some of them anonymously calling him "Comrade."

The most memorable response occurred when a dummy was found hanging from a tree near Alpha Hall one morning with a placard attached reading "PROF. KREIDER." The effigy was quickly removed. There was no official administrative response to the act, and *The Etownian* did not report the incident, but several letters recorded the aftermath. One from James Hilton, the president of the Elizabethtown College Student Association, criticized the manner in which those responsible condemned Kreider's opinions.

Another letter from James Seaton '65 also criticized the hanging in effigy, observing that "Such action does injustice to a person who holds a minority opinion [and] can do irreparable harm to the student body and the College." Student Corrine Bennett criticized those students who refused even to listen to Kreider's remarks: "Those who paraded out of assembly were either seeking attention or were so uncertain of their own views that they were afraid to hear any opposing views."[30]

A month later in the "Faculty Forum," history professor Richard L. Mumford, who would three years later teach a course on the history of Vietnam, opined that U. S. troops should remain in Vietnam, primarily for humanitarian reasons. Mumford felt that the communists would, in the absence of American forces, slaughter the South Vietnamese and then move into other countries in Southeast Asia.[31]

For the next few months, however, the College was concerned less with Vietnam and more with its own future. On January 17, 1966, Dr. Jacob E. Hershman, who had become dean of the College at the time McAuley was made president, resigned his position effective July 1.

Several months later, on April 25, Roy McAuley resigned the presidency to become effective the last day of August. "In any administrative position," McAuley was quoted as saying, "a time is reached when a president has done all he can do. He should then move out and let a man come who has fresh ideas."[32]

McAuley had accomplished a great deal for the College. In their resolution, the trustees remarked that in McAuley's ten years as dean and president, the College more than doubled in the size of enrollment, physical assets, and campus area, and grew greatly in public esteem. In McAuley's words, it had become a "demand institution" with a young and aggressive faculty. Even with the growth, McAuley's administration had always stayed within its budget, while keeping tuition costs average or below. Moreover, the first phase of the Pathway to Fulfillment had been successfully completed.

McAuley intended to return to teaching: "I feel that teaching English is one area where you get to know students well on the creative, personal, and emotional levels. You are then dealing with the fundamental creative areas of students."[33]

During the 1966–67 academic year, McAuley became a professor of English at Central Missouri State College in Warrensburg, Missouri. The following year he was appointed the humanities division chairman, and in 1968 became academic dean of the college. In 1971 the College reorganized as a university with five different colleges, and McAuley was named vice-president for academic affairs. He held that position until 1983, when he returned to his beloved teaching, retiring in 1990. He then became pastor of Cumberland

Presbyterian Church in Warrensburg for seven years, retiring for a second time in 1997.

McAuley's successor at Elizabethtown was, for the first time in the College's history, a person who had no former connection with the school. After a number of interviews with educators connected to the Church of the Brethren, Dr. Morley J. Mays was chosen on July 11, 1966, as the new president.

Mays was born on December 13, 1911, in Johnstown, Pennsylvania. He was a *cum laude* graduate of the Juniata College class of 1932, received his master's degree from the University of Pittsburgh in 1936, and his Ph.D. in 1949 from the University of Virginia. He taught English at the University of Chicago and at Bridgewater College, where he was head of the English department and assistant to the president. He then moved to Juniata College, where he taught philosophy and became the school's first academic dean, as well as vice president for academic affairs.

Mays was a published author, active in community affairs, and chaired committees of the Middle States Assocation, which gave him valuable experience in evaluating academic programs. He was also an active churchman, serving as secretary of the Church of the Brethren's annual conference and as chairman of the board of directors of Bethany Theological Seminary. He was married with two children. All in all, it was an ideal background for the presidency of Elizabethtown College, in spite of the fact that Mays had no previous connections there.

Mays had determined, however, what he considered to be the best ways to help the College, and change, or at least the promise of change, was to come swiftly. A firm hand was seen in his first written address to the students in the September 16, 1966, "Faculty Forum" in *The Etownian*. "I want to encourage you," he said, "to look upon your college years as opportunity… Society has too much invested in education and its expectations are too high to tolerate shoddy results. Our image is marred when we give the impression that we are irresponsible, purposeless, or frivolous."[34]

That same issue, however, included a tongue-in-cheek response to one of Mays's remarks: "Dr. Mays comes to us with the auspicious words of 'greeting, encouragement, and promise.' For those of us who ended last semester with despair and despondency, this presents a hopeful change."[35]

One would not have to look far to read a thinly veiled hostility in the comment. Mays was replacing a well-liked former dean who had become a well-liked president, and as far as many students were concerned, he was going to have to prove himself fit for the task.

Mays started quickly. His first public appearance after being named president in July was at the annual faculty and staff dinner. There he announced his plans to ask the trustees at the October eighth meeting to appoint a committee to study the purpose of the College and clarify its objectives. Mays had also come up with a name for the undertaking: EPIC, an acronym for "Elizabethtown Plots Its Course."

He began with four basic presuppositions, the first of which was that the College's survival would be determined by its educational quality. "No other qualities will assure us of our place in the educational sun," Mays explained. "Our business is education." The second concept was that the instructional faculty had a corporate responsibility: "It must have a voice in and a responsibility for the policy and program within which it teaches."

The third was that the College needed to re-examine the grounds of Christian commitment. "We can no longer expect to certify our Christian character by prescribing an inventory of do's and don'ts for student behavior."

The final presupposition was that students would be vocal and demonstrative. "We need them to engage in taking responsibility for their own education."

Mays stressed that the College would have to be able to compete with the coming wave of community colleges. "I am not an alarmist," he said, "but this is not only a question of finding our place or fulfilling our mission, but a question of survival. Complacency could be our worst enemy."[36]

Despite his organizational strictures, Mays was anxious to solicit the opinions of others in the College community. At a trustee meeting in July, he had said that he was eager to have the faculty become responsible for the academic planning and programming of the College, and in October he activated the Campus Council, which brought representatives from the student body, the faculty, and the administration together to discuss problems and concerns. He also set up a program in which he would have a meal with five students chosen at random, and the students could discuss whatever they liked with him.

Dr. Mays did on occasion indicate an aversion to some changes. At one meeting in which a faculty member announced an upcoming "faculty social," Dr. Mays was heard to remark, "I thought that 'social' was an adjective."[37]

The editors of *The Etownian* praised Dr. Mays for his openness as well as his willingness to listen to different points of view. He would need such openness in the months and years to come, and seemed to realize it. His first written address to the alumni, penned four months after taking office, was entitled "An Adventure in Accommodation," and talked about the difficulties of accommodating all the different constituencies that are a part of the College. He discussed the recent dismissal of Dr. Clark Kerr, former president of the University of California, a situation in which "these forces became contenders with each other, and then turned on the man in the center."

Mays's strategy was to start an immediate dialogue. "Everyone with a valid concern should enter it in the dialogue in the confidence that it will find its place along with other interests and that as a consequence a higher level of competence will result than if the dialogue had not occurred."[38]

Dr. Wayne L. Miller joined in the dialogue by being named dean of the College faculty on January 9, 1967, replacing Jacob Hershman. His duties began on July 1. Miller, like McAuley, was a graduate of McPherson College, and was teaching there before he came to Elizabethtown.

President Mays's inauguration took place on April 15, 1967. The newly designed College flag was used in the ceremony, and the new president received a silver medallion bearing the College seal, which was to be worn by him and successive presidents on ceremonial occasions.

While the inauguration may have been pleasant for Mays, the rest of the week could not have been. A full-fledged protest had taken place just three days earlier, but not by the students.

The situation was the result of a proposed visit by Russian churchman Metropolitan Nikodim of the Russian Orthodox Church. Dr. Carl McIntyre, president of the ultra-conservative International Council of Christian Churches, protested the visit by picketing the College, along with a group of his followers. They marched between the Church of the Brethren and Royer Hall, holding signs proclaiming, "NIKODIM IS A RED AGENT," "THE VIET CONG ARE KILLING OUR BOYS," and "THE RUSSIANS ARE OUR ENEMIES."

The truth was that Nikodim never arrived in Elizabethtown, nor ever got out of Russia, because he and his entourage were unable to secure visas for the trip. The fact that there was nothing *to* picket did not stop McIntyre, who simply told his followers that the Russians were being hidden on campus. The march continued.

Another contretemps occurred that same week, when several students wearing masks broke into long-haired student Larry Myers's room and forcibly cut his hair. A letter from Bible and philosophy professor Eugene Clemens called the act "barbarous, cruel, and morally bankrupt," "a most grave act of inhumanity," and "morally abhorrent."[39]

The editorial addressing the incident was headlined, "Bigots Commit Atrocity In 'Liberal' Community," and deplored it as "an outrage" and an example of "brutality and insensitivity," adding, "In an academic community where liberal thinking is supposedly the byword, we certainly have some hypocritical Pharisees."[40]

It was a far stronger editorial response than the silence with which the hanging of the Kreider effigy had been met the year before. The attitudes of many in the country had changed in that year and would continue to do so.

The following fall, the draft became a greater concern for male students. All those who wished a student deferment had to obtain a copy of Selective Service Form SSS104: Request for II-S.

In October, students initiated "Project Vietnam," an open forum intended to develop awareness of and interest in the country and the conflict taking place in it, with the further purpose of having "the students express their concerns in a commitment to some form of action."[41] The idea for the project began when student John Cassell worked with John Gosnell, Minister of Education at the Elizabethtown Church of the Brethren, on a program in Harrisburg called "Vietnam Summer."

Project Vietnam held a forum entitled, "Profs Speak Their Mind on Vietnam" in Esbenshade Auditorium. A number of professors spoke, nearly all of whom were against American involvement. Scott T. Swank of the history department said that the real threat to Vietnam was not communism but the United States; English professor Carl J. Campbell said that the United States was guilty of crimes of aggression, and compared President Lyndon Johnson to Hitler and Napoleon; Eugene Clemens said the country was on the wrong road: "I love my country...but my country is wrong."[42]

Students also heard a report from John Brinley, who had attended the previous weekend's Peace-In in Washington, D. C., along with 250 other Elizabethtown College students and faculty members. The number of participants indicates a vast difference in campus attitude toward the conflict since Professor Kreider's poll results the previous year. Of that Peace-In, the *Etownian*'s editorial said:

> One widely-known and respected statesman in the United States has called the Washington peace-in "an American tragedy."
> The tragedy was not the protest but the fact that United States policy makers in the 1960s have retained a 19th century myopic view of imperialistic, protective diplomacy and foreign policy.[43]

Both sides of the issue were presented by Project Vietnam. At the following forum, Dr. Elizabeth M. Garber, head of the political science department, and John Tulley, the College's athletic director, gave students a look at the U. S. State Department's policy in Vietnam, and explained why they supported American involvement.

Other subjects proved of less interest to students. When the College's Women's Auxiliary presented a symposium on "The Education and Roles of Women in the Last Quarter of the Twentieth

Century," the attendance was so low that letters were written to the College paper commenting on it.

Although the women's movement and its goal of sexual equality had not yet made its presence known, the concept of racial and religious equality certainly had. In the second semester of the 1967–68 school year, the administration of the College was in effect accused of discrimination in hiring, accusations that came from within the College itself.

The problem arose as the result of a January 20 meeting between President Mays, Dr. Wayne Miller, and members of the psychology department, of which Dr. Antonio Felice was the chair, as well as the chairman of the Personnel Council. Mays later stated that he was concerned with discontent in the department and had called the meeting in "a sincere effort to reconcile whatever differences existed." But then Mays went on, "Instead of being conciliatory in tone, the Administration was subject to a four-hour attack, largely personal in nature."[44]

The criticism was based on an opening in the biology department that had occurred the previous spring. "There was a proposal," Mays explained to *The Etownian*, " that I hire a Hindu. I had already hired a Moslem in another department. Being aware that the Board of Trustees was sensitive about the number of non-professing Christians on the faculty, I felt I could not now hire a Hindu. At the same time I felt we had a qualified candidate who was offered the position and accepted."[45]

In response to Mays's explanation, Dr. Felice replied in a public letter that he had had conferences concerning the matter with Dean Miller prior to the meeting with Mays, and that the meeting was not called solely by Mays but by mutual consent, the reason being that:

> …in April 1967 a Hindu with a Ph.D. and college teaching experience was not hired on the faculty simply because he was a Hindu…the Personnel Council, of which I am chairman, began to study the formulation of an employment policy statement in the early fall of 1967 only after being instructed to do so by a majority of faculty members."[46]

The policy statement, written by a faculty committee, read as follows:

> *Elizabethtown College shall hire new faculty members on the basis of academic and professional qualifications without reference to race, color, creed, or national origin. It is understood, of course, that all faculty members will respect the goals and purposes of the institution.*[47]

Dr. Felice told the paper that the first reaction from the administration was "somewhat unfavorable," even before Presidents Mays made his initial comments in a story which began, "Rumor and allegations, accompanied by slander and potentially violent student discontent, eclipsed the campus of Elizabethtown College last week."[48]

Mays went on to tell *The Etownian* that a committee of two trustees and two faculty members were reviewing the policy statement. He concluded his interview by stating, "The personal religious preferences of any member of the faculty are not at stake. The only question is whether members of the faculty, having accepted a position here, are willing to respect the purposes of the institution, one of which is religious."[49]

In April, the administration offered a revised policy statement on hiring. It was nearly four times as long as the original, and read in part:

> *Elizabethtown College, being church-related, seeks to bring an additional dimension to college life, and therefore is vitally interested in the total impact of its staff upon its students. Thus it is important that Elizabethtown College employ faculty whose personal values contribute to its purposes.*
>
> *...the faculty...shall include a preponderance [sic] of persons who come from non-Christian backgrounds. All faculty members should reflect in life and attitude the goals and purposes of the College.*
>
> *The president of the College, in consultation with the Dean of the Faculty and the appropriate*

Department Chairman, shall have the freedom to exercise his best judgment in consideration of new faculty members in the light of these guiding principles...[50]

The faculty rejected the statement. The editor of *The Etownian* wrote an extremely critical editorial, accusing the administration of playing semantic games. In an article about students' favorite professors which appeared on the same page as the editorial, it was announced that Dr. Felice was resigning his post at Elizabethtown College. It appeared that President Mays, like the American government in Vietnam, was "waist-deep in the Big Muddy," immersed in his first great crisis of "accommodation." There would be others to come.

≈§—§≈

In 1968 politics continued to be widely discussed and debated on campus. History professor Richard Mumford decided to give a course on the history of Vietnam from 1941 to 1968, and though he expected only fifteen to twenty students, seventy-six signed up, and two sections were offered.

On April 4, 1968, Martin Luther King was shot to death in Memphis. The next issue of the College paper contained a report by student Lee Griffith, who was in Washington, D. C. just after the riots that followed King's death. It was a sympathetic view toward Dr. King and those ravaged by the riots, ending with a quotation from the U. S. Riot Commission report: "Segregation and poverty have created in the racial ghetto a destructive environment totally unknown to most white Americans."[51]

That same issue contained a "Student Reaction" to the assassination by Thomas Poulin, which seemed to damn with faint praise, and began oddly by comparing the efficiency of two recent assassins:

> *The assassin...did an efficient job with much better equipment than Lee Harvey Oswald in his assassination of President Kennedy a few years ago...[King] was not a perfect leader for the Negro race, but he was perhaps the best that they had...he expressed opinions at times which were not the most rational in the world ...on things (such as Vietnam) that he was not quali-*

fied to voice an opinion on. But on the whole he was more rational at all times than, say, H. Rap Brown, or Stokely Carmichael.[52]

There was also the concern expressed that the assassination would not lead to "more insane gun legislation." Needless to say, the official editorial on the assassination was, like Griffith's report, far more sympathetic.

In the forthcoming presidential election, there were reports of rallies on campus for Eugene McCarthy, and a parody interview of George Wallace in *The Etownian*, where he was quoted as saying, "I have the cross of our dear Lord burning in my soul, and in my heart, and in my mind, and sometimes in the meadow I own down near Selma."[53]

Still, in the campus poll, George Wallace outpolled Democratic candidate Hubert Humphrey, getting fifty-nine votes to Humphrey's fifty-seven. McCarthy received thirty-one votes, but the pack was easily outrun by the actual 1968 winner, Richard Nixon, who received 57.1 percent with a total of 233 votes.

Besides politics and Vietnam, another area of concern on the nation's campuses involved the use of mind-altering drugs and the philosophical impact of the hippie lifestyle. *The Etownian* ran an ad for the Lancaster "Trip Psychedelic Shop/Hundreds of posters, buttons, gifts, light boxes and mind blowing items./This is a true psychedelic community with happenings for electric bodies and minds."[54]

Even the state of Pennsylvania got into the "groovy" act. An ad from the State Department of Commerce advised, "If you'd rather join a job-in than pull a cop-out, there's a groovy state where the bag is work, and tuned in swingers turn out happenings. Pennsylvania's where it's at, and if you're ready to be zapped with a turn-on scene, take a trip to Pennsylvania, and check out the chances you have to do your own thing."[55]

The Etownian itself was not immune. In the fall of 1968, the usually sedate masthead was replaced with the lamp from the seal spewing out psychedelic smoke. The reality belied the image, however, with only 5.8 percent of Elizabethtown College students admitting to having tried drugs. Since 33 percent said that they knew at least five students who had taken hallucinogens, one can only assume that these acquaintances must have attended other schools. An adventuresome 20 percent, however, said that they would try marijuana if given a chance.[56]

Whether willing to try drugs or not, the general feeling of many students was definitely anti-establishment. Popular music, movies, and some of the more hip television shows preached a gospel of rebellion, of, in LSD guru Timothy Leary's words, turning on, tuning in, and dropping out. Student publications reported this rebellion more honestly and fearlessly than ever before.

An *Etownian* editorial entitled, "They Call It The Establishment" boasted:

> *We students aren't acting very "'nicely" these days. We have been called "sore losers." We are "spoiled." We have not learned to hate as patriotically as we should. As a result we have been ostracized from the Establishment.*
> *Thank God.*[57]

The College "establishment" was changing one of its leaders at a critical time. J. W. Kettering, who had been chairman of the Board of Trustees of the College since 1954, chose to step down from the chairmanship and become an honorary trustee.

His replacement as chairman was elected on December 12, 1968. Aaron G. Breidenstine was a graduate of Elizabethtown College, and had earned his Master's and Doctorate degrees at Temple. He had been on the faculty of Elizabethtown College, had served as dean at Hershey Junior College and Franklin & Marshall College, and as dean of academic affairs at Millersville State College. He was also Acting and Deputy Superintendent of the Department of Public Instruction for the Commonwealth of Pennsylvania from 1966 to 1968.

When he accepted the post, Breidenstine observed rather realistically "It is going to be somewhat difficult to chart the course for the next ten years, because I think institutions such as Elizabethtown College will not escape some of the great difficulties that are present in higher education... Our uniqueness must be the product of a coordinated team effort involving trustees, faculty, alumni, students, our church constituency, and others…"[58]

Coordination between the different segments would be difficult. The adult disenchantment with youthful rebellion that was such a defining element of the late 1960s seemed to affect the faculty as well. When the campus paper asked faculty members what they thought of Elizabethtown College students, 18 responded, but of that number, "only four praised the caliber of students attending E-town. The rest thought the students lacked everything from enthusiasm to intelligence."[59]

The students found a defender in President Mays, who stated in an interview, "Our students are well above average. It can be proved by statistics — the college boards' scores are considerably above average."[60] Students might have hoped for a more emotional response.

The winter of 1968–69, however, brought about a period of *sturm und drang* that would involve President Mays, the campus, and Elizabethtown itself. Though in retrospect it may seem like the proverbial tempest in the teapot, it infuriated and polarized segments of both the College and the community, and sorely tested the limits of campus power and the concept of free speech. It also brought about the realization that an engine to provide a reasoned dialogue between these ever more disparate segments was desperately needed.

The battle was openly waged in the pages of *The Etownian*, and the first shot came in the December 13, 1968 issue, which carried a special announcement by the masthead:

> *The administration lately may be 'diplomatically' trying to censure some of this newspaper… Also, students might be interested in knowing that through pressure of the administration many of the comments in this week's Would You Believe column would have been deleted. In fact, the whole column (editor's decision) didn't appear this week.*[61]

If the paper's annoyance with the administration wasn't obvious enough, the editors made a point of referring to the administration as "the establishment." A very lengthy report from the Academic Facilities Committee was introduced as the report of "The Establishment's Academic Committee."

It was not until the January 10, 1969, issue that the full story was told. An editorial entitled, "Censorship Continues: Straightening the Record," explained that *The Etownian* was printed on the press and at the offices of the *Elizabethtown Chronicle*, a community newspaper owned, published, and edited by Ray Westafer.

According to the editorial, Westafer felt that many of the items in the December 13 issue of *The Etownian* were "in bad taste," and phoned President Mays. Mays then phoned the editor of *The Etownian*, Gary Mantz, explained the situation, and said, "he [Mays] would prefer if the questionable articles would not appear." Mantz decided not to run the column, admitting that it was partly out of fear and partly because Westafer refused to print it.

A meeting was held after the decision, attended by Mays, several student senators, Mantz, the unnamed writer of the column, James Yeingst, director of public relations, and Eloise Aurand, director of public information. The meeting, the editorial charged, was unsatisfactory and inconclusive. Mantz asked Mays, "What would have happened if I had printed the column?" The president gave an "evasive answer to the effect that certain articles which the president did not agree with had already appeared."

Mantz concluded the editorial by saying, "It's a shame that a college that preaches a liberal, mind-disturbing education is so afraid of letting the students read some liberal, mind-disturbing material."[62]

President Mays attempted to explain his decision by issuing a statement printed on the front page of the same issue. The statement affirmed that students already had free speech, but with free speech came responsibility. It was the paper's responsibility to present "all the facts that pertain to a given situation," with "a respect for the sensitivities and the rights of others," and without "slander and libelous reference" or "obscenity and profanity."[63]

The contretemps was far from over, and Westafer attempted to explain his side of the situation with an editorial in the *Chronicle* that was later reprinted in *The Etownian*. It read:

> *About one-fourth of the content of The Etownian*
> *...was devoted to criticism of the **Chronicle** editor and*
> *the College administration.*
>
> *A portion of the copy which was slated for a pre-*
> *ceding issue...was a series of "jokes" about Christmas.*
>
> *Several of them weren't too funny in the*
> ***Chronicle** editor's judgment, and he flatly refused to*
> *print these portions in his plant, feeling they were not*
> *in good taste, to say the least.*
>
> *Now some of the students are crying "suppression"*
> *and "generation gap."*
>
> *It certainly is a trying time - this transition from*
> *childhood to the responsibilities of adulthood.*
>
> *Looking back, though, we realize that we had to*
> *go through the same transition. We'll guess that 90 per-*
> *cent of them will turn out all right.*[64]

Westafer's editorial could not have been more provocative if he had called every Elizabethtown College student a filthy, long-haired pinko hippie. By referring to the students as just coming out of their "childhood," he had insulted their maturity. By his implying that turning out "all right" meant turning out like himself, the man who had censored their newspaper had only poured more fuel on the fire.

English professor Jobie E. Riley wrote, "Apparently unsatisfied with being the editor of one paper, Mr. Ray Westafer has now taken upon himself the responsibilities of editing the college paper. He has also assumed the role of conscience for the college, of protector of collegiate morals. This is not his job."[65]

Nor did President Mays escape unscathed. Student Bruce Hutcheson's letter criticized Mays for censoring the piece in question for being blasphemous, not for being obscene or profane.

Westafer shot back at Riley in the following issue, insisting that:

> *As owner we have the undisputed right to refuse*
> *any printing job.... We still have the galley proof of*
> *that particular column, with the (to us) objectionable*
> *items circled in red. We invite Mr. Riley to come to our*
> *home and read it. If, after seeing what we insisted be*

*deleted, he still terms it overstepping our authority...
then we feel he's in the wrong business.*[66]

Professor Riley apparently declined Mr. Westafer's no-win invitation.

During all this uproar, President Mays must have felt that he'd been thrown into a hornets' nest. Things could not have improved when, a month later, the Student Senate voted itself out of existence. Senior Martha Douple, academic vice-president, made the proposal because she felt that elections had become "a farce" with no alternatives or choices. "If students," she said, "are not behind their government — and there is no evidence of their present support — it has ceased to function as a governing body."[67]

The proposal, after being passed by the Student Senate, was then presented to the student body for their vote. The next few issues of *The Etownian* were filled with arguments for and against the Senate, along with an ever increasing number of articles criticizing the administration for a number of reasons, including tuition hikes and the current grading system. When the final vote was tallied, the students voted overwhelmingly to "keep and expand" the present senate.

If the senate would survive, however, many students felt that it and the student body it represented needed to have more clearly defined rights. To this purpose, in April 1969, a Student Bill of Rights was presented to the Campus Life Council. The document included the right of free speech, the right to privacy, the right to form student organizations, the right to bring speakers onto the campus, and the right of due process.

The Campus Life Council had been created at the request of President McAuley in 1963 to provide better communication between students, faculty, and administration, but meetings had been so infrequent that none were held in 1965. Its function was to make recommendations concerning non-academic programs and policies, but its decisions were subject to veto by both the president and the Board of Trustees.

At the same time the Student Bill of Rights was submitted to the Campus Life Council, a petition signed by over 500 students was also presented calling for a community government, "the shared decision making by representatives of all segments of the college community."[68] President Mays responded by calling for the first "All-College Assembly" to discuss campus issues with representatives of seven interest groups — trustees, administration, faculty, students, alumni, the Church of the Brethren, and the Parents' Association, an organization that had been formed by Mays the year before. This attempt to accommodate all constituencies was not particularly attractive to the activist students, greatly outnumbered as they were by what they considered "the establishment."

John Ranck, an Elizabethtown graduate with a Ph.D. in chemistry from Princeton, gave one of the most reasoned pleas recommending a community dialogue. He admitted that both sides had been at fault, and that proposals from all sides should be:

> ...*judged in the light in which they were offered — as possibilities set forth for consideration by the community, for criticism of the weaknesses contained therein and not of the integrity of the author, and for the ultimate strengthening of the community.*
>
> *I especially urge students to realize that changes in direction to accommodate ideals (or for any other reason) have many implications in many functional areas and that proper planning and groundwork are necessary for any successful accomplishment of any program. I urge faculty and administration not to get "hung up" on "the way things have been done in the past" and to consider what could be and why it would be good to be so.*
>
> *Above all, our dialogue must be conducted in such a way as to validate the principle that rational men and women can reason together to arrive at understanding...*[69]

Understanding between students, faculty, and administration would have to wait, however, while two factions of the student body battled over another free speech issue. Only a few weeks after junior Lee Griffith had been elected the new president of the Student

Association, senior Jeffrey Byrem was circulating a petition for Griffith's recall.

The reason was that Griffith, who had been a vocal critic of U. S. policy in Vietnam, had recently participated in a campus peace demonstration. "Even though," Byrem argued, "the president of the student senate may express his views apart from his office, his very presence unconsciously and inadvertently gives impetus to the movement to which he associates himself, an impetus which acts as an unfair deterrent to an opposing view."

Griffith responded, "Under no conditions will I keep quiet about my convictions on any matters.... I am weighing all of the possibilities, including resignation, if it is deemed necessary by the student body." He went on to ask precisely what he could or could not do. "Do I or do I not have the right to wear a peace badge? Do I have the right to be a member of either the Democrat or Republican Club? Do I have the right to express my opinion in Ethics class?"[70]

In spite of the attempt to unseat him, Griffith retained his office and presided as president of the senate the following year. Griffith listed his goals for the College and the students at the start of the 1969–70 school year with a "Campus Position Paper." The paper set forth Griffith's views on a number of issues, including the elimination of compulsory classes and convocation, longer hours of library operation, a deeper financial commitment to the College from the Church of the Brethren, and recognition of the Student Bill of Rights.

Adoption of the bill was passed by a student vote in October, although only 20 percent of the students voted in the referendum. The Student Senate adopted it the following month. That same October, the College participated in an event that drew students, faculty, and administration closer together while estranging it from many members of the Elizabethtown community.

A nationwide Vietnam Moratorium was held on October 15, when citizens were asked to pause and reflect on the war. At Elizabethtown, activities were planned in association with the Church of the Brethren. Although many individual Brethren supported U. S. involvement in the war, the official church stance was against it. The Eastern Pennsylvania district even published a newspaper advertisement in 1967 calling for a cease fire and an immediate cessation of bombing, an end to troop movements to Vietnam, and a request for all parties to negotiate in good faith.[71]

C. Wayne Zunkel, a pastor at the Elizabethtown Church of the Brethren, edited the newsletter of the Brethren Peace Fellowship, a group made up of veterans of alternative service who were against the war. The head pastor at the Elizabethtown church, Nevin Zuck, gave a public statement about the war, part of which stated that the church needed to be "the conscience of the community and the nation."[72]

Church and college joined together on October 15 to be part of that national conscience. The day was filled with debates, speeches, and discussions, although classes remained in session for those wishing to attend. Those who participated in the moratorium would be dismissed without having their grades endangered. That evening a memorial service was held in the Church of the Brethren, led by C. Wayne Zunkel. President Mays also spoke, calling the day an educational experience in which many different ideas were shared.

Before that service there had been a candlelight march of 275 students, faculty members, and administrators. As *The Etownian* reported, "The quiet, solemn group marched two by two each carrying a lighted candle. As the procession reached the presidential mansion, Dr. Mays emerged from the house to lead the procession."[73]

Louise Baugher Black, who at that time was teaching at the College and had a son serving in Vietnam, recalls:

> We came down College Avenue at night, carrying candles, led by Morley Mays and some trustees. We got downtown, and the American Legion knew we were coming. They lined the square, and shouted some pretty nasty things. We just kept walking. The relations between the town and the College at that time were pretty strained. Some of the more radical students had erected a Hanoi City of tents and flew the North Vietnamese flag, and those things just didn't sit well with the town at all.[74]

Although some townspeople were in sympathy with the marchers, those who were not were the more vocal. Many in the community, according to Mrs. Black, "linked pacifism to communism. You were either a loyal American or you were a communist."[75]

Several members of the town fire department were so irate over the march that they plotted to drench the marchers with their fire hoses, and were fueling themselves for the attack at the Black Horse, a Market Street tavern. Communications professor Donald E. Smith, then a new member of the faculty, prevented this occurrence by slipping fifty dollars to the bartender and quietly instructing him not to let a fireman's glass get empty. The strategy worked. The firemen stayed nestled snugly in their pub, and the marchers stayed dry.[76]

In the square, the marchers found enough enmity without fire hoses. One middle-aged couple holding flags said, "We're protesting the protestors. We're behind the president [Nixon] all the way." A local veteran remarked, "I think it's a tragedy. I lived here all my life...and for years that college has been a hot bed for slackards. Sure, they're pious, but I've seen them sneaking in the back door at the Black Horse. I say, if you don't like this country, then leave."[77]

When President Mays attended the next meeting of the local Rotary Club, he found himself the target of several verbal attacks from fellow Rotarians for participating in the march, and was greatly shaken by the angry comments. "America — Love it or leave it" was the cry of the majority in the community, regardless of education or church ties.

Many of those at the College, however, had decided to try to work within the system to change it rather than desert it. That same philosophy was reflected in the students' approach to compulsory convocation (formerly chapel). Less than a week after the Vietnam Moratorium, the Student Senate urged a boycott of the IBM cards used to check convocation attendance. Attend whatever convocations you wish, the senate advised students, but don't hand in your cards.

Several dozen students emulated the current practice of burning draft cards in protest by burning their convocation cards in a campus parking lot. Nevertheless, the controversy over convocations would go on.

⋖⋗

Amid all the unrest on campus in the late sixties, many students went on with college life as usual, or at least attempted to.

The feelings of these students paralleled sophomore class president Thomas G. Elicker's as expressed in a letter to the newspaper: "It seems that in recent weeks all of Elizabethtown's news has been concentrated in the area of anti-Vietnam War protests, gross-outs, panty raids, and arson, all of which has upset and disgusted most of the people on this campus." Elicker then praises all those students who worked for what he felt were constructive campus events, and adds that, "In the fall our class sponsored a mum sale, put together a float, and tried to organize a tug-of-war three times!"

The sixties were filled with such activities, along with sports, music, clubs, and all the other usual college pastimes, including the popular Sadie Hawkins Day, a female-empowering social event based on Al Capp's *Li'l Abner* comic strip. In 1960, students socialized in a new "Jay's Nest," complete with vending machines, coin changer, and an electric oven for making toasted cheese sandwiches and hot dogs. Starting in 1962, students with a literary bent contributed work to the new campus literary magazine, *The Elm.*

Students sang in the new Men's and Women's Glee Clubs, or played in the new string orchestra. There were also hootenannies on campus, at which such folk groups as The Wayfarers and The Plainsmen, made up of Elizabethtown College students, sang.

There was outside entertainment as well. The College brought in The Lettermen, a hit vocal group of the era, to perform at the local high school auditorium, as well as The Highwaymen, famous for their rendition of the folk song, "Michael."

Students could get more music at the College bookstore, which, beginning in 1965, sold LP records. They could also go to The Jabberwock, a campus coffeehouse, which offered folk music and poetry readings

Others became involved with WWEC-AM, a college radio station that broadcast forty to forty-five hours a week. It featured music, frequent news breaks, live reporting of sports events, and, an *Etownian* story reported, "special events such as Dr. Schlosser's lecture on the poetry of Tennyson and Browning."[78]

It's likely that the Kirby Stone Four's song, "The Eyes of Texas," got a lot more airplay than Dr. Schlosser. The vocal quartet's song used the lyrics, "The 'A' is for Amherst, The 'B' is for Brown/ The

'C' is for Colgate, Then Dartmouth comes around./You know the 'E', why, that's for E-town!"

In an *Etownian* editorial, the editor complained that many people were amazed by the use of E-town, which, the editor suggested, showed a lack of school spirit. Rather ask why *not* pick E-town. There were 70 other colleges, the editor observed, that started with E, and many with two syllables. However, what the editor did not mention was that it was also a matter of rhyme. The quartet was limited to a college that started with "E" and rhymed with "Brown" and "around." Still, it was an unexpected, novel, and flattering national mention of the school.

The College gained far more meaningful national recognition when the 1963–64 men's basketball team, coached by Donald Smith and captained by John Neely, became the Middle Atlantic Conference champions, and finished second in the NCAA playoffs. That same year, the baseball team won an unprecedented MAC triple crown, and the soccer team brought home their second MAC championship.

The soccer team would amass an impressive record during the decade. Coached by Owen L. Wright, Elizabethtown's soccer team won the MAC championship for six straight years from 1962 to 1967. They also won the NCAA Atlantic Coast Regional Co-Championship in 1966 and Championships in 1967 and 1969.

The 1960–61 school year was a great year for both soccer and women's field hockey. The soccer team once again won the MAC crown and went to Slippery Rock to vie for the NAIA championship. There they tied Newark College of Engineering and became NAIA co-champions.

Although the women's field hockey team was not yet competing for national titles, it had an amazing season, including a perfect one defensively with eight wins, no losses, and not a single goal scored against them. Linda Eshelman Hopple, center forward, made a record 18 goals and was named to the Mid-East All-Star Team. She was also named to the Central Penn All State Team, as were Captain Lois Herr and Sally Wenger Hoober, who scored 12 goals during the season.

Romance seemed a byproduct of victory, and several members of those winning soccer and field hockey teams married each other and made further contributions to the College. The soccer-playing

Hershey brothers, Al and Carroll, respectively married hockey players Linda Eshleman and Naomi Lucabaugh, who is now Reference Librarian at High Library. Ellwood Kerkeslager, currently a trustee, wed Lois Herr, who would also be a trustee and is now Director of Marketing and Public Affairs for the College. Soccer player Ron Shubert became the Chair of the Mathematics Department at Elizabethtown College, while hockey goalie Martha Eppley presently serves as the College's Associate Dean of the Faculty and Registrar.

While the school had its share of team accomplishments in the sixties, two individual athletes stood out. One became known for his activities after leaving the College, and the other for his triumphs while a student. In the spring of 1965, freshman Eugene Garber was drafted by the Pittsburgh Pirates before he ever had a chance to play baseball for the College. He had a 20-year career in the major leagues as a relief pitcher, leaving the game with a total of 218 saves and an average ERA of 3.34. He is probably best known to baseball fans for stopping Pete Rose's challenge to Joe DiMaggio's record of hitting safely in 56 straight games.

The other standout was Earl Brinser. In 1968, his junior year, Brinser was named to the College Division NCAA Wrestling All-American Team. He thus became the first Elizabethtown College athlete to receive national recognition in an individual sport. He placed sixth in national competition in his 152-pound weight class.

"Educate For Service" continued to be a deeply felt reality for many students. By 1964, four former Elizabethtown students, Jay Buffenmyer, Belva Cassel, Beth Deibert, and Jean Zettlemoyer, were serving in the Peace Corps.

In 1965, members of the Elizabethtown College Christian Association (ECCA) participated in an experimental program in Harrisburg. There they conducted two-hour classes for teenagers in the neighborhood of the Church of the Brethren, teaching drama, needlework, recreation, radio electronics, and wrestling. ECCA members had a special treat when Rebekah Schaeffer returned to address their annual banquet on April 29, 1964. The much beloved teacher, who had left Elizabethtown in the early 1940s, had retired in 1958 after forty-two years of teaching. Since her retirement, she had spoken to over 750 groups.

Over sixty students volunteered their time to a campus service project group. They helped set up an elementary and secondary school tutoring service, attended a weekend work camp in Maryland, where they processed relief goods, and organized a Community Action Program (CAP) in Elizabethtown as part of a national organization which helped communities mobilize their resources to combat poverty.

As at all colleges, there were students whose activities were at the opposite end of the spectrum. The 60s saw a number of suspensions for violation of campus drinking rules. As the decade came to an end, there was a notorious "panty raid" and some cases of suspected arson, incidents that would have been unthinkable a decade or two before.

But the times and society had changed. The idea of students asking for a bill of rights and burning their convocation cards would have been equally unthinkable in the 1940s and 1950s. Although the changes that Elizabethtown College experienced through the 1960s were quite painful at times, they turned out to be growing pains that were both necessary and inevitable. The College would be all the stronger for them in years to come.

In a 1969 editorial, junior Marlene Decker expressed the sense of this growth somewhat naively, but sincerely and accurately:

> After a long cold winter, "came spring…" has finally arrived at Elizabethtown…This year has seen many changes at Elizabethtown College. We have finally started to awaken from the long apathetic sleep that had encased the campus for years…
>
> Not only has Elizabethtown College gotten awake but it has gained a voice, an expression of its own. The College community should be thankful that this is not the expression of one group, ultimate in power, but a joint expression, a two-way thing.
>
> Students should be glad that we have had this chance at expression offered to us, that we have not had to fight for it. The chance has always been there but it was up to us the student body to take it. Since

*the administration has offered this chance they should
be willing to listen, perhaps even to change if necessity
demands it. Either way, however, it is a two way street.
Came spring has indeed finally come to
Elizabethtown. Change has begun and it is hoped will
continue to grow and flourish...[79]*

1 The *Etownian*, January 9, 1960, p. 2
2 The *Etownian*, October 22, 1960, p. 1
3 The *Etownian*, May 20, 1961, p. 1
4 The *Etownian*, July 17, 1961, p. 1
5 Grubb was the husband of Grace Ober, daughter of H. K. Ober.
6 *Elizabethtown*, Winter 1987, p. 16
7 Ibid.
8 The *Etownian*, November 16, 1962, p. 2
9 *History of Elizabethtown College 1899–1970*, p. 236
10 Ibid, p. 248
11 The land, located on both sides of East High Street, was used by the College as farm plots for college staff. A lottery system determined who would farm which plots. The land was sold in the
   1980s, and is now occupied by housing developments.
12 The *Etownian*, October 28, 1966, p. 1
13 The *Etownian*, April 8, 1961, p. 3
14 The *Etownian*, March 22, 1963, p. 3
15 The *Etownian*, November 6, 1964, p. 3
16 The *Etownian*, November 5, 1960, p. 1
17 The *Etownian*, February 25, 1961, p. 2
18 quoted in The *Etownian*, December 8, 1961, p. 4
19 The *Etownian*, October 18, 1963, p. 3
20 The *Etownian*, December 6, 1963, p. 2
21 The *Etownian*, November 22, 1963, p. 1
22 The *Etownian*, December 6, 1963, p. 1
23 The *Etownian*, September 25, 1964, p. 2
24 The *Etownian*, October 9, 1964, p. 2
25 The *Etownian*, November 19, 1965, p. 2
26 The *Etownian*, December 3, 1965, p. 2
27 Ibid.
28 The *Etownian*, December 16, 1965, p. 1
29 Ibid.
30 Ibid.
31 The *Etownian*, February 25, 1966, p. 2
32 The *Etownian*, May 20, 1966, p. 1
33 Ibid.
34 The *Etownian*, September 3, 1966, p. 2
35 Ibid.
36 Ibid., p. 3
37 Recollection of Dr. Jobie E. Riley, February 23, 1999.
38 *Elizabethtown College Bulletin: 1967 Alumni Edition*, p. 10–11
39 The *Etownian*, April 14, 1967, p. 2
40 Ibid.

41 The *Etownian*, October 27, 1967, p. 1
42 Ibid.
43 Ibid. p. 2
44 The *Etownian*, February 22, 1968, p. 1
45 Ibid.
46 The *Etownian*, March 8, 1968, p. 2
47 The *Etownian*, February 9, 1968, p. 2
48 The *Etownian*, February 22, 1968, p. 1
49 Ibid.
50 The *Etownian*, April 26, 1968, p. 1
51 The *Etownian*, April 19, 1968, p. 3
52 Ibid.
53 The *Etownian*, September 20, 1968, p. 4
54 The *Etownian*, March 22, 1968, p. 3
55 The *Etownian*, November 22, 1968, p. 3
56 The *Etownian*, April 19, 1968, p. 3
57 The *Etownian*, September 20, 1968, p. 2
58 *History of Elizabethtown College 1899–1970*, p. 294
59 The *Etownian*, May 10, 1968, p. 1
60 The *Etownian*, September 27, 1968, p. 1
61 The *Etownian*, December 13, 1968, p. 1
62 The *Etownian*, January 10, 1969, p. 2
63 Ibid., p. 1
64 *Elizabethtown Chronicle*, January 16, 1969, p. 2
65 The *Etownian*, January 17, 1969, p. 2
66 The *Etownian*, February 7, 1969, p. 2
67 The *Etownian*, March 7, 1969, p. 1
68 The *Etownian*, April 18, 1969, p. 1
69 The *Etownian*, April 25, 1969, p. 2
70 The *Etownian*, May 2, 1969, p. 1
71 *Moving Toward the Mainstream*, p. 213
72 quoted in *Moving Toward the Mainstream*, p. 214
73 The *Etownian*, October 17, 1969, p. 1
74 Interview with Louise Baugher Black, May 28, 1999
75 Ibid.
76 Interview with Donald E. Smith, September 6, 2000
77 The *Etownian*, October 17, 1969, p. 1
78 The *Etownian*, January 1, 1963, p. 1
79 The *Etownian*, May 9, 1969, p. 2

Chapter 10

1970–1980

"We now have a sense of purpose..."

Change would continue to flourish, but there would be more winters of discontent between the springs of every year. For Elizabethtown College, the 1970s would prove to be even more turbulent than the preceding decade, as once again the school was faced with questions of its very survival.

While President Mays and his administration had gained favor with the students for supporting student sentiment against the war in Vietnam, they were losing the battle in other areas, just as the United States was losing the battle for the hearts and minds of the Vietnamese people. Many students rejected the role of the College as a wise and guiding parent who dictated to the students when to come and go. One of the most obvious and long standing results of this parental role was mandatory convocation, a requirement that many felt was more restrictive than ever in the light of the student protests and rebellions of the 60s.

Yet, as the College entered 1970, the Board of Trustees made it clear that no changes in convocation would be considered, reaffirming their dedication to the program as it stood. They were rewarded for their stand with an *Etownian* editorial on "Communications Breakdown,"[1] two words that would become a catchphrase frequently heard in the months and years to come.

Most often, the administration would find itself embattled by either the students or the faculty. During 1970, the administration was attacked for not paying attention to the needs of Fairview Hall residents, who claimed the condition of the building was sub-par. Then an April editorial accused the administration of being a "dictatorship" by compiling a list of magazines that could not be sold in the College bookstore. When questioned, the administration officiously replied that the magazines listed were "not in keeping with college policy."[2] The list of titles was not offered.

However, it was the administration's perceived apathy toward minorities on campus that would cause the year's major crisis. In a March issue of the student paper, student Pete Pero criticized the College for having less than a 1 percent enrollment of African-Americans, and called for an expanded admissions program. In his support, Professor Louise Black was quoted as saying, "Elizabethtown has the reputation of being the 'Birmingham' of the North among many Harrisburg Blacks."[3]

The charge led President Mays to issue a statement on racism and social intolerance, which said in part, "We have made available financial assistance designated specifically for minority groups to enroll here. Further, we intend to pursue this program with added emphasis in time to come."

In its two pages concerning student financial aid, the 1969–71 *Elizabethtown College Bulletin: Catalogue Number* says nothing about grants or scholarships intended for minority students, only "disadvantaged" ones.[4] Nor would the 1973–75 Bulletin include any such notice. Finally, the 1975–77 catalogue stated that "Special programs are available for Minority-Group students and athletes."[5]

The perception that the College was not doing enough for minorities persisted, so on May 5, 1970, African-American students presented a list of eighteen demands to the administration. They included scholarships for all incoming and present black students, active recruitment of black students in inner-city areas, the hiring of more black faculty and staff, the guaranteed admission of at least 200 black students, and, more unexpectedly, the removal of three deans and a faculty member. An editorial appearing in the same issue of *The Etownian* that reported the story expressed disapproval of the demands.

The demands had been signed by eighteen students, only seven of whom were African-American. This figure constituted a majority of the thirteen registered African-American students, five of whom were on scholarships for the "disadvantaged." The demands were presented in President Mays' absence to Dean Wayne Miller, who told the petitioners they would have to wait for an official response from Mays.

On May 21, the President submitted a letter to the signers stating that he was immediately rejecting five of the demands, including those concerning large amounts of financial aid, as they "seem to exceed the fiscal capability of the institution."[6] Likewise, the demands asking for the removal of personnel would not be discussed: "The College cannot accept those items," read the letter, "which bypass normal administrative procedures. Appointments follow recommendations from supervising administrators and involve professional judgment."[7] Negotiations on the other demands would, he went on, take place in the appropriate committees and offices which were intended for such purposes.

The College, Mays said, "cannot entertain matters presented under the veil of threat, either implicit or explicit," but added that "the College recognizes the right of petition for the purpose of expressing a request and/or point of view."[8] He concluded by reiterating his earlier statement: "The College stands ready and eager to work in any practical and constructive way with those students who are interested in promoting greater understanding and acceptance among the races."[9]

The department of philosophy and religion, always in the forefront of any struggle for social justice or human rights, found their own "practical and constructive way" to contribute to the welfare of African-American students. A faculty-sponsored Black Scholarship Program was begun, and the department added to it a $500 teaching award they had received from the College.

Dr. Stanley T. Sutphin, associate professor of religion and philosophy, was the informal chairman of the program. He announced that eighteen faculty members had also pledged $200 a year over the next four years to underwrite the fund. The total of nearly $15,000 would still not be enough to provide full scholarships for two students, so Sutphin requested further donations from other faculty members, as well as alumni and friends of the College.

The following fall, a further response to the students' demands was given in the form of the newly created Commission for the Advancement of Racial Equality (CARE), founded to deal with the more general demands and concerns of African-Americans on campus. Only a few weeks after CARE's founding, controversial comedian and writer Dick Gregory spoke to a huge crowd on campus, presenting an African-American viewpoint with wry and witty intensity.

Other black speakers were invited to campus, and the fall of 1972 saw the College's first Black Cultural Weekend, complete with speakers, a soul food brunch, and a showing of the film, *A Raisin in the Sun*. The weekend became a popular and continuing tradition.

❧—☙

White students as well as black were continuing to question and to resent authority at Elizabethtown College. Such a student response was inevitable, considering that many colleges had recanted the role of parent, granting students the right to live their personal lives as they pleased. This desertion of *in loco parentis* was in many ways a betrayal of the long-lived concept that colleges were expected to teach moral as well as academic lessons, creating the whole person. There were few places where this was as true as at Elizabethtown College.

From its start, the object of the school had been "a harmonious development of the physical, mental, and *moral* powers" of the students. The very motto, "Educate for Service," reflected a moral and spiritual purpose behind a college education. During the 1970s, however, the College would begin to learn the lessons that would take it many more years to fully discern — how to mold character without preaching, how to create morals without moralizing, and how to change the concept of service from something one was required to do to something one *wished* to do.

But in order to reach such a state, the first decision that was needed was to let go, something which most administrators were loathe to do, both for fear of antagonizing the constituency of the College, and out of mistrust of those whom they considered their charges.

Though the process was slow, there were signposts along the way. In 1970, the Campus Life Council passed a resolution stating that "each resident hall will determine its own living regulations in keeping with the ideals of Elizabethtown College and in keeping with local, state, and federal laws."[10]

A new self-regulated hours policy was introduced in the fall of 1970. A female student was permitted to sign out a residence hall key to return after hours, but only with the permission of her parents. The same semester saw men and women living in the same building, the Living-Learning Complex, albeit in separate wings. The idea of open dorm hours would not even be considered by the trustees until 1975, when its executive committee rejected the idea.

Students were still concerned with issues that affected their own freedoms in a broader sense. The Vietnam war was still very much a presence in the early 70s, but students who were against the war found firm allies in the College and its spiritual partner, the Church of the Brethren. A full page ad in *The Etownian* made the church's stance perfectly clear. It showed a drawing of Christ before Pilate, and the copy read:

> *I reel at the atrocities in Vietnam, Yet the atrocity is war itself. I shudder at killing villagers one by one, Yet bombers do whole villages at a time.*
>
> *I cringe and say "no" to war, Yet my taxes pay for it. I would put an end to war, Yet my children play it. Who is on trial? I am. I am on trial for a war crime. We believe that God is the Father of all. If this be so, then all war is between brothers and all war is wrong. The present mood is to Vietnamize the war, but a Vietnamized war is still war. Historically, we have said "no" to war. Say "no" with us.*
>
> *— The Church of the Brethren*[11]

The College's Board of Trustees continued its resistance to war by approving a policy to allow military recruiters to visit the campus and hand out materials, but specifically forbidding them to enlist students.

In May of 1971, an event was held in the Dell to raise awareness of the Vietnam situation. Students set up tents and camped there, flying a North Vietnamese flag, as well as a U.S. flag flown upside-down. Speakers at the event included professors Kenneth Kreider and Eugene Clemens, both of whom had been early critics of U.S. policy in Vietnam. They were joined by professor Richard Mumford, who had changed his mind concerning his early support of U.S. involvement.

Several townspeople, possibly those who had protested the College's earlier candlelight vigil, were infuriated by what they took to be a demonstration of treason in their own community, and several complained to Director of Development and Public Relations James L. M. Yeingst, warning that there might be trouble as a result. There was none.

Students continued to be vocal about the war. They planned to demonstrate at a 1972 speech on campus by Curtis W. Tarr, head of the country's Selective Service System, but Tarr's speech was cancelled due to Senate hearings, and was not rescheduled.

The protestors had a second chance a week later, when the U.S. Air Force Band and the Singing Sergeants gave a concert at the College. Several hooded students interrupted the concert, carrying a banner that read, "Sing a song tonight, drop a bomb tomorrow."[12] They were removed by police.

Another *cause célèbre* related to the war was the trial of the Harrisburg Seven, a group of anti-war protestors who were accused by the government of plotting to bomb a heating system in a Washington, D. C. building and kidnap Henry Kissinger. The group included a member of the Church of the Brethren from Lancaster. The first three months of 1972 saw many stories concerning the case in *The Etownian*, including an interview with Harrisburg Seven member Ted Glick, as well as an account of activist Tom Hayden's visit to the College in support of the group.

Other national issues gained the attention of Elizabethtown College students. Feminism received a boost with the visit of Ti-Grace Atkinson on February 16, 1971. Atkinson was considered a radical feminist who criticized marriage and the nuclear family, along with violence to women, and preached Simone de Beauvoir's concept that gender was not a biological fact, but a social construct. The fact that Russell Kirk spoke on campus about American conservatism during the same month clearly demonstrates the wide range of ideas the College was making available to its students.

Women's liberation was one of several topics of concern at the College's next "Tent City," held in April 1972. The actual camp was rained out, but the planned seminars were held as scheduled in the Alumni Auditorium. Along with feminism, participants discussed resistance, political trials, Angela Davis, and abortion. In the fall of 1973 a group of students organized a discussion of women's problems. It would take another few years, however, for the subject to reach the highest offices of the school.

The controversial subject of abortion, one of the topics of the 1972 Tent City, returned to campus in the fall of that year. A seminar on sexual behavior was conducted by Ron Lutz of the Germantown Church of the Brethren and Mary Tyson, Chairperson of Clergy Consultation Agency in Philadelphia, with both participants urging "free choice."[13] An opposing view was later presented by Dr. Robert Lombard, who spoke against abortion at a meeting of the Biology Club, thus bringing to the campus a societal disagreement that, nearly thirty years later, shows no sign of resolution.

Students and faculty also chose sides in a more political controversy concerning President Richard Nixon's involvement in the cover-up of the break-in at the headquarters of the Democratic National Committee in the Watergate apartment complex. Nixon, partly because of his escalated bombing of Vietnam, as well as ordering U.S. incursions into Cambodia and Laos, was far from the darling of many anti-war faculty and administrators. An ad that appeared from "Faculty and Administrators for McGovern-Shriver," Nixon's challengers in the 1972 election, carried 33 signatures.

When the Watergate hearings began, *The Etownian* ran many opinion pieces, including "Conservative vs. Liberal" columns on how "Watergate Affects America." One unsigned piece entitled "One View of Impeachment" erroneously predicted that impeachment proceedings would occur, since the writer found it impossible to imagine Nixon resigning.[14]

There were a number of angry outbursts from students in the letters column. The year 1970 saw a small contretemps over the use of a "Hell, yes" cheer at athletic events. Another free speech issue arose the following year when a student posted in the window of her residence hall room a line from a Jefferson Airplane song, "Eskimo Blue Day," that read: "It doesn't mean s___ to a tree."

The student was ordered to remove the sign, and when a number of students criticized the administration's action as censorship of free speech, Dean John Taylor adroitly responded that it was rather a matter of consideration for others, including alumni and townspeople who would see the sign. He added that by taking the line out of the context of the song, the student had left only the vulgarity.

The greatest student outcry, however, was over the quality of the cafeteria food. Lengthy articles were published on the subject, as well as reports of a fact-finding committee and their proposals for improvement.

There was a small minority of students whose expressions of dissatisfaction were less civilized. Four bomb scares requiring building evacuations occurred from late 1970 to early 1971: two were at Myer Hall, one at Royer, and another at Schlosser. Fortunately each incident proved to be a hoax.

The spring semester of 1973, however, saw what Gordon Bateman, Director of Housing, called "the worst case of malicious mischief I've seen in my tenure here."[15] On the third floor of Founders Hall's B-wing several male students had spread eggs, syrup, flour, feathers, ammonia, garbage, and other materials on the walls and floors, causing $1200 worth of damage. It was the most destructive act of student violence ever, only to be surpassed by the notorious snowball fight of 1991.

❧—☙

Despite such acts, the College continued to function as usual. The way the school functioned, however, was becoming a major concern of students, faculty, and administration. By the start of the

70s, there were still enormous questions about the governance of the College that required discussion and resolution.

A petition signed by five hundred students had been presented to President Mays, asking him to appoint representatives from the students, faculty, and administration to form a Constitutional Assembly. Its purpose would be to structure a Community Government for the school, which would allow student voices to be heard more clearly.

President Mays presented the task of writing a document that would create such an organization to the faculty, and appointed chemistry professor John Ranck as chairman of a committee whose goal was to create a faculty consitution for the governance of the College. The committee presented the text of the proposed constitution of the Community Congress in March of 1970, and it was ratified by the student association and the administration. The Board of Trustees approved it on April 25, and the Community Congress became a reality. The *Elizabethtown College Review* explained it in the following way:

> *The Community Congress will consist of four divisions — one from each academic area on campus and a student division — and the administrator group...*
>
> *The Student Congress, to number between 35 and 40 persons, will replace the Student Senate. [It] will be elected on a representative basis from residence and departmental units rather than at-large...*
>
> *The administrator group...has the option to act as a division or remain apart from the normal legislative channels.*
>
> *...Students and administrators will share voting membership with faculty in the new government.*[16]

In short, the new congress would be responsible for making all academic, professional, and social policy, "subject," the *Review* reminded its readers, "to the review and approval of the Board of Trustees as determined by President Morley J. Mays."[17] Ranck admitted that:

> *The proposed Constitution does not give each member of the College community a vote on every issue, as did some of last Spring's proposals for Community Government, though it does embody much of the spirit and many of the principles of Community Government.*
>
> *The test...will not be in any particular structures that it does or does not establish, but in the willingness of students, faculty, and administration to accept each other's concerns for conditions at Elizabethtown College as born out of institutional love and loyalty, and in their willingness to cooperate toward mutually accept-able solutions to our common problems.*[18]

There were other changes in the works as well. The 1970–71 academic year would see a major change in the office of the presidency. President Mays would now spend most of his time on long-range planning and fund-raising. Since he would be absent from the campus most of the time contacting foundations and other sources of financial support, the four administrators directly under him were given more direct responsibility for the day to day operations of the school.

The trustees' executive committee had recommended the change, and Chairman of the Board Breidenstine explained that the College was at a moment of decision, in which "careful, long-range planning" and "finding more adequate means of support"[19] were the essential elements. Further aid in daily operations was given by Wayne Miller, who, in the spring of 1971, was named Executive Vice-President of the College.

During the remainder of Mays's tenure, several new majors were added to the curriculum. Among them were Early Childhood Education, Occupational Therapy, Music Therapy, and Physical Therapy, all of which became strong and in-demand programs. The Music Therapy program received accreditation by the National Association of Music Therapy in 1979, and the College's Social Work program, exemplifying the College's creed of "Educate for Service," was granted accreditation by the Council on Social Work Education of New York City.

The 70s were the dawning of the digital age, and by 1976 there was a great demand among students for a computer science major. A number of courses were offered, and an *Etownian* story supporting a major stated that, "Local businessmen have found Etown computer graduates to be especially satisfactory."[20] Although an official proposal for the major went before Academic Council, it would have to wait for the time being.

≈§—§≈

During the 1970s, the campus grew physically as well. The first week of the new decade saw the dedication of a building that was the fulfillment of a fifty-year dream when 276 alumni began to raise funds to erect a gymnasium. The Alumni Physical Education Center, later known as the Thompson Gymnasium, was officially opened on January 7, 1970. The hexagonal building covered over an acre of land. The gym, given to the College by Dr. Troy M. and Elsie Thompson, held a large floor with two sets of folding bleachers that sat 3300. When the bleachers were closed, the floor could hold three basketball courts. The building also contained badminton, handball, and volleyball courts, a wrestling room, training rooms, a remedial gym, locker rooms, physical education classrooms, a laundry, ten offices, a lobby, and storage rooms. It also connected with the Baugher Student Center and its swimming pool and bowling alleys. The huge edifice has served the College well ever since.

While the College received a new and much-needed building, another was badly showing its age. Fairview Hall, the men's residence built in 1920 as Fairview Apartments, was in such disrepair that its residents frequently complained about their living conditions. In April 1970, the trustees agreed to end its use as a residence hall and turn the building into faculty offices. Faculty members voiced few complaints, since they would be leaving South Hall, one of the army barracks erected as dormitories after World War II, and a far worse office environment than Fairview. (West Hall, another post-war barracks building, burned beyond repair in 1972, the victim of faulty wiring.)

Fairview Hall found a champion in John E. Fetzer, who was the owner of the Detroit Tigers baseball team. Fetzer, a descendant of one of three men named Christian Wenger who settled in Lancaster

County in the 1700s, pledged $40,000 to the Fairview Hall renovation on the condition that other members of the Wenger family could match it with an additional $60,000. The Wengers proved more than generous, and the renovated building was renamed the Christian Wenger Center for the Humanities, housing offices and seminar rooms for the departments of English, history, and religion and philosophy.

The autumn of 1970 saw students moving into the "Living Learning Center," a newly built residence hall. It contained four wings, two with seventy-six students in each and two with eighty-eight in each, as well as a large central lounge. It was planned so that students would live in groups of sixteen and be taught interdisciplinary courses in seminar rooms attached to the living areas. The layout was also intended to make the students more independent. Those who lived together would be totally responsible for the care of their own suite.

In 1972, two years after construction was completed, the complex was christened Founders Hall, and the four wings were named for men who had been instrumental in founding the College: Falkenstein, Beahm, Ziegler, and Hertzler. The central lounge was dedicated to Dr. and Mrs. Horace E. Raffensperger, alumni and founders of the Continental Press.

A new social sciences building was needed, and a two-story structure was planned that would house the departments of education, sociology, political science, and the new Center for Business Studies. The building was dedicated on May 5, 1973, and would later be named Nicarry Hall after Mr. & Mrs. Wayne Nicarry.

The final building project of the Mays administration was a major addition to Esbenshade Hall to house the biology department. The Board agreed to the addition in February 1974, and it was completed in time for the fall 1975 semester at a cost of $700,000.

Unfortunately for the College, more money was often going out than coming in. The bad news hit the campus in February, 1973, with a front-page *Etownian* headline: "Budget Crisis Strikes E-town." In the story Dr. Wayne Miller stated that the College was "on the brink of a financial crisis."[21] The immediate problem was a deficit of $820,000 in the 1973–74 operating budget.

By April, the budget had been successfully balanced, but the College still stood in a precarious financial position. It may have been financial consideration that led to a special session of the Board of Trustees in August, where they discussed changing the school's charter in order to put the College wholly in the hands of the trustees rather than the Church of the Brethren.

The close ties with the church, some feared, might violate the rules of separation of church and state, a consideration since the College received federal assistance. If such assistance were lost due to a federal ruling against the College, the monetary loss would be disastrous in light of the current state of finances.

The proposed changes in the charter were submitted to the Atlantic Northeast and Southern Pennsylvania districts of the Church of the Brethren for their consideration. The crux of the change would be an end to ownership of the College by the two districts, and the reduction of trustees directly elected by the church to twelve out of a total of thirty, making church-elected trustees a minority for the first time.

The Atlantic Northeast District Conference was to be held at Elizabethtown College on October 12–14, 1973, and it was expected that the proposal would be considered at that time. The issue of *The Etownian* that appeared shortly before the conference offered an in-depth look at both sides of the issue.

The advocates for the change claimed that it was needed to prevent the erosion of state and federal funding on which the College depended. If the College moved further away from the "church help" relationship, the reasoning went, it would be less likely to lose those funds.

A second reason, advocates claimed, was that qualified trustee candidates could not always be found. Trustees were required to be members of the Church of the Brethren, and it was not always possible to find Brethren with the requisite skills.

Opponents to the changes accused the administration of failing to tell the whole story. Eugene Eisenbise, former Planning Advisor for Higher Education for the Commonwealth, and the Reverend Wayne Zunkel, moderator of the conference, met with state personnel who were responsible for college charters and scholarship funds.

These state officials told Eisenbise and Zunkel that scholarship aid was granted to *individual* students, and could be used at any accredited school. To deny such aid on the basis of the College having a church relationship would affect twenty-five to thirty colleges in Pennsylvania, and the officials viewed such an occurrence as highly unlikely. While it was true that some schools had lost funding, it was because of sectarian requirements for faculty and students, a condition which did not exist at Elizabethtown.

A view on federal funding was offered by Dr. Jacob E. Hershman, a former dean at Elizabethtown College. Hershman was presently an administrator for the Department of Health, Education, and Welfare, which was responsible for federal funding of colleges across the country. He felt that it would be a mistake to think that the federal government would jeopardize grants because of church-college relationships, and stated that Elizabethtown's future could be linked to maintaining its church ties — ties which gave it a distinctive personality among colleges.

The unnamed reporter for *The Etownian* probed more deeply into the issue, and found:

> *The changing of the charter represents a long-time goal of President Morley J. Mays. Early in his administration he told a small group of faculty members that one accomplishment of his ten years would be to separate the College from the church. Once in the Spring issue of "Brethren Life and Thought" he said, "One wonders what the church can continue to contribute to higher education." He further questioned whether Elizabethtown's relationship to the church can be continued "without compromising the legitimate educational aspirations of the College."*
>
> *Tension has been building over the proposed revisions. The executive committee of the trustees has complained that some members of the board are "treasonous" for not supporting the board's proposal.*
>
> *Some of the members of the administration, faculty, and trustees feel strong pressure has been applied to them to support the decision.*[22]

At the October meeting of the district conference, Dr. Mays presented the resolution, but when it came up for a vote, conference members expressed strong opposition and it was defeated. The relationship between Elizabethtown College and the Church of the Brethren would not change for nearly another twenty years.

There was no question, however, that state and federal funding for Elizabethtown College would be secure. But the question remained, as it had through the College's first seventy-five years, of how to ensure its financial position. The cost of tuition had consistently climbed over the College's lifetime, but the challenge was to keep it equivalent to price increases in general, and not to have tuition inflation outstrip the rest of the economy.

One strategy was the "Decisive Years Fund," a three-year capital gifts campaign begun in early 1974 with a goal of 3.1 million dollars. The initial responses topped one million; by year's end the response was so positive that the hoped-for endowment portion of 1.5 million dollars was doubled to $3 million.

There was no doubt, however, that money was tight, and cost-cutting affected nearly every level of the College. President Mays requested Dean of the Faculty Robert V. Hanle to furlough three faculty members. Even the cheerleaders were hard-pressed enough to stage a strike. Since they could no longer afford the supplies and travel expenses that came out of their own pockets, they hoped to get the squad declared a club and eligible for Student Activities funds.

Another remedy to the school's woes was the creation of the new post of Director of Government Relations, "in recognition of the need for a central clearing house for exchanges of ideas on federal and state funding."[23] Edmund M. Miller was appointed to the office.

A financial turnaround, however, would have to wait for a new president, and some of his tactics, though necessary, would prove unpopular with many.

⋑—⋐

The early 70s saw a number of college milestones. Vera Hackman retired in the fall of 1973. She received an honorary Doctorate of Humane Letters from the College in 1978, and kept her retirement years filled with activity. Her work teaching English to immigrants won her the Jefferson Award in 1984, and on February 2, 2000, she was one of thirteen individuals chosen to receive a Centennial Medal from the College, honoring those people who had a profound impact on the institution. She died on September 8, 2000, at the age of ninety-seven.

Besides Miss Hackman's retirement, the early 70s also saw A. G. Breidenstine's resignation as chairman of the Board of Trustees, after six years in the office.

His successor was Clifford B. Huffman '47, a trustee since 1967. Huffman worked as area loan manager for the Equitable Life Assurance Society of the United States, which he joined two years after his graduation from Elizabethtown College. He was active in the Church of the Brethren as chairman of the District Board and moderator of Lancaster Church of the Brethren. A past president of the Lancaster Council of Churches, he conducted a weekly radio program "Religion in the News" under their sponsorship.

Huffman's radio career began when, as a boy, he played harmonica in a group called the Blue Ridge Mountaineers on the radio. The music led him into radio announcing, and he worked his way through college by announcing for WGAL Radio in Lancaster and WHP in Harrisburg.

⌇⌇

Outreach to the Elizabethtown community gained momentum with new two programs in 1972 and 1973. The first was the "Golden Agers" program, which offered senior citizens the opportunity to audit courses of their choice for a five dollar fee per semester. Fourteen seniors attended eight of the seventeen courses made available to them. The second program was the Center for Community Education under the direction of Dr. James Berkebile. Separate from the residential college, the experimental agency offered 'open-university' type degree programs.

A cooperative education program was announced in 1976, the result of a $14,000 federal grant. Under the program, students could take a full-time academic study program for a certain period of time, alternating with periods of educationally related work.

By then, Dr. Mays' term was nearly over. He had lost his wife, Lucinda, on April 13, 1975, following a lengthy illness. Less than a month later, Executive Vice-President Wayne Miller, who had been responsible for much of the administrative work at the College, resigned to take a deanship at Laverne College in California.

In April of 1976, President Mays announced his plans to retire at the end of the 1976–77 school year, when he would reach mandatory retirement age. During his retirement he took a second wife, Lettie Willis Terry, served briefly as interim acting president of Albright College, and died in Lancaster on July 4, 1998.

The person chosen as Dr. Mays' successor in January 1977 was familiar to many at Elizabethtown College. Mark Ebersole, a 1943 graduate of the school, entered the office on June 30, 1977. At the time, Dr. Ebersole was dean of the graduate school and associate vice-president for academic affairs at Temple University.

Had the University of Pittsburgh not dropped its ice hockey program in the late 30s, Ebersole, who had originally received a hockey scholarship there, might never have come to Elizabethtown College. He transferred from Pitt, and then earned degrees from Elizabethtown, Crozer Theological Seminary, the University of Pennsylvania, and Columbia. Elizabethtown had granted him an honorary Doctor of Laws degree in 1969.

Ebersole's teaching career began at Elmira College. He held both teaching and administrative positions at Bucknell, and had been at Temple since 1971. He served on evaluation teams for The Middle States Association, was president of the Northeastern Association of Graduate Schools, and chairman of the membership committee of the National Council of Graduate Schools.

He was married to Dorothy Baugher, one of the daughters of A. C. Baugher, with whom he had two sons — Philip, a history major at Dartmouth, and Stephen, a business major at Indiana University.

In the announcement of Ebersole's appointment, Clifford Huffman said, "To say that we feel privileged to have Dr. Ebersole as our president-elect would be an understatement. He is a distinguished alumnus of the College who has earned a wide reputation as a scholar and an administrator in higher education."[24]

In a public statement, Ebersole remarked that he foresaw a future for small colleges, and that among Elizabethtown's assets were a "long tradition of combining liberal studies with professional studies, its handsome physical plant and fine academic facilities, and its physical location amid a thriving business and industrial region." Among Ebersole's concerns:

> *...to do all we can to strengthen faculty develop-*
> *ment, to shore up public relations and fund raising,*
> *and to make sure we are maintaining liberal studies*
> *and professional studies within the curriculum.... Top*
> *priority must be given to continuing the College's move-*
> *ment toward great academic strength and stature....*
>
> *We must provide faculty members with opportuni-*
> *ties for scholarly work and study leaves, maintain*
> *appropriate criteria for granting tenure and promo-*
> *tions, and recruit, when there is occasion to, outstand-*
> *ing faculty members, provide them with adequate*
> *compensation, and assure them the freedom to practice*
> *their procedures. [We must] expand and intensify our*
> *fund raising efforts and do so promptly, for without*
> *money we can't even maintain our current problems,*
> *much less improve them....*
>
> *The job of the undergraduate college is to either*
> *prepare students for graduate school or to prepare them*
> *to be able to work in some form of professional work.*
> *If this goal is not met, then the school is not fulfilling*
> *its mission to its students.*[25]

President-elect Ebersole would find these tasks approaching the Herculean. The College remained in precarious financial condition, and at the same time some faculty members were expressing concern about the caliber of some incoming students. In March 1977, Acting English Department Chairman Carl J. Campbell bewailed the lack of grammatical skills and writing ability of incoming freshmen. "Pathetic," he termed it. "As many as one third are at a fifth or sixth grade reading level."

Freshmen who did poorly on screening tests were given General Studies to bring their basic skills to the point where they could take English 105, Introduction to Literature. More and more were being placed in the remedial course. Many faculty felt that academic excellence was taking a back seat to other considerations.

Among the first requests to cross President-elect Ebersole's desk, however, concerned sexual equality. In March, a statement signed by forty-three administrators, faculty, and staff was sent to Ebersole. It asked the search committee to consider a qualified woman for the open post of dean of the College. Ebersole responded by saying that "the committee will, indeed, seek and give serious consideration to women candidates who meet the specified qualifications for the position."[26] However, a few weeks later senior Deborah C. Bruno, a member of the selection committee, revealed the intrinsic pro-male assumptions when she said, "We would like to have *him* [italics added] appointed by the time Dr. Ebersole takes over."[27] The following autumn, Dr. Bruce L. Wilson became the new dean.

A fact-finding survey conducted by the College's Caucus for Women's Issues that fall found that "men hold virtually all the positions of authority, prestige, and leadership" in the College community. In response, the new president promised to try and redress the imbalances.[28]

In September of 1977, President Ebersole addressed the Community Congress for the first time. He rejected the idea of a nursing major, which many students had requested, since it "would shift the center of gravity too far from the College's liberal arts tradition." It would also be "the most costly single department in the entire College, and it could alter substantially the character of the College."[29]

Ebersole also postponed a final decision on the addition of a computer science major until the following February, saying, "In the long run it is not how much we do that counts, but that what we do, we must do well."[30]

His decision to ensure that the quality of liberal arts was strengthened before new majors were added was not to the liking of all students. Senior business major Lisa Marx responded in a letter that claimed, "Business is where the jobs are. Why develop an area which people are not going to be employed in?"[31]

Another of Ebersole's concerns was student attrition and student life. He referred to the turbulent era of the 60s as a reminder that "students dislike being treated as a nuisance."[32] He also planned to increase the endowment, and hoped to increase faculty salaries based on performance. He also expressed the hope that retrenchment through dismissal of tenured faculty or the elimination of departments would not be necessary. Retrenchment, however, was a word and a concept that would become all too familiar to those at Elizabethtown College in the next few years.

❧—❧

By the end of 1977, deeper cracks were starting to show in the financial status of the College. *The Conestogan*, the College yearbook, was $3000 in debt, and for the first time in many years, students would have to pay for their yearbooks rather than have the cost included in their activities fees.

Earl Kurtz, treasurer of the College for twenty years, had announced his retirement at the fall meeting of the trustees, to be effective in June 1978. At that same meeting, finances were discussed, and President Ebersole told the board that "Deficit budgeting alarms me. Somehow we must balance our budget by the end of this year."[33]

Less than a month after President Ebersole was inaugurated on November 5, "retrenchment" began. Fred M. Rice, counselor and Director of General Studies, was dismissed. *The Etownian* reported: "Rumors are circulating through the college that other employees may be dismissed in the near future."[34]

Dr. Ken Zirkle, dean of student affairs, spoke for President Ebersole, saying, "The President is trying to keep room, board, and tuition as low as possible for students. As a result, we must evaluate whether we are operating at peak efficiency…'Retrenchment' is a very normal procedure during a new administration suffering from budget difficulties."[35]

Some students were not so easily mollified, however. An editorial the following week, "Why, Dr. Ebersole?" took the president to task for dismissing Rice on short notice while paying his salary through the end of the year. There would be further questions.

In mid-December, President Ebersole announced more imminent retrenchment moves that would involve the dismissal and/or relocation of possibly five more administrators. By the end of January,

1978, *seven* more had been dismissed. Ebersole explained that the number of administrators in comparison with faculty members was considerably out of balance. One of those administrators who left immediately was Director of Alumni Relations Albert W. Peterson, who commented, "I hope that eventually Dr. Ebersole will be proven right in what he is doing."[36]

The stories on the first page of *The Etownian* that reported Peterson's dismissal seemed to underline the College's need for greater fiscal responsibility: tuition was rising again; there would be no further issuance of emergency loans from the Alumni Loan Fund; there would be a campus musical, but *How to Succeed in Business Without Really Trying* had been chosen because it was the least expensive to stage.

The same issue ran an article on student attitudes toward the new president. Many felt he was being too secretive, not letting students know what was happening, nor the reasons behind his actions. He had defenders as well, such as student Kathy Liberatori, who said, "I heard that he is going to different organizations to raise money for the school, while the other presidents really didn't try to." Craig Clinger was the first to express an opinion that would be echoed frequently in months to come: "A lot of these things should have been done a long time ago."[37]

Cost-cutting continued. Due to a projected decline in enrollment, student cooperative housing was to be phased out. "The plan," Dr. Zirkle said, "is to bring students back to the residence halls so they will be operating efficiently...There is not one thread of anything in this beyond financial concerns. Right now one of the most important situations facing the college is fiscal. We must remain solvent."[38] The houses would not be sold, but would be rented to non-students, so that co-op living could eventually be reinstated.

The one area where the Ebersole administration refused to compromise was academic excellence. Despite the need for increased student enrollment, the Academic Standing committee reviewed the academic performances of twenty-three students in early 1978, and refused to grant them further enrollment. After a year, they would have the right to appeal their dismissals and reapply for admission.

There were some, however, who welcomed the administrative pruning. Dr. Carl J. Campbell in a letter to *The Etownian* spoke for many of the faculty when he said, "Faculty morale has improved greatly rather than declined [as a result of retrenchment]. After years of wasteful expenditure and drifting, we now have a sense of purpose...[improving] the former absurd situation where we had one administrator for every two faculty members."[39]

Another letter from "Cum Laude, Class of '68" took an even harsher view of what had occurred at the College before President Ebersole arrived:

> Many of us who graduated during the 'sixties and early 'seventies became very demoralized in recent years by the failure of the previous (Mays-Hanle) administration to maintain the academic standards of the institution.
>
> "Academic excellence" had become an archaic phrase, uttered only in private. The only admission criterion had become a check which did not bounce. Grades of "A" were handed out like gold stars in elementary school, and a "C," which supposedly meant average, had become tantamount to a failure. Pass/fail courses, no-work internships, and "testing-out" had transformed the College into the Lake Placida Country Club...In short, our hard-earned degrees were cheapened.
>
> ...I am most pleased with the new (Ebersole-Wilson) administration. They are chopping away the deadwood. They are upgrading the academic program. They are fostering the betterment of the institution and laying a firm foundation for the College's second century.
>
> I fault them only for something beyond their control: they arrived five years late.[40]

At the end of March, all academic and administrative departmental budgets were frozen until June 30, the end of the College's fiscal year. Another new strategy adopted to conserve funds involved a stipulation in freshman housing contracts that stated that students must live in campus housing for all four years. The reason was to avoid having empty dormitory rooms from which the College would derive no income. The measure proved unpopular among students; the following semester, the Student Senate advised new students not to sign their room contract, considering it an infringement on the students' rights.

Still, the news was not altogether gloomy. The careful handling of finances had brought about some results, and at a meeting with the faculty, President Ebersole stressed that the College was not in a permanent financial crisis. There had been a substantial increase in endowment, and Ebersole announced a new campaign to raise $500,000 to endow a professional chair in the name of accounting professor Edgar T. Bitting. "We're in relatively good financial shape,"[41] Ebersole told the faculty.

The positive financial news continued. An increase in the Presidential Scholarship Program brought the number of $1000 scholarships from twelve to twenty-four. In April, Ebersole announced that a total of $950,000 had been bequeathed to the College as a result of his personal visits to individual college supporters. That same month, the Armstrong Cork Company of Lancaster donated $32,000 to renovate the Baugher Student Center.

In a public statement, President Ebersole reflected on his first year in office: "We went through the painful process of making the change to a different financial base. We may need to make other changes, but we are started in the right direction."

Of fund-raising, he stated that he liked it more than he had thought he would: "I've met a lot of very bright, very successful people, and I've been encouraged by the understanding support many of them have for the college."

Ebersole expressed regret that his program for improving the College's financial status required dismissing nine administrators. "I found it very painful to carry out that particular task, but I saw it as absolutely necessary for the future of the college."[42]

⊷§—§⊶

The fall semester of 1978 saw the announcement of a major gift to the College. Drs. John F. and Shirley W. Steinman presented Elizabethtown College with $550,000 to renovate the Gibble Science Hall and make it the Steinman Center for Art and Communications.

It was, at that time, the largest single gift ever received by the College. (The center was not dedicated until September 7, 1985. Those unable to be seated in the packed Brinser Lecture Hall viewed the proceedings on closed circuit television operated by communications students.) The Steinman Foundation would prove to be a good friend to the College in the future, making a 1997 pledge of $500,000 to the endowment campaign to update the Department of Communications and its curriculum.

In February of 1979, the Middle States Association's evaluation team presented their report. They suggested that the College improve its catalogue and strengthen its Adult Continued Education Program. As for the faculty, it recommended that merit pay be established, that the faculty should become more involved in student recruitment, and that funds should be provided for the faculty to study computer science. The team felt that the bookstore needed to be enlarged, that chemistry facilities needed to be improved, and that a zero-based budget should be implemented. Few, if any of these recommendations could be implemented without money.

But money was the farthest thing from the minds of those on campus on March 28, 1979, when the nuclear plant at Three Mile Island, only six miles away from the College, experienced a failure in the cooling system of its Number Two reactor. As a result, the uranium core partially melted, coming within thirty minutes of a large-scale meltdown, which would have released major amounts of radiation into the atmosphere. As it was, there was a minor release, and fears of a large release or even a total meltdown caused many people to desert the area for several days.

The College took no chances with the health and lives of its students. As Barry J. Llewellyn '79 recalls:

> *Professor Richard Koontz was late for class. He was never late. When he arrived...he began to speak, very slowly and deliberately. He announced to the class that there had been another accident at TMI. He said that the president of the College was closing the school indefinitely and asking all students to evacuate the campus as quickly and as orderly as possible...*

> *As I rounded the corner of the building...I saw stu-*
> *dents leaving from another doorway. Most of them were*
> *running. Several girls clutched their books above their*
> *heads as they ran by me in a state of terror, trying to*
> *shield themselves from some sort of invisible threat from*
> *the sky...I wondered if I would ever be able to return to*
> *this place which had been such a haven for me.*[43]

Some faculty and administrators remained, while others evacu-ated their families from the area. It was a time of uncertainty and fear, but by mid-April, Dr. Donald B. Kraybill and his students were gathering information on the incident. Kraybill was an associate pro-fessor of sociology and director of the College's Social Research Center. He and his students conducted the first survey of area resi-dents, using phone polls to gauge the attitudes of those who lived within a fifteen-mile radius of TMI.

Schedules were chaotic upon the students' return to campus, with the postponement of a number of athletic and social events. In May, President Ebersole sent a letter and a resolution adopted by the College's Community Congress to Walter M. Creitz, President of Metropolitan Edison, the company that owned and ran Three Mile Island. The resolution urged that TMI be permanently closed, and that a moratorium be placed on all future nuclear power plants. Creitz's response predictably called nuclear power an "indispensable source of power," and made the unproven claim that such plants had "an excellent safety record... No one suffered personal injury or damage to property as a result of the accident at TMI."[44]

The College would not win any battles with Metropolitan Edison, so it continued instead the battle of the budget. Since the cost of maintaining the Cameron Estates had risen every year and become a major drain on the College's budget the property was put up for sale in the winter of 1979 at a price of $325,000.

In early 1980, the position of Director of Athletics was consoli-dated with that of Chairman of the Department of Physical Education. As a result, John M. Tulley, Director of Athletics at the College for sixteen years, was told on January 29 that his contract had not been renewed, and that he would have to leave the campus by February 1. The Dean of Student Affairs stated that the dismissal was due to retrenchment, and that: "retrenchment has nothing to do with competency."[45]

Nevertheless, Senior Class President Bradley S. Poore sent a letter to the dean resigning his office due to Tulley's dismissal, as well as the dismissals of two other professors and the denial of tenure to an assistant professor, along with what he saw as low standards in many areas. The Dean of the Faculty responded that two of the professors had not been dismissed, but rather had resigned to accept other faculty positions.

Concerning the faculty member who had not received tenure, President Ebersole stated that tenure recommendations were made by the Professional Standards Committee, which was elected by the faculty and not appointed by the administration. "I rely heavily upon their judgment," said Ebersole, "and have no reason not to accept the recommendation of the committee and the dean."[46]

President Ebersole had weathered the financial storm that threatened to capsize the College as it had in the 1930s. As the school entered the 80s, a new capital gifts campaign was launched, intended to raise $5.5 million: $325,000 was targeted to build and maintain a new chemistry building, and another $1,250,000 was sought to endow five professorships — the A. C. Baugher Professorship of Chemistry, the Horace E. Raffensperger Professorship of History, the R. W. Schlosser Professorship of English, the Carl W. Ziegler Professorship of Religion, and the Edgar T. Bitting Professorship of Accounting.

As the campaign entered its initial phase, forty per cent of the funds were already in hand or had been pledged.

❧—❧

In spite of the problems faced by the College during the 1970s, student athletic and social activities continued to flourish. One of the College's major traditions began on the weekend of April 5, 1974, with the first "Thank God It's Spring" (TGIS) weekend. Organized by Director of Alumni Relations Albert Peterson, it originally combined the school's Spring Weekend with Alumni Day and Freshman Parents Day.

The weekend theme spread, and by 1979–80 the students were enjoying Baseball Weekend, Royer Country Western Weekend, Ober Christmas Weekend, Brinser Winter Carnival, Myer 50s Weekend, and Ivy League Weekend.

The decade saw such clubs and organizations as the Aeroclub for student pilots, Scuba Club, Alpha Psi Omega (national dramatics fraternity), History and Political Science Club, Social Work Club, Speech Club, Computer Science Club, History Club, and many more. Abraxas and Sigma Lambda Sigma, the men's and women's honor societies, merged in 1979 as the Elizabethtown Academic Honor Society.

Musical groups offered opportunities for instrumentalists and vocalists alike, and included Brass Ensemble, Clarinet Quartet, Chorale, Choral Union, Community Orchestra, Concert Band and Choir, Jazz Band, and Woodwind Quintet.

Sports continued in popularity in the 70s, and Etown athletes made a number of impressive showings. In 1970, Mike Yassim, a 22-year-old sophomore from Sierra Leone, was named the College's first All-American in soccer since Al Hershey in 1963. Another foreign student, Glasgow's James "Jamie" O'Donnell, was honored as a soccer All-American in 1977.

In 1970, the College boasted its first All-Americans in swimming: Jim Gingerich, Don Schaeberle, Dave Anstine, and Robert Sahms. The swim team also won its first Mid-Atlantic Conference championship, breaking nine MAC records while tallying 111 points.

The 1971 soccer team was another MAC champion, but the days of a dynasty were still in the future. The 1973 Blue Jays, though seeded number two in the NCAA playoffs, didn't make it to the national championships.

Wrestler Eric Mast compiled a perfect 18–0 season in 1974, the best individual wrestling season in the program's history.

But it was the end of the decade that saw the greatest flurry of athletic success. In March of 1979, Coach Don Smith was named Middle Atlantic District Coach of the Year by the National Association of Basketball Coaches. That year, his men's team won the MAC Northern Division championship, and went on to the NCAA eastern Regional playoffs.

In May 1979, Kathy Keller and Nancy Wilkins became MAC champions in tennis doubles, and in March of 1980, the College wrestling team won its first MAC team title with a 12–4–1 season.

There were other, "unofficial" athletic achievements in the 70s. On November 5, 1975, senior Lloyd B. Negoescu broke the world's record for the longest stationary handstand, balancing for three minutes and eight seconds in front of faculty witnesses. Negoescu officially increased the time to 3:34, and had an unofficial time of 4:32.

Another sport that didn't qualify as an official track and field event was streaking, an early 70s fad that consisted of running through a public place naked. Elizabethtown College was not immune, and on March 7, 1974, a "Streak-in" was held on campus with several participants that *The Etownian* did not identify.

By far the decade's greatest athletic addition to the College was the establishment of the Elizabethtown College Athletic Hall of Fame. Dedicated to Coach Ira Herr, ten charter members were inducted on Homecoming Weekend in the fall of 1975. The honorees were:

* Warren Angstadt '30, who played on the first basketball team and was an outstanding tennis player.
* Guy R. Buch '45, who participated in three sports, and was an outstanding basketball player who, in his senior year, led the nation's small college scorers.
* Joel D. Chase '67, a premier Blue Jay soccer team goalie.
* Warner Cheeks '61, baseball player and All-American soccer goalie who led the Jays to a four-year record of 32–7.
* Ray R. Diener '65, star soccer goalie, a center/forward in basketball, and a baseball pitcher with a three-year record of 14–5, who later signed a pro contract.
* William E. Foster '54, who tallied 1148 points in his college basketball career, and who became Duke University's basketball coach.
* Alvin E. Hershey '64, an All-American in soccer with 61 goals in four years, and a baseball player who batted over .300 in three of his four years.
* Linda Eshelman Hershey '63, an All-American field hockey star, who led the undefeated 1961 team and made 64 goals

in four years. She also helped establish women's tennis at the College and was the first woman to serve as executive director of the Middle Atlantic Conference.

✳ Frank W. Keath '49, who played baseball, soccer, and basketball, in which he became the all-time Blue Jay scoring leader with 1872 points in four years, set the state small college scoring mark with 564 points in his junior year, and was twice selected All-State.

✳ Sal L. Paone '57, a sharpshooting basketball guard who scored 1408 points in four seasons, ranking fifth among college scoring leaders.

There would be much more athletic glory in the 1980s. The financial security and academic grounding that President Ebersole's administration had reestablished for the College seemed to bring a new vitality and spirit to all campus activities and functions.

Although a number of painful decisions and sacrifices had been made, the College had a balanced budget and would remain on a solid financial footing through Ebersole's term as president. Admission standards would grow tougher, and the hiring of faculty ever more selective, with a constant search for professors who would challenge students to do their very best.

Elizabethtown College was quickly becoming a school in which the expectation of victory, both on the playing fields and in life, was becoming the norm.

1 *The Etownian*, January 16, 1970, p. 2
2 *The Etownian*, April 10, 1970, p. 2
3 *The Etownian*, March 6, 1970, p. 2
4 *Elizabethtown College Bulletin 1969–71*, p. 111
5 *Elizabethtown College Bulletin Catalog Edition 1975–77*, p. 14
6 *Elizabethtown College Review*, June 1970, p. 5
7 op. cit. p. 6
8 op. cit. p. 5
9 op. cit. p. 6
10 *The Etownian*, February 20, 1970, p. 1
11 *The Etownian*, March 13, 1970, p. 6
12 *The Etownian*, April 28, 1972, p. 1
13 *The Etownian*, November 3, 1972, p. 4
14 *The Etownian*, November 9, 1973, p. 2
15 *The Etownian*, May 4, 1973, p. 1

16 *Elizabethtown College Review*, April 1970, p. 1

17 *Elizabethtown College Review*, May 1970, p. 4

18 *Elizabethtown College Review*, April 1970, p. 2

19 *Elizabethtown College Review*, September 1970, p. 1

20 *The Etownian*, April 2, 1976, p. 1

21 *The Etownian*, February 9, 1973, p. 1

22 *The Etownian*, October 5, 1973, p. 1

23 *The Etownian*, September 17, 1976, p. 1

24 *The Etownian*, January 28, 1977, p. 1

25 Ibid.

26 *The Etownian*, March 25, 1977, p. 1

27 *The Etownian*, April 15, 1977, p. 1

28 Presently, the College has more women in staff positions than ever before, though no women currently are full professors.

29 *The Etownian*, September 16, 1977, p. 1

30 Ibid.

31 *The Etownian*, September 23, 1977, p. 2

32 *The Etownian*, September 16, 1977, p. 1

33 *The Etownian*, November 4, 1977, p. 1

34 *The Etownian*, December 2, 1977, p. 1

35 Ibid.

36 *The Etownian*, January 27, 1978, p. 1

37 op. cit. p. 5

38 *The Etownian*, February 3, 1978, p. 1

39 op. cit. p. 3

40 *The Etownian*, March 3, 1978, p. 2

41 *The Etownian*, March 31, 1978, p. 1

42 *The Etownian*, April 28, 1978, p. 1

43 *Elizabethtown Magazine*, Summer 1999, pp. 22–23. Llewellyn now works as a chemist/waterlab supervisor with GPU Nuclear.

44 *The Etownian*, November 9, 1979, p. 2

45 *The Etownian*, February 8, 1980, p. 1

46 *The Etownian*, February 22, 1980, p. 1

Chapter 11

1980–1990

"A raising of our standards..."

S tudents who attended Elizabethtown College in the 1980s might well remember the decade as the beginning of the glory years for sports. Elizabethtown had had outstanding players and teams in the past, but the 80s and 90s saw a large number of milestones in athletics.

The streak began in the summer of 1980, when the women's tennis team, coached by Yvonne Kauffman, won the Division III Eastern Regional Championship sponsored by the Eastern Association for Intercollegiate Athletics for Women, and placed fourth in the National AIAW Championship Tournament. Sophomore Beckie Donecker was named to the Women's All-American Tennis Team, the first time an Elizabethtown College woman had joined an All-American team.

Honors went to soccer coach Owen L. Wright the following fall, when he coached his team to his 200th win in a victory over Gettysburg College. His twenty-year record at the college was

200–65–22, making him the first soccer coach in the Mid-Atlantic Conference ever to win 200 games.

Coach Kauffman was chalking up some triple-digits herself. Her basketball team had reached 100 wins the previous year, and her 1980 field hockey team achieved that milestone in the fall. Such sports successes gave E-town's cheerleaders plenty to cheer about, and 1980 saw the first male cheerleaders, brothers Craig and Rick Beittel, John Palmer, and Don Warner.

By the end of the 1980–81 basketball season, another record had been set. Geri Bradley, in only her second season, became the first woman in Elizabethtown College's history to score 1000 points, reaching the mark in only 45 games. She helped the team to a 27–3 record, its best season ever. As a result, Coach Kauffman was named Regional Coach of the Year.

The following year the women's team was ranked number one in basketball. The ranking proved prophetic as the team defeated Greensboro 67–66 in the finals of the NCAA Division III Championship Tournament, becoming the first team to win a women's NCAA basketball championship, and the first team since the 1960 men's soccer team to bring home a national championship.

It was a great year for Coach Kauffman. Only a month later, in April, 1982, her tennis team reached its hundredth win. In her thirteen years of coaching the sport, her record stood at 100–16.

In both 1983 and 1984, her basketball team was national runner-up, and she won both Division III and College Division Coach of the Year awards in 1984. Whatever team Coach Kauffman handled, it came out smelling like the 1927 Yankees, at least in terms of success.

The men proved their mettle in 1986, when the soccer team won its first MAC championship since 1979, beating Johns Hopkins in a tight 1–0 match-up. But the best of the decade for both men's and women's sports was saved for the last year of the 80s.

Coach Kauffman's women had a 29–2 record in 1989, and the team went to the NCAA playoffs at Centre College in Kentucky. Their first game was against Centre, with senior center Maria Pioli sinking a basket at the buzzer for a 57–57 tie. Etown won with a 16–7 overtime run for a final score of 73–64.

The title match-up was against California State at Stanislaus, who had three players over six feet tall. At the half, the score stood 34–28 in favor of Cal State, but the Etown women battled back. In the last minute of the game, the score was tied 65–65. After an attempt and a rebound, sophomore Sue Krieder was fouled, and stepped to the line for two foul shots. Kreider, a sophomore, was considered a poor foul shooter, but with two seconds left on the clock, she made her first shot, making the score 66–65. She missed the second, but only needed the first. Cal State's desperation shot missed, and the Elizabethtown women were, for the second time in a decade, NCAA Division III Champions.

Eight months later, on November 18, 1989, the men's soccer team, coached by Skip Roderick, went after *their* championship. They had been underdogs in the preseason, but had stood the league on its head as they set NCAA single season records with 24 wins and 96 goals scored.

In the semifinals, they beat the University of California at San Diego, the defending champs, 1–0, and Greensboro defeated top-ranked RIT 2–0. It was Etown versus Greensboro for the championship.

At the end of the first half, there was no score. But at 79:00 of the ninety-minute game, Tim Jones passed to Mark Pratzner, who booted a goal. Five minutes later Robbie Martin passed to Pratzner for a second goal, and Etown goalkeeper Jay Varrato continued to keep Greensboro scoreless for the rest of the game. The Blue Jays had won the NCAA Championship 2–0.

❦

Just as it was a feel-good era for sports, the 80s tended to be a feel-good era in other ways. The 70s had seen student protests, an increase in drug use, a lengthy energy crisis, and the ignoble withdrawal of American troops from Vietnam. At the turn of the decade, American response to the Soviet invasion of Afghanistan was President Jimmy Carter's decision for the U. S. to boycott the 1980 Olympic Games. The Iran hostage crisis in which 52 Americans were held hostage for a total of 444 days was another indication of American weakness.

The country was ready for a change, and it came in the form of presidential candidate Ronald Reagan, whose "Morning In America" campaign struck a chord with the electorate in general and Elizabethtown students in particular. In a campus poll, Reagan outdrew Carter by two to one, and even the third party candidate John Anderson scored higher than the incumbent.

The election of Reagan was enough in itself to make many Americans optimistic, and Elizabethtown College was off to an equally bright start. In early 1981, the National Endowment for the Humanities awarded the school a $250,000 challenge grant to be matched with $750,000 by the college. The funds would establish professorships that included chairs in history, English, and international studies.

In the spring of 1981, the decision was made to create a full four-year computer science major, to begin the following fall. By September, the curriculum had been completed, a full computer science faculty positioned, and hardware upgraded.

V. Lester Schreiber was elected chairman of the board of trustees, succeeding Clifford B. Huffman. Schreiber, a native of Quarryville, was graduated from Elizabethtown College in 1939, and received his M. Ed. from Temple. He was active in public education, serving as principal in the East Lampeter and Solanco school districts until 1948, when he joined Sperry New Holland and eventually became director of marketing and training.

Schreiber was long involved in college affairs, and became a trustee in 1967 as a district representative of the Church of the Brethren. The college recognized his contributions to education by presenting him with an Alumni Citation Award in 1964, and an honorary degree of Doctor of Humane Letters in 1990. "I certainly feel that as a board," Schreiber said, "we should listen carefully to our various communities — students, faculty, administration, and alumni — to the extent that the board's policy would be tempered by their needs and wants."[1]

In his annual fall report to the board of trustees, President Ebersole reported that the college had increased its endowment from 2.5 to 4.3 million dollars, a significant increase, and that the construction of a new chemistry building should remain the school's top priority. He addressed another subject, the so-called "Religious Right" movement that had been growing stronger in the country, and particularly in Lancaster County:

> *I suspect many of us have noticed in the last year or so, that there has been born again in the land a certain intemperate religious zeal which would presume to dictate loudly to others its views on all kinds of matters — moral, religious, social, and political. In such a climate I think it is best to state clearly the proper relations between Church and College, since church-related institutions are, understandably perhaps, often misunderstood by the public.*
>
> *In its early history as a protesting church and in its strong stand in the peace tradition, the Church of the Brethren at its best has always supported the power of the individual conscience, the importance of independent thought, and the integrity of action that proceeds from both.*
>
> *Accordingly, it is imperative that if Elizabethtown is to achieve its high educational goal it must persuade learning within the tradition of free open inquiry, critically and creatively examining everything that is worthy of study. No outside force, neither political ideology, nor religious bias, nor currents of anti-intellectualism can be tolerated. For any force that dares to suppress, overtly or covertly, the intellectual exploration of the great ideas and issues of life constitutes a violation of our educational mission, a violation, indeed, of the very values that undergird College and Church alike.*[2]

That same month, President Ebersole wrote a brief editorial for the *Elizabethtown College Bulletin*, which further presented his views on the firm but changing relationship between college and church:

> *Both now understand, I think, that a college is neither a cloister nor church — its mission is to expose our*

*young people to the world of ideas, not to "protect"
them from it. And certainly the Church has come to
understand that no religion gains a meaningful membership through coercive indoctrination.*

*...the fundamental characteristic of a liberal arts
college is that it seeks to produce free people, people
who are not only free to consider and choose their des-
tinies, but who are also able to exercise that choice —
free not only abstractly, but in fact. We want to produce
not small men and women, but courageous and
thoughtful ones; not stiffnecked ideologues, but tolerant
and knowledgeable individuals who accept — indeed,
celebrate — diversity. We want to produce not men and
women who are moralists but who are intensely moral.*[3]

While conservative Ronald Reagan's election may have provided a more sympathetic political environment for those "stiffnecked
ideologues" and practitioners of "intemperate religious zeal," the
new president's hawkishness certainly caused a reconsideration of
the nuclear arms race on campus. Reagan's warrior views, which
led to his depiction of the USSR as "the evil empire," and the proposal of the "Star Wars" nuclear defense plan, was partly responsible for peace being discussed further in this peace college.

In the fall of 1981, professors Donald Kraybill and William
Puffenberger team-taught a seminar on "The Nuclear Arms Race."
In February, 1982, thirty faculty members and administrators participated in a colloquium on nuclear weapons, which resulted in a
statement of concern against "nuclear weapons as an instrument of
foreign policy."[4]

The actions of the Reagan White House would trigger more ani-
mated responses over the next few years. *The Etownian* ran articles
criticizing Reagan's Nicaragua policy, along with many cartoons.
One pictured Reagan's Secretary of the Interior James Watt despoil-
ing federal lands, while another showed Reagan opening several
doors for a woman. The doors were labeled "Job Discrimination,"
"Sexual Harassment," and "Unfair Pay."[5]

Reagan's policies hit even closer to home. Director of Financial Aid Gordon Bateman wrote a letter to *The Etownian* urging all readers to write their congressmen concerning the Reagan administration's federal budget, "severely slashing five U.S. programs aimed at helping students pay for college and university educations." The cuts "signal that the White House is reneging on a major national commitment to postsecondary education opportunities."[6] It seemed that Morning in America came at a stiff price.

Despite such proposed cuts, the board of trustees gave their approval to a new chemistry building at a projected cost of $2.2 million. Construction began the following October.

That fall found the campus more crowded than ever. With a total enrollment of 1402, 45 students were assigned temporary housing, using lounges as bedrooms.

In January 1983, while the chemistry building was still under construction, the board decided to name the building after Dr. Benjamin G. and Vera Shoop Musser. Both had been graduated from Elizabethtown in 1942, and were considered two of the college's most loyal alumni. Dr. Musser, a nephew of former college president Ralph W. Schlosser, had been a trustee since 1966, was national co-chairman of the Annual Fund campaign, and was a recipient of the alumni association's Educate for Service Through Professional Achievement Award. He would receive an honorary doctoral degree from the college in 1986. Mrs. Musser was active for years as a member of the college auxiliary. Musser Hall was dedicated on October 29, 1983.

1983 saw another new building, or rather an old building put to new use. The two-story colonial co-op house that had most recently been called Sigma House was completely refurbished and made the college's admissions building. It was named The Leffler House, in honor of Carlos R. and Georgianna Leffler, long-time supporters of the college. Mrs. Leffler was on the executive board of the college auxiliary, and Mr. Leffler had been a board member since 1968, board secretary since 1979, and was the national chairman of the Design for Excellence Capital Campaign.

Lake Placida saw some changes as well. In an effort to make the lake deeper, an attempt to drain it had been made in the spring, but the heavy rains made it impossible. In the summer, the lake dried out, and layers of silt were removed to deepen it. Unfortunately, when it was time for the lake to be refilled, the weather was again uncooperative, and the county was in one of its driest periods in years. Finally the rains came, and the lake was refilled.

At the beginning of 1984, President Ebersole announced his intention to resign, officially informing the trustees on February 11th. In the statement to the faculty and administration, he said, "I came to Elizabethtown because of the challenge and I have enjoyed very much my work here...My interest in the College will by no means diminish. I shall continue to be loyal to the College and keenly interested in her progress in the years ahead."[7]

After leaving Elizabethtown, Dr. Ebersole came to the rescue of many institutions, serving as Interim President of Maryville College from 1986–87 and 1992–93, Interim President of Webb School of Knoxville from 1987 to 1988, Interim Headmaster at Cambridge School from 1988–89, Interim CEO and Headmaster at Linden Hall School from 1991 to 1992, Consultant and Interim Chief Academic Officer of Mount St. Mary's College from 1994 to 1995, and Dean and Interim Vice-president for Academic Affairs at Saint Joseph College in 1996–97 and 1999. He now resides in East Petersburg, Pa.

Before Dr. Ebersole departed from Elizabethtown, however, another college stalwart took his leave. Edgar T. Bitting retired, and was honored with a retirement dinner on March 24th. Hundreds of Bitting's friends, colleagues, and former students were on hand to say goodbye and hear of the official establishment of the Edgar T. Bitting Chair of Accounting.

President Ebersole's final year in office was relatively peaceful. The financial crisis was over, coop housing was offered again for seniors, and placement for graduates was high, with 96% of the class of 1983 finding employment.

The announcement of Ebersole's replacement was made in March, 1985. The new president, Gerhard E. Spiegler, would take over the office on July 1st. Spiegler was formerly Provost of Haverford College, and was currently chairman of the department of religion and of graduate studies at Temple, after having been university provost for academic affairs and health sciences there.

A native of Lithuania, Spiegler was born in 1929 in the Baltic port of Klaipeda, a disputed area between Germany & Lithuania from 1919 to 1939. As Spiegler grew up in the 1930s, the Lithuanian government pressed citizens to "Lithuanianize" their lives. The territory had been granted certain rights of independence by the League of Nations, so many residents resisted this pressure. Spiegler's parents, who were German, were among them, giving him and his sister German names.

Germany took over the port in 1939 and used it as a submarine base, taking control of Lithuania from the Soviet Union in 1941. In 1944, Germany shipped Spiegler's high school class to central Lithuania to do military defense work. He was fourteen at the time, and lived in a barn with his fellow classmates, eating only bread and soup, arising at 4:00 A.M. every day to do construction and build fences.

When Russia advanced to reclaim Lithuania, Spiegler was marched back to his hometown, only to be to evacuated with the women and other children. His family gathered in Potsdam in 1945, eventually went into a British refugee camp, and were shipped west.

Spiegler, who became a U. S. citizen in 1958, attended Roosevelt College from 1952 to 1954 before earning his Bachelor's Degree at the University of Chicago. He took advanced study at the University of Bonn in Germany, returning to Chicago to complete work on his master's degree and his doctorate, granted in 1961. He served as a visiting professor of historical theology at the University of Tubingen in Germany, of contemporary theology at the Graduate Theological Union in Berkeley, CA, and in various professorships of religion at Haverford.

He and his wife, the former Ethel Maldonado, had three children: Karin, who was at the time a graduate student in speech pathology and linguistics at Temple, Eric, a graduate student in psychology at San Diego State University, and Mark, a senior at Tyler School of Fine Arts, majoring in ceramics and painting.

V. Lester Schreiber, chairman of the trustees, said of the transition between presidents:

> *Under Dr. Ebersole, the college has made consider-*
> *able strides. Enrollments are stable, the quality of our*
> *students is up, and the college is in excellent financial*
> *shape. The Board of Trustees is confident that, under*
> *the leadership of Dr. Spiegler, Elizabethtown College*
> *will build upon this sound base and increase its aca-*
> *demic stature as an institution of higher education*
> *devoted to excellence both in the liberal arts and in pre-*
> *professional training.*[8]

In his first remarks to the college, Spiegler said: "Elizabethtown, in facing its centennial not too far in the future, also faces the challenge of the 21st century. The next decade clearly will see major changes in education. The recent critique of college education in particular has made clear that the public, and parents, will demand greater quality control and assurance that they will get for their children what they are paying for...."

As Spiegler saw it, Elizabethtown College had to address three curricular issues in preparing students for the next century:

> *First, we must combine in an intelligent way*
> *career and liberal arts education, and aspire to a rais-*
> *ing of our standards. Secondly, if we do our job well,*
> *the excellence of our product ought to be made known*
> *in an active campaign which will make Elizabethtown*
> *one of the important colleges of Central Pennsylvania.*
> *Third, in heading for its centennial, the college effort to*
> *raise its endowment must be increased.*[9]

Spiegler did not take long in starting to make the changes he thought necessary. His first proposal proved to be one of his most controversial. He wanted nothing less than to abolish the college's Community Congress. At the time, the congress was composed of representatives from the Student Senate and the faculty. They would make proposals for changes in curricular and campus life policies, which the administration would either approve or return.

Spiegler wanted to replace this arrangement with a non-voting discussion body in which the faculty would make proposals on academic affairs and the Student Senate would make proposals on campus life matters. These proposals would go directly to the president for his review and recommendation, if warranted.

"The Community Congress," Spiegler claimed, "has not functioned as an effective governance instrument for many years. It met rarely and when it did meet it often met very briefly...it diffused governance responsibility."[10]

There was another reason for change. Spiegler felt the current Community Congress was overstepping its bounds. "[Its] role in matters of academic and curricular policy," he went on, "does not seem to be appropriate. The responsibility for shaping the curriculum and for educational policy issues such as grading must be placed squarely with the faculty."[11]

The dissolution of the Community Congress was quickly accomplished. The board of trustees' executive committee approved it on October 5th, using the rationale that the last Middle States evaluation team had called the current structure "bizarre," and had given the college until November 1986 to resolve the issue.

At the October 26th meeting of the trustees, the academic affairs committee recommended a revision of the current governance structure. The board unanimously decided to abolish the Community Congress. The Student Senate and Faculty Meeting would continue to exist as the major governing bodies, reporting directly to the president. At the same meeting, the board approved a provision for faculty merit pay, "based on excellence in service."[12]

The Student Senate president, Jim Foresman, claimed to be excited about the new changes in governance. "Students," Foresman said, "will increasingly have more influence in matters of campus life as they are held responsible for their social actions and services."[13]

It seemed that Brian Cassel too had a change of heart. In a February 1986 editorial, "We Have a Voice," he said, "...The idea is that the Big Guy [Spiegler] makes these decisions by himself; the only choice we have is whether to trust or distrust him. For what it's worth, I trust him."[14]

"The Big Guy" became Spiegler's nickname among the student body, more for his take charge attitude than for his size. In spite of his sometimes imperious manner, he was starting to win over many of the students, and in April 1986 an article, "The Big Guy: The Man, The Myth, The Legend," appeared in *The Etownian*. Somewhat tongue in cheek, it was still filled with admiration for what Spiegler had accomplished in a brief time, as this passage makes clear:

> *There are still rumors floating around [in] which the President is featured as a diabolical fiend who is taking over Elizabethtown and remaking it Gerhard U. It is true that in just this year, the college seal and mascot were both redesigned, Community Congress was dissolved, we had our first Booster Day, the Core Curriculum is being revised, an honor code is being studied, the administration was reorganized, a merit pay system was established for the faculty, etc.*[15]

That redesigned college seal received excellent exposure on April 5, 1986, the day of Spiegler's inauguration as the twelfth president of Elizabethtown College. He wore a new chain of office and medallion with the redesigned seal. The sterling silver medallion bore the seal, the name of the college, and the founding date on a blue enamel band. On the reverse were the names of all the past presidents.

Spiegler's next area of concern, as Cassel had foreseen, was the core curriculum. "We have substituted a smorgasbord for a well-thought-out curriculum," Spiegler had stated shortly after taking office. "There is no substitute for hard thinking, and that is what we need...The responsibility is ours to determine what we want the degree from Elizabethtown College to represent."[16]

The faculty, however, did not prove as cooperative as the trustees. At the final faculty meeting of the Spring 1986 semester, the entire core revisions proposal was defeated by a margin of 2–1.

The reasons given by Professor Fletcher McClellan, chairman of the academic council, were that the process was too quick, many departments were not ready to readjust and reevaluate, and, in the words of *The Etownian*, "McClellan indicated, in a year of turmoil and unilateral decisions, some faculty may have seen the issue as the first major change backed by the administration for which the faculty had a vote...perhaps some faculty saw it as '...a way to tell the [administration that change] cannot be made unilaterally."[17] Although McClellan did not actually say it, the defeat was nothing less than a slap on the hand from the faculty to the president, warning him not to go too far too fast.

The faculty was having its own problems with the students in the spring of 1986. On April 15th, student journalist Brian Cassel was asked to leave the scheduled faculty meeting when a vote showed that at least one faculty member objected to his presence. The Student Senate was meeting at the same time, so Cassel approached them and told of his ejection.

The senate immediately voted and approved a protest, and went *en masse* to the faculty meeting. There they remained, demonstrating against "the faculty's lack of response to Senate inquiries concerning the right of students to observe faculty meetings,"[18] and refused to leave unless ejected by force. A motion was made asking the chairman of the faculty, Dr. Jobie Riley, to reconsider the original decision not to admit Cassel. It was discussed, but was defeated by secret ballot 30–31, and the meeting was adjourned.

The following September, the faculty voted by a 2–1 margin to allow officers of the Student Senate to observe faculty meetings, with speaking but non-voting privileges. In turn, the faculty elected a representative to attend meetings of the Student Senate.

A month later, another student-faculty bridge was built with the "Invite a Prof to Dinner" program. If a student was on a meal plan, he or she could invite a professor to lunch, with the prof eating for free.

～§—§～

President Spiegler had major plans for Elizabethtown College. When he had first applied for the job, he had frankly told his interviewers that if they were looking for someone to maintain the status quo, he was not their man. If on the other hand they wanted to move the college forward academically and realize a capital campaign of between $25 and $30 million dollars, then he was interested.

In Spiegler's years at Elizabethtown, the college's endowment grew from $8 million to $24 million, it further increased the quality of its students and faculty, and a building program brought both beauty, utility, and a sense of heritage to the college. The Brethren tradition of Elizabethtown College greatly appealed to Spiegler, and he was a driving force behind a building that is now considered one of the college's unique treasures, the Bucher Meetinghouse and Young Center.

A Meeting House Study Center was first proposed in October 1985 by the Church/College Mutual Expectations Committee. It would be modeled after the original 1721 meetinghouse in Germantown, PA, the Church of the Brethren's first established place of worship in America. It would have a library for religious research, with a concentration on Anabaptist and Pietist studies, display space for historical artifacts, and space for conferences and seminars. Its cost was projected to be $500,000, and from the beginning it was planned to be named after Rufus P. Bucher, one of the "Faithful Six," and chairman of the board for many years.

By the following spring it was decided that the meetinghouse would also be a full-fledged center for Anabaptist and Pietist studies, and that Dr. John A. Hostetler, Elizabethtown College's first scholar-in-residence, would be the director, assisted by his wife, Dr. Beulah Hostetler. Ground was broken in April of 1988, and construction soon began, with funds raised through Brethren groups, not through student fees and payments.

The Rufus P. Bucher Meetinghouse and the adjoining Galen S. and Jessie B. Young Center for the Study of Anabaptist and Pietist Groups were dedicated on October 28, 1989. Embedded in the meetinghouse's interior walls are a stone from the original Germantown Meetinghouse, as well as stones from the Eder River in Schwarzenau, Germany, where the founder of the Brethren movement, Alexander Mack, baptized his followers.

At the dedication, Dr. Joan Austin, the college chaplain who had strongly promoted the meetinghouse, called it, "something for all members of campus. It is not just a Brethren, Mennonite, Amish, and Anabaptist meeting place."[19]

The meetinghouse provided a new structure rich in the heritage of the college. But at the same time it was being erected, plans were being made for the destruction of the campus's second oldest building. Rider Memorial Hall, built in 1906, was nearing the end of its days. Although photographs show a stately building with an attractive exterior that included a shockingly bright red roof, the interior needed major renovation.

In 1987, two options were offered: either completely renovate Rider or demolish it. In the opinion of President Speigler, the cost of renovation would not be worth it, especially as the college intended to build a new auditorium/performing arts/chapel complex.

Every year, the community's "Arts on the Square" program honored an historic Elizabethtown building by placing an illustration of the building and its history on a stoneware mug released in conjunction with the festival. In June, 1989, Rider Hall was the honoree. But it would not be long before the mug and photographs were the only evidence of Rider Hall's existence. By the fall of 1989, its fate was sealed.

The building would be demolished, and the music department would move into the former Zug Library after the new library was finished. John Shaeffer, the college treasurer, was asked by *The Etownian* about the building's sentimental value. "Life must go on," he answered. "We're doing this to improve ourselves."[20]

The new library would certainly add to that improvement. It was part of an overall ten year building plan announced in the fall of 1987 that included not only a new library but a new fine arts building (which would be incorporated into the new chapel), an addition to Thompson Gym, the elimination of Baugher Avenue, and a major parking lot expansion. The library alone was to cost $12 million, and would be a state of the art facility.

On October 26, 1987, the college received a contribution that once more broke the record for the largest single gift ever. The High Foundation of Lancaster contributed $1.5 million to be used toward the new library. S. Dale High, president of High Industries, was a 1963 graduate of the college and a trustee. In presenting the gift, he expressed his feelings that High Industries was a far better company because of the twelve Elizabethtown College graduates it employed.

Ground was broken for the new library building on March 14, 1989. The dedication took place on September 22, 1990, after the symbolic "book walk" of the previous month, in which over 200 faculty members, students, administrators, and friends of the college had carried over 5000 volumes (specifically, the 900 section) from the old Zug Library to the new High Library, named in honor of the High Foundation.

The High Library contained four stories capable of holding over 250,000 volumes, and was filled with study and conference areas. The building honored the past with the Brethren Heritage Room, into which were placed the college archives, and looked to the future with its emphasis on technology, including computer terminals and a computerized library catalogue.

Though most campus denizens were pleased with the building and environs, the distinctive bench at the base of the steps leading to the building was looked on askance by some. An *Etownian* cartoon shows "Gunther the Canine Art Critic" disparaging the construction of rock chunks and marble slab in a way that most likely would have appalled the college's founders, not to mention *Chronicle* editor Ray Westafer.

⋙—§—⋘

The social changes that occurred throughout the eighties changed the face of the school as much as did the new technologies that were making their presence felt on campus. There was more of an emphasis on student placement and the job market in the 80s, and many articles on those subjects appeared in *The Etownian*. Students who had come of age during the "Me Generation," in which self-fulfillment was a basic need, were not shy about making known their desire for success.

Students became more sexually active, if campus polls could be believed, and birth control became a serious area of discussion. The November 15, 1985 issue of *The Etownian* offered a front page article, "Birth Control: The Choice Is Yours," with a photograph of a display of condoms taken at a local drugstore. "Chances are," the text read, "that during your college career, you have, will, or are currently involved in some form of sexual relations." In an odd juxtaposition, an article on the same page, "Why the Brethren Church?" explained the relationship between the college and the church.

In 1988, Planned Parenthood offered to provide free condoms to the college's Health Center to either distribute free or sell to students. The Health Center wanted to accept the offer, but President

Spiegler rejected the idea, despite the desire of many students to procure condoms on campus from either machines or the bookstore.

In 1990, however, an AIDS task force was established on campus. The sexually transmitted condition had become an extremely serious public health problem, and a team of eleven administrators, faculty and students joined together to promote AIDS education among the student population.

There were other changes of attitude and policy on campus that would have astounded many of the college's early founders. What had formerly been compulsory "Chapel" and "Convocation" had become "Monday at 10." In early 1989 the alcohol policy changed drastically. Students who were twenty-one would have a stamp placed on their ID card showing that they were permitted to drink in private places. Those under twenty-one would continue to be denied any alcohol. Infractions, however, continued.

Back in 1979, the college had developed its own way of dealing with alcohol possession and other infractions. Instead of official disciplinary action, many student offenders were given up to ten hours of hard labor picking up trash, digging ditches, planting, trimming bushes, cleaning vehicles and buildings, and painting. It was a punishment that the founders might well have approved of.

Academically, the college continued to improve. By 1988, *Barron's Educational Series* had upgraded Elizabethtown from a "competitive" to a "very competitive" college, basing the change on an increase in students' average SAT scores and high school rankings, as well as in the number of applicants to the school.

That same year the college earned two other honors. It was included in *Peterson's Competitive College Guide*, which listed 350 of the best schools in the country, and *U.S. News and World Report* rated Elizabethtown the 12th best small comprehensive college in the nation.

The faculty boasted its own Fulbright scholar, Dr. Carmine Sarracino of the English department, who in 1985 traveled to Sri Lanka, India, and Nepal to lecture on American literature.

During the 1987–88 school year, the college had another Fulbright scholar in residence, Dr. Jon Serveas, a professor of communications from Belgium who had been researching the effects of the media on the world situation, and was rather critical of his host country. "In general," he observed, "most American students seem to be interested in education mainly as a means of making money... Americans are not willing to understand other cultures. This is due to the environment and attitude with which most have been raised."[21]

In this statement, critics could see a rough parallel to the subject of minority representation at Elizabethtown College, which was still minimal. A 1989 *Etownian* piece on recruiting minorities began: "What has nine Blacks, four Hispanics, and twelve Asians? The answer is Elizabethtown College."[22]

An article on the subject written two years earlier was headlined, "A Private Boarding School For Rich White Kids?" Because of such an image, it reported, the admissions office had become even more committed to recruiting more minorities. Still, the problem did not end at recruiting:

> *After the minority student is recruited to Elizabethtown, it is hard to retain the student. Behrs [David Behrs, Associate Director of Admissions and Chair for Minority Recruitment and Retention] says the perception by the faculty is that most minority students won't pan out at Elizabethtown. There is a sense of apathy from the faculty. Students do not respond favorably either. The Hillel Club has disappeared, people laugh at the Black Student Union... Right now there is only one black professor on campus.*
>
> *[Behrs:] "As an administrator, my vision is to make Elizabethtown College more diverse. We're talking about changing the history and fabric of the school, and change is hard to achieve here."*[23]

In 1988, the college had only eleven African-American students, a ratio of 100–1. There were few minorities represented among the faculty and administration. The 1988 *Conestogan* shows only one African-American faculty member, economics professor Dr. Maurice Hoppie. Besides the small number of students, only one other African-American face is seen, a member of Building and Grounds.

September 1989 saw the hiring of a new dean of college life, Dr. Ronald R. Brown, who was an African-American, but after eight months he resigned, due to an "illness in the family."[24] He was replaced by Richard R. Crocker.

Even as recently as the late 80s, the Elizabethtown area could not have been the easiest place for African-Americans to make their home. It remained quite conservative and overwhelmingly white, and despite the values of religious and racial tolerance that were so much a part of an Elizabethtown College education, what Dr. Serveas had called "the environment and attitude with which most [Americans] had been raised" was responsible for unpleasant occurrences.

In the 1989–90 school year, two racial incidents took place on campus. Racial comments were made that then led to physical confrontations.

Fortunately for the college, the vast majority of the students deplored such incidents. Social consciences were still strong, and, with an increasing emphasis on the college's heritage of peace and social justice, would continue to thrive. In the early 80s, weekly religious activities included meetings of the Brethren Identity Group, the Newman Club, Bible Study, E.C.F., a Catholic mass in Rider Chapel at 5:00 Saturday afternoon, and a church service there Sunday morning.

In 1987, the college hosted a theology conference "to promote a greater understanding among the three major western religions."[25] Representatives of Judaism, Christianity, and Islam all spoke.

Dr. Kenneth Kreider, along with other members of the faculty, proposed in 1988 a Peace and Conflict Studies program. It would begin as a minor and later become a major, and was intended to be interdisciplinary, with many departments offering related courses.

In such a campus atmosphere, it was only natural for students to be aware of social concerns. The dismantling of South Africa's apartheid policy was called for in *The Etownian*. Students slept outside in refrigerator boxes in a "Cardboard Village" to increase awareness of the plight of the homeless.

They participated in candlelight vigils, one of which recognized "the newfound freedom for the citizens of East Germany."[26] Another was held in memory of the six priests and two bystanders killed by political death squads in El Salvador on November 16, 1989. That same winter 43 Elizabethtown College students were part of a 300,000-person pro-choice rally in Washington, D.C.

Some causes were closer to home. In 1986 a proposal came before Mount Joy Township to change zoning, clearing the way for a $150 million incinerator to be built by the Lancaster Area Refuse Authority. The college joined the community in opposing the plan.

Students continued to channel their social concern into other, more productive actions. The decade saw CROP volleyball marathons to aid world hunger, and the college supported the Heifer Project International, sponsoring a Holiday Hunger Fair in 1988 to raise funds for a program that provided aid and training for farmers overseas to fight hunger, malnutrition, and poverty.

Other students helped Habitat for Humanity. In 1990 fifteen students spent three and a half days in John's Island, South Carolina helping demolish a burned-out family home so that it could be rebuilt the following week by a new student team.

The problems of the physically handicapped were another area of campus concern. A 1989 issue of *The Etownian* ran two full pages of articles on handicapped accessibility at the college. Even though the college was calling itself handicapped accessible, it was the judgment of the students that it was not. Many of the campus buildings were not accessible at all to those in wheelchairs, and the administration assured the students that proper steps would be taken. The subject even entered the curriculum, with the occupational therapy department having its students conduct a wheelchair experiment in their sophomore year.

Another concern that had increased over the years was sexual equality on campus. A 1989 article pointed out the low number of female faculty members. Only 20% of the teaching staff were women, and most of them were in the lower echelon of teachers. Of the 34 full professors, only two were female, and of the 42 associate professors, there were only four women.

Provost and Dean of the Faculty Dr. Frederick E. Ritsch said, "We are trying to increase the number of female professors, but we really have to hire the best qualified candidate." He further explained that many male professors had tenure, causing a situation in which there were fewer openings for women. Also, there were more males in the specific job market, and in certain fields few women were getting doctorates.

Dr. Jacqueline Jones, chair of the department of occupational therapy and chairperson of the Task Force on Women's Issues, countered: "One of the problems this campus has had, though, is that there has been no wave of sentiment for the issues of women, no real effort to form a group to deal with this."[27]

There had, however, finally been enough concern to deal with the long discussed honor code. Such a code had been considered during the 1985–86 school year, and had been reviewed from time to time ever since. In the winter of 1989–90, the Student Senate at last passed and sent to the faculty a proposal to implement a partial honor code the following semester. All freshmen seminars would require students to sign a pledge promising that they "neither gave nor received any unauthorized aid" on work turned in to a professor.[28] They would not, however, be required to report any academic dishonesty on someone else's part.

⊷§—§⊷

Despite social and political concerns and the day-to-day academic work, students still found time for other activities during the eighties. There were sixteen sports teams, including men and women's basketball, soccer, cross country, swimming, and tennis. Men also participated in wrestling, baseball, and golf, while women played field hockey, volleyball, and softball.

The end of the decade also saw nearly two dozen other clubs and social organizations, as well as the many musical and performing groups on campus, including S.T.E.P (Student Team of Entertainers and Performers), a 70-member group that began in the early 80s and put on an annual variety show.

There were many other student productions, and outside performers who entertained students on campus included James Taylor, the Charlie Daniels Band, Doc Severinsen (accompanied by the Pittsburgh Symphony), and Vincent Price, guest of honor at the 1984 homecoming festivities, where he gave a seminar on the fine arts. "Mr. Television" himself, Milton Berle, spoke about "The Golden Age of Television Comedy" on campus, using old film clips that delighted the audience, and sexual innuendo that, according to a report, shocked others.

Elizabethtown College was one of 15 colleges in the nation to participate in an entertainment first. On October 30, 1982, in Thompson Gym, it showed the first live 3-D concert transmitted by satellite. The concert, headlined by the rock group DEVO, was not a total success, owing to a number of technical glitches, and many students, 3-D glasses in hand, left with more of a headache than a sense of having made history.

Students found more hassle-free entertainment in their own campus television station, and in 1986 the college produced its first show for cable TV, *Talk of the Towns*. Its quality was recognized by Alpha Epsilon Rho, the National Broadcasting Society, who voted it Best Student-Produced Television Public Affairs Program in the country two years in a row. The student radio station, WWEC, finally went from AM to FM in the fall of 1990, using the new call numbers 88.3.

There were other venues for student entertainment off-campus, including The Carpenter's Inn in downtown Elizabethtown, which held a special College Night every Thursday for students 21 and over. Reviews of local restaurants and taverns ran regularly in the college paper, and an "Etown Pizza Report" ranked North Market Street's Pizza Town first, with a 4.0 GPA (Great Pizza Average), followed by Brothers Pizza with a score of 3.6 and Pizza Hut at 2.7.[29]

Some student's gastronomical outings may have been individually financed by Sera-Tec Biologicals in Harrisburg, a company whose ads ran regularly in *The Etownian* through the 70s and 80s, offering students money for their blood plasma. Sera-Tec offered to pay for gas, and even targeted campus organizations, offering $1750 to clubs that could supply 40 people to donate plasma for two weeks. By 1990, the Sera-Tec ads were gone, and parents no longer needed to fear that their sons and daughters would trade their blood for beer and pizza money.

But as the college entered the 90s, other, more treasured traditions were gone as well. Times had changed and left behind May Day dances[30], required chapel services, and literary societies. Gone too were sewing courses, annual cantatas, and faculty members who wore Brethren beards and dress. Gone were *Our College Times*, the Candles, and so much more, relegated to the past, existing only in photographs and memories.

Though the College Seal remained intact, a new official logo was created in 1988, not by anyone associated with the college, but by The National Institution for Organizational Research and Problem Solving. The graphic design consisted of a blue oval with a large capital E surrounded by the name of the college and the date, 1899, a date that reminded everyone who saw it that in less than a decade, Elizabethtown College would enter its centennial year.

Academically and financially, the school was in a better position than ever before. While looking toward the future, it had become more and more in harmony with its heritage. Elizabethtown College was poised to enter the 1990s and begin its second century.

---

1 *Elizabethtown College Bulletin,* Winter 1981, p. 22
2 *The Etownian,* November 6, 1981, p. 1
3 *Elizabethtown College Bulletin,* Winter 1981, p. 33
4 *The Etownian,* February 12, 1982, p. 1
5 *The Etownian,* September 30, 1983, p. 2
6 *The Etownian,* February 19, 1982, p. 6
7 *The Etownian,* February 4, 1984, p. 1
8 *The Etownian,* March 22, 1985, p. 1
9 Ibid.
10 *The Etownian,* September 20, 1985, p. 1
11 Ibid.
12 *The Etownian,* November 1, 1985, p. 1
13 op. cit., p. 4
14 *The Etownian,* February 14, 1986, p. 2
15 *The Etownian,* April 4, 1986, p. 4
16 *The Etownian,* October 4, 1985, p. 1
17 *The Etownian,* September 5, 1986, p. 1
18 *The Etownian,* April 18, 1986, p. 1
19 *Elizabethtown College: The First Hundred Years,* p. 81
20 *The Etownian,* November 3, 1989, p. 4
21 *The Etownian,* April 29, 1988, p. 1
22 *The Etownian,* March 17, 1989, p. 5
23 *The Etownian,* March 27, 1987, p. 1
24 *The Etownian,* April 27, 1990, p. 1
25 *The Etownian,* March 20, 1987, p. 1
26 *The Etownian,* November 17, 1989, p. 1
27 *The Etownian,* November 17, 1989, p. 2
28 *The Etownian,* February 23, 1990, p. 1
29 *The Etownian,* November 20, 1981, p. 2
30 The last May Day celebration had taken place in 1969.

Chapter 12

1990–2000

"The union of the world of the spirit with the world of work..."

The early 1990s brought back to the campus a personality that had last been influential there in the late *18*90s. J. G. Francis, the man who had started the movement for a Brethren college in eastern Pennsylvania, made his return to the campus in bronze.

In the fall of 1991, it was announced that friends of the college would donate a garden to stand where Rider Hall had stood. The garden would honor the memory of J. G. Francis, and would have a sculpture of the young Francis with bicycle (his mode of transportation while soliciting churches) and camera (with which he took photographs of the churches he had visited).

The idea was that of Robert Odean, assistant to the president, and the statue would be done by Arizona sculptor Snell Johnson. "There was nothing physical that gave witness to the founding [of the college] by the Brethren," Odean explained. "They had left no trail behind."[1]

The recognition of J. G. Francis set the tone for Elizabethtown College in the 1990s. The heritage of the school would be recognized and honored more than any other time in its history. The approach of the college's centennial was partly responsible, as was a shift in society back to a more peaceful, generous nature. Despite the military triumph of the Gulf War, which had opened the decade, by 1992 President George Bush was promising a kinder, gentler America in his hoped for second term, while Democratic challenger Bill Clinton was telling the country that he could feel its pain. The sentiments of both men were right in line with the Brethren traditions of peace and service.

In the fall of 1990, the alumni began the "Educate for Service" awards. At that homecoming and at every homecoming since, three awards are presented to individuals for service to humanity, service to the college, and service through personal achievement.

Current students as well as alumni reached out to others. Big Brother/Big Sister Day was held on November 3, 1990, with 55 students and 65 children from Harrisburg, aged 5 to 15, participating. 1990 was the first year that the program was held every semester rather than annually.

Only a few weeks later, the college's education department brought in fifteen Chapter One students from Fairview Elementary School in Elizabethtown. The college and elementary students spent a morning of reading, sharing, and learning in connection with American Education Week's Readers' Day.

Habitat for Humanity continued to involve students. In 1991, students held a benefit auction for the organization, and a group helped to build a house in Chattanooga, Tennessee over Easter break. Further building was done in subsequent years, and the Church of the Brethren became involved in its own project in 1993, when two students spent two weeks of their winter break in Florida under the auspices of the church, constructing new roofs for houses that had been damaged by Hurricane Andrew.

The continued need for service resulted in the final report of the college's Task Force on Community Service, created by Dean of College Life Richard R. Crocker, in order to evaluate the proper place of community service. The committee recommended that the college encourage community service, but not require it, recommending further that a committee carefully study the policy issues of such a program.

Another outreach program was the college chapter of SIFE (Students in Free Enterprise). Begun in 1989, it was an economic organization that promoted awareness of the nation's current economic situation and the American free enterprise system.

The dining hall performed its own services for the community. Starting in the fall of 1992, leftover food was given to volunteers from Water Street Rescue Mission and Elizabethtown's Community Action Board to distribute to the hungry.

Service to the campus and community took a giant leap forward in 1992 with the establishment of the Student Directed Learning Center program (SDLC). First directed by Dr. John R. Saddlemire and later by Shirley A. Deichert, the program would serve both campus and community by allowing groups of four to eight students to live together in college-owned houses and create, organize, and participate in a service learning project. The projects included SMACC (Students Making a Cleaner Community), LIGHT (Lasting Impacts by Giving to the Hungry Today), KIC (Kids in the Community), TEAM (Together Everyone Achieves More: providing middle school tutoring), SHARE (Students Helping to Advance Relations with the Elderly), Saturday's Special (providing activities for local children), Ohm Sweet Ohm (bringing computer knowledge to the community), and The Harmony House (bringing music therapy to students and the elderly).

And the list went on. SMILE (Students Making Individual Lives Enriched) started to sponsor Daffodil Days for the American Cancer Society. 35 members of Habitat for Humanity traveled to Florida for the 1993 spring break to rebuild houses damaged by Hurricane Andrew.

Clearly, the concept of service had been embraced by the campus. Nowhere can this be seen more clearly than in a document drafted by the college's resources and planning committee as the framework for a five-year plan. While predictably addressing such concerns as campus upkeep and several other specifics, the document went on:

We must plan to create an ethos and an atmos-
phere at Elizabethtown College in which all members of
the community share a common sense of purpose....
Elizabethtown College was founded by members of the
Church of the Brethren, a small religious group with
firmly-held beliefs. One of their fundamental beliefs
was in the union of the world of the spirit and the
world of work. For them there was no distinction
between a college degree and a lifetime of service. For
them a college degree was not a ticket to a better job,
but preparation for a leadership role in a community
dedicated to serving God and humanity; hence the
College motto, "Educate for Service."

Elizabethtown College is firmly rooted in the belief
of its founders in the union of the world of the spirit
with the world of work. Most of its curricula combine
the liberal and the practical — what is necessary for
the spirit and what is necessary for service...This
strong combination has been a direct result of the reli-
gious beliefs of the founders of the College and it is a
distinguishing characteristic of Elizabethtown
College...The first step in our five-year plan is for the
community to understand and reaffirm the founders'
premise in the union of the world of the spirit and the
world of work. We all must wholeheartedly embrace
this part of our heritage and actively capitalize on it.
We must recognize the distinction between
Elizabethtown College's historic view of learning and
today's general societal view and become a community
dynamically engaged in learning, not simply a place
where students obtain a college degree.[2]

Although the college grew closer philosophically to the spirit of
the Church of the Brethren, the 90s saw it grow further away from
the church officially. Like a child who had learned the wise lessons
its parents had taught it well enough to be successful on its own, the
college was now further than ever from the church in a legal sense.

On December 3, 1992, a Mutual Expectations Committee made up of members of both the college and church communities produced a "Statement of Basic Understandings." It reads in part:

> *Though Elizabethtown College no longer serves only a Church of the Brethren constituency...it still continues to maintain a covenantal relationship with the Atlantic Northeast District and Southern District of Pennsylvania Church of the Brethren by honoring and giving witness to the tradition, spirit, and values of the Church of the Brethren.*
>
> *In keeping with the changing conditions in higher education and in church life, it is important to recognize that the present relationship between Church and College is foremost a covenantal relationship and not a legal one. The Church cannot and should not control the College, and the College cannot and should not expect the Church to totally finance its operations and assume all of the legal responsibilities of ownership.*[3]

The remaining five pages of the document list the basic understandings that underlie the relationship between the two institutions, including separate and joint missions, and both the college's and the church's roles in detail. Among the objectives are providing a climate to develop wholeness, giving witness and testimony to the tradition and values upon which the college was founded, increasing the number of Brethren students, strengthening the school's financial base, and making facilities and personnel available to each other. The church would also develop service opportunities for students and offer hospitality to foreign students.

In terms of governance, the College was expected to "recruit a Board of Trustees that actively supports the mission of the College through financial support, active participation and wise counsel, that affirms the religious, historical and cultural roots of the College and its Brethren tradition..."[4] The church's role in governance was "to help identify committed and resourceful members of District churches for consideration as Trustees of the College."[5]

On October 23, 1993, less than a year after the drafting of this document, the board of trustees voted to approve a measure that would amend the college's Articles of Incorporation, giving the board itself sole power to elect board members. The Atlantic Northeast District and the Southern District of the Church of the Brethren, those directly involved with the college, would no longer be able to elect trustees, but would retain nominating power over 12 of the board's 27 seats. A majority of the board, as before, would have to be Brethren.

In order for the amendments to be passed, however, they first needed the approval of the two church districts by a 2/3 majority vote. The Southern District delegates voted to approve by a three to one margin, but the Atlantic Northeast District only passed the amendments by one vote.

Elizabethtown Pastor Daniel L. Poole said, "I think the vote sends a message from the district that you may move ahead, but do so very cautiously. Technically you do run things, but don't forget that the College was begun by the Church of the Brethren and that we still have an interest in that."[6]

The College would continue to maintain its covenantal relationship with the church. In reporting on this relationship as spelled out in the Statement of Basic Understandings, *The Etownian* observed that the statement merely put into words what had been the reality for many years. By 1993, the student body was less that 5% Brethren, and most faculty members did not belong to the church. Church financial support stood at $130,000 per year, a small fraction of the college's $30 million budget. The church had not hired faculty, determined curriculum, or been involved in the school's day to day operations for at least 30 years. Another benefit of the statement and of the amendments was the assurance that no government body would try to withdraw funding on the basis of the college being under church control.

Despite the amendments, Brethren ideas would continue to be respected. No military recruiters were permitted on campus, the college did not condone the use of alcohol and would have enforced alcohol regulations even if state law had not required it to do so, and the school still retained "Educate for Service" as its motto, and firmly emphasized the qualities of peace and social justice.

The Young Center for the Study of Anabaptist and Pietist Groups also continued to honor the college's religious heritage under the direction of sociology professor Donald B. Kraybill. Kraybill, under whose leadership the center gained a reputation for international scholarly research, grew up in a Mennonite family, began teaching at the college in 1971, started studying the Amish in the early 80s, and was named director of the Young Center in 1989. He has written many books and articles about the Amish, including *Old Order Amish, The Amish and the State, Mennonite Peacemaking,* and *The Riddle of Amish Culture.* In 1990, he won Professor of the Year, Teaching and Leadership. In 1996, he left Elizabethtown to become provost at Messiah College.

The re-emphasis on the College's heritage created a more sedate and peaceful environment on the campus, but academic growth and improvement continued at a rapid pace. The college had more faculty members with a Ph.D. than ever before. In the 1987-88 year, 56.2% had doctorates. In the ensuing four years that percentage increased, until by 1991–92, 67.3% had doctorates, and 70% had achieved a terminal degree.

During Dr. Spiegler's term, the college also added several new majors, among them Environmental Science, and by the spring of 1992, the library had gone on-line. All items had been barcoded, and students' ID cards also functioned as library cards. The library also benefitted greatly from the formation of Friends of the High Library, a support group that raises funds for the library and sponsors events such as lectures, readings, trips, and exhibits.

In September 1991, the new Academic Code of Integrity was established, with freshmen signing a pledge that stated, "On my honor, I have neither given nor received unauthorized aid on this work."[7] In March 1995 this was replaced by a Pledge of Integrity, which freshmen were asked but not forced to sign.

The college continued its physical growth. In the fall of 1991, announcements were made for an addition to the Baugher Student Center. The plans included a large multi-purpose room for dances, a theatre in the round, a new Jay's Nest, a dry, student-run pub, student meeting rooms, a large lounge, and a recreation area with pool and ping pong tables.

A month later, in November 1991, the campus received the news that a new chapel was also being planned at an estimated cost of $4.5 million. It would also provide a location for large group assemblies and concerts. Though the chapel would eventually prove to be the architectural jewel in the college's crown, its road to construction was fraught with pitfalls.

By January 1992, construction had begun on still another project, a quadrangle intended to house 120 seniors and two faculty families. The 30 apartments would each house four students, with the remaining two units for faculty. When the quadrangle was dedicated on October 24, 1992, it was named the V. Lester Schreiber Senior Townhouse Quadrangle, after the former chairman of the board of trustees, who had died on April 6, 1991, following a heart attack.

Wayne A. Nicarry, who had first been elected a trustee of the college in 1969, was chosen to replace Schreiber as chairman of the board. Nicarry was past president of Grove Manufacturing Company, originally a fledgling, three-person company that manufactured farm wagons in a rented garage in Shady Grove, Pennsylvania, but which grew into a major, multi-national business. He was ordained a free minister of the Church of the Brethren in 1946, and remained deeply committed to the church.

Though he desperately wanted to attend Elizabethtown College, the Depression prevented him from doing so. His years of service to the school, however, earned him an honorary Doctor of Science degree from the school in 1986. "It is one thing I'm very proud of," he said. "I waited fifty years to earn it."[8] He served as chairman until 1997, and remained on the board until 1999.

While the Schreiber Quad memorialized Nicarry's predecessor, still another memorial was planned for the college in the early 90s, a garden with a black granite marker memorializing the names of all those who had died while students at Elizabethtown.

In the midst of all this planning, however, the state of Pennsylvania reduced its grant to the College from $395,000 a year to $365,000, and also eliminated a $40,000 capital equipment grant. The country in early 1992 was in a minor recession, and by March, budget cuts had forced the dismissal of one counselor.

The following fall, an article appeared in *The Etownian* headlined "Financial Aid Slows in Three Major Areas." In the article, Director of Financial Aid Gordon Bateman said that the recession had caused problems in three major sources of financial aid funding: the federal government, the state government, and the private sector, which seemed to cover the entire spectrum.

Major gifts, however, were still being received. In 1991, Dr. William H. Lodge and his sister, Sara Lodge, bequeathed $1.7 million to the college. William had attended the school in the early 1930s, and Sara was a 1941 alumnus. In 1992, Armstrong World Industries donated an annual $10,000 scholarship, along with an additional $100,000 to the library and the scholarship fund.

1993 saw a large gift from Walter Annenberg, who donated a million dollars to Elizabethtown College in honor of Phares Hertzog, who taught Annenberg in high school. The money was placed in two endowed funds, one for scholarships and the other for faculty development. The college wanted to name the new annex to the Baugher Student Center in Annenberg's honor, but at first he asked the college not to use his name, since he was already inundated with requests from other colleges for contributions and dedications. Nevertheless, he eventually relented, and the annex became the Annenberg Center, opening on February 14, 1993.

The College also received a large number of generous contributions toward the newly planned chapel. The first of these was a $250,000 grant from Texaco, which was given in five yearly increments of $50,000. The gift was an endowment, and the college would spend only the interest, about $17,000 a year, on the performing arts.

Among the many controversies over building in the early 90s, the first came with the announcement that Dr. Spiegler's house would receive a major addition. Spiegler was in Germany at the time, teaching, writing, and doing research at the University of Hamburg as part of a sabbatical that lasted from January to July 1993. During his absence a two-story addition was made to his house.

The back porch, which had been damaged by termites, was replaced, and a large expansion of the existing kitchen and a breakfast area were added to the first floor. The second floor gained a master bedroom suite with walk-in closets and a private bath. Although Robert Odean stated that the cost would be $80,000, rumors soon priced the addition between $100,000 and $200,000. Trustee Richard E. Jordan II said that the addition made "good business sense...the home is used principally to entertain visiting speakers as well as members of the community asked to contribute to the college."[9]

Some students, however, saw the addition as another wing added to the palace at Versailles. A full page ad paid for by the Student Senate Executive Board appeared in the April 23, 1993 *Etownian*, in which the board expressed concern about "the lack of funds allocated to student needs...our funds are limited and constrained...Because of these concerns, the administration was confronted on how our money is spent and they were unwilling to talk about facts or figures."[10]

The ad stated that student activity fees amounted to $600,000, of which the Student Senate received $30,000, the Activities Planning Board $70,000, and the Residence Life Council $2000. Where, they asked, was the remaining $500,000? "Why and how was President Spiegler's two-person house (in which only two people reside) expanded and renovated while classes are being cut? Why are new buildings being erected when the newly constructed High Library has empty shelves?"[11] The ad concluded by urging students to join a demonstration the following day, when the trustees were all on campus for their meeting.

The 11:00 A.M. demonstration drew between 100 and 150 protesting students, who called for more information and closer contact with administration. They did not receive an answer about the student activity fee until the following March, when the administration explained that the fee covered only half of the yearly costs, many of which were not even considered by the students, while the other half came from tuition fees.

Student annoyance now extended to the chapel project, with many students complaining about the huge amounts that were being spent. The college's answer to this was that no tuition money was being used to build the new chapel. Instead, it was being paid for through contributions given specifically for it, such as the $400,000 donation from the Kresge Foundation in early 1994.

Even before it was completed, the new chapel was proving its mettle as a performance venue. In the fall of 1994, the college began a relationship with Music at Gretna, a performing arts venue offering summer outdoor concerts at the nearby Chautauqua community of Mount Gretna. Using the chapel as their off-season home, Music at Gretna would be able to present concerts year round, while bringing world class performers to Elizabethtown.

The chapel was finished and dedicated on January 28, 1996, and was named the Leffler Chapel and Performance Center after trustee Carlos R. Leffler, who had envisioned such a chapel before his death in 1994, and his wife Georgiana. At the dedication, Linda Castagna '67, a daughter of the Lefflers, said that the chapel was a dream come true for her late father, who had tried to bring a chapel to campus for the past twenty years. "He knew in his heart," Castagna said, "that life without the church and without faith is empty."[12]

Besides the massive lobby and the awe-inspiring sanctuary/performance hall, other features of the chapel include the Lyet Gallery, an art gallery made possible by a gift from Dorothy Lyet, and the Chapel Prayer Tower and third-floor prayer room, the result of the generosity of Mrs. Esther S. Winters '31. The college's heritage is further seen in the fact that the stained glass windows in the prayer room were taken from the prayer room in Rider Hall, which had been razed five years earlier.

⟶⟶⟵

The final half of the Spiegler presidency saw other changes and improvements to the college. In 1990, the campus became smoke-free, in response to a Pennsylvania law which required all organizations to reduce the possibility of second-hand smoke, though private residences, including dormitory rooms, were excluded. That same semester, the campus became *Coke*-free. Pepsi was chosen as the cola served in the cafeteria, saving the college $3000 a year through an arrangement with the Pepsi-Cola company.

Lake Placida had become an unofficial waterfowl refuge, with ducks and geese taking it over to such an extent that the college banned all feeding of the birds. In 1992, two Royal Muted Swans joined the Placida menagerie, the gift of librarian Naomi Hershey and her husband Carroll, who bought the two cygnets from Millersville University. Though the staff called the swans Fred and Fern, they had no official name. *The Etownian* remarked that, "Suggestions for official names have ranged from Axl and Cher to Louis and Rich. The swans would not comment on the suggested names."[13]

There were other distinctive, non-monetary gifts to the college, among them the presentation by Robert F. and Annette R. Nation of thirteen art works by the famed Lancaster artist Charles Demuth, a trove that included five watercolors and eight drawings.

Of less financial value, but certainly more apparent was the gift from the Class of '92 of a new college sign on the corner of College Avenue and Mount Joy Street. The gift has become as much a part of the college as the Class of '52's famous gate.

As the College grew, so too did the need for parking. That need caused a minor town-gown rift in 1992, when the Elizabethtown Borough Council considered reducing the number of non-family members living in one house from four to three, partly due to parking problems and partly in response to complaints from townspeople about the noise from houses that students were renting.

Some students' neighbors complained of drinking and noise at all hours. Others defended the students, admitting that while they might keep late hours and have parties, college wouldn't really be college without such activities.

As finally written, the borough zoning ordinance did not affect the College, as it contained a "grandfather clause" stating that current buildings housing four unrelated people would not be affected unless they were vacant for one year or the zoning status of the structure itself was changed. For the most part, the college and its students were good neighbors to the community, economically as well as socially. A study that resulted in a pamphlet entitled "The Economic Impact of Elizabethtown College" showed that the college spent $45 million a year in Lancaster County, and that students spent $2.2 million.

The students, faculty, and staff of the College became even better neighbors in 1994, when the first "Into the Streets" program took place. When the program was announced, *The Etownian* stated that twenty students and seven faculty members would be participating, but a month later, on October 29, 1994, the number had increased to nearly 400 students helping to meet the community's needs.

The program was started by Dean Richard Crocker and Shirley Deichert, Director of the Learning Center, as part of a national campaign to promote service learning. That first year, students helped with a day care center, tutored younger students, and put on community programs. The second year saw over 600 students participating in 19 separate projects, including painting buildings, working with children, and offering workshops in communications and computers. The program has become an annual tradition for the college.

Unfortunately, there were some incidents that proved the antithesis of such positive behavior. During the early morning hours of March 15, 1991, a snowball fight between residents of Brinser and Ober Residence Halls turned into a destructive melee, expanding to Founders Hall as well. It began at 12:30 A.M. and ended at 3:00 A.M. after order was restored by police from Elizabethtown Borough, Mount Joy Township, and West Donegal, as well as a K-9 unit.

"The battle got out of control," said David G. Rich, RA on Brinser 2-North. "It was total chaos, bordering on a riot."[14] Nearly 40 windows were broken, and $3000 worth of damage was done. The involved students were to pay triple costs. Dean Richard Crocker observed, "As adults, we should be able to find a better tradition for the College."[15]

Shortly after the incident, the Activities Planning Board went on strike, canceling a number of scheduled campus functions, including a dance and the screening of a movie. In a letter, the board called the cancellations "a result of difficulties encountered this past year, for example, drunkenness to the point of being rude, violent behavior, and vandalism."[16]

In spite of such problems, the college made it apparent that it would deal with the perpetrators in its own way. When, in the fall of 1992, the Liquor Control Enforcement office of the State Police asked the college to issue ID cards to their undercover officers, the administration refused. Bruce Holran, Director of College Public Relations, explained that if the agents were not taking any courses, the IDs would be false documents "The way they want to operate," Holran said, "is unethical and wrong and contrary to the way we want to operate on this campus."[17]

Fortunately there was no repeat of the snowball fight after the blizzard the following March, which brought enough trouble of its own. The storm of '93 made it necessary to cancel classes for the first time in ten years, though there was minimal damage from the heavy snow and high winds. Two trees were damaged, and a number of ceiling tiles fell in Thompson Gym, but the campus was otherwise unscathed.

The following year the college acknowledged changing times in a number of ways. All employees, including faculty and administrators, were required to attend summer seminars on sexual harassment, and in the fall of 1993, the school announced new full-tuition scholarships to students of color. Eight of these "Build the Bridge" scholarships, worth more than $13,000 each, would be offered to the following year's freshman class.

There was also a New Business Scholarship introduced in 1993. A joint idea of local businesses and the college, it allowed the businesses to contribute to the scholarship and then meet the recipients at an annual reception.

On April 23, 1994, the board of trustees voted to accept a Five Year Plan that had been formulated by the college's Resource Planning Committee. It was a strategic plan of where the committee felt the college should be headed, prefaced by the vision statement, "Elizabethtown College is a community dynamically engaged in learning."[18]

Further proof of that statement was seen when senior John H. Leaman was named a 1994 Rhodes Scholar, the college's first, and one of 34 students in the United States to be so honored. A biology major, Leaman had a GPA of 3.94, had been an RA for three years, captained the cross country team, and participated in many volunteer and service activities, doing independent research at Hershey Medical Center and volunteering at church and at work missions in Central America.

Born in Ethopia, Leaman expressed his desire to return there after finishing medical school. "I'd like to go back and serve over there," he said, "working in a rural hospital. With a degree in public health, I could train doctors and nurses." Of his honor he said, "the reward is individual, but it reflects on the whole school — my friends and my teachers. Without them, this wouldn't have been possible."[19]

Leaman spent two years studying at Oriel College in Oxford University, where he also became president of the school's basketball team. He is currently a medical student at the University of Pennsylvania.

At the end of January 1996, Dr. Spiegler surprised the college community by announcing that he would resign as president of the college effective August 31, 1996. Only a few days after this announcement, on February 6th, the Faculty Assembly held a special meeting, at which faculty members presented a two-page motion asking for a sense of "shared governance" with the administration. "It is time," the motion affirmed, "to exercise our rights as shared managers of this college and to help guarantee its future, while at the same time guaranteeing our own rights."[20]

The motion, which was signed by 29 faculty members and would be voted on at the February 20th faculty meeting, also criticized the college's use of funds: "there have been, for nearly ten years, rumors of extravagance and possible mismanagement with regard to various major and capital projects undertaken by the institution."[21]

In the same issue of *The Etownian* that reported the motion, Dr. Spiegler discussed what was now called his "retirement decision." He said that the recent conflicts between administration and faculty had nothing to do with his decision to retire, and stated that there was a clear division of responsibilities at the college. While the trustees might listen to the faculty's advice, it was Spiegler's opinion that the trustees were ultimately responsible for the college's fiscal matters.

Spiegler hinted that he would have retired earlier, but had remained longer than he had intended in order to finish certain projects. His best experience, he said, was early on, when he worked with the student body to move "what was a very externally-directed student life to an internally-directed student life, which is now enshrined in the structure [of the college]."[22]

At their February 20th meeting, the faculty learned that John Ranck and Anthony Matteo, respectively president and vice-president of the faculty, had met with Dr. Spiegler and reached some agreements relating to shared governance. The agreements were sufficient to table the governance motion indefinitely.

One final charge of Dr. Spiegler to the college that he had served for the past eleven years was a new endowment campaign. As of 1996, the endowment stood at $23.8 million. It was the goal of the new campaign to nearly double that amount by 1999, with a cash goal of $9 million and a planned/deferred gift goal of $11 million in future gifts.

Since his retirement, Dr. Spiegler has periodically taught graduate courses in religion to doctoral students at Temple University, where he also serves on several dissertation committees. He travels frequently to Europe, has revisited his native country of Lithuania, and serves on the Boards of Trustees of the Graduate Institute and Global Ethics, both located in Philadelphia.

In 1996, another person retired who had been with Elizabethtown College far longer than Dr. Spiegler. Otis D. Kitchen had begun teaching music at the school in 1965. He received his education from Bridgewater College and the Navy School of Music, and his master's degree from Northwestern, and ran the Army Band School at Fort Jackson, South Carolina.

For many years, Kitchen directed the College Concert Band, and founded the College Jazz Band, the Elizabethtown College Community Symphony Orchestra, and the Lancaster County Music Camp at the college. The master of nearly every instrument, he specialized in woodwinds, and has guest conducted all over the world.

In 1999, several years after his retirement, Kitchen, as coordinator of the prestigious New Year's Music Festival in Vienna, invited the Elizabethtown College Concert Choir and Jazz Band to perform at the festival over the Christmas vacation.

⋞§—ჵ⋟

On June 18, 1996, the new president of Elizabethtown College was chosen. He was Dr. Theodore E. "Ted" Long, provost and vice-president for academic affairs at Merrimack College near Boston. A Lutheran, he was only the second non-Brethren to become President of the college. Dr. Long had been born in Steubenville, Ohio in 1944, but grew up in Austin, Texas. He was a 1965 graduate of Capital University in Columbus, Ohio, where he majored in sociology and philosophy. Long earned a master's degree in sociology from Duke University in 1968 and a doctorate in sociology from the University of Virginia in 1979. He also attended the Institute for Education Management at Harvard in 1992.

His first faculty position was as a visiting assistant professor of sociology at Georgetown University in 1969–70. He taught sociology at Hollins College from 1970 to 1980, and was department chair in 1974–75. In 1980 he went to Washington and Jefferson College, where he was associate professor and chair of the sociology department until 1989, when he joined the staff at Merrimack as dean of arts and sciences and professor of sociology. He became provost and vice-president for academic affairs in 1991.

Dr. Long's writings have appeared widely. He has authored chapters for books such as *The Handbook of Cults and Sects in America, Religion and Global Order*, and *The Politics of Religion and Social Change*. With Jeffrey K. Hadden he co-edited *Religion and Religiosity in America* and two special journal volumes on religion in America.

Dr. Long is a member of the Evangelical Lutheran Church of America, and has been active in local and regional church bodies. He and his wife Betty have two grown children, Edward, who lives in Pittsburgh, and Rachel, of Boca Raton, Florida.

Senior Robert Miller, who served on the presidential search committee, told *The Etownian* that of all those considered, Dr. Long exhibited the energy and qualifications the College was searching for. "A lot of people...wanted to be Presidents of colleges," Miller said, "but Dr. Long wanted to be President of Etown."[23]

In accepting the position, Long said, "In addition to its academic excellence, I am impressed with the College's historic commitment to education for service, its strong infrastructure, and the vibrant sense of community among its people."[24]

Several years later, Dr. Long recalled being impressed by "the sense of solidarity in the community, the sense of care for one another, the affection that people have for the institution, the sense of possibility, and the strong connection between faculty, students, and staff."[25] Dr. Long chose to be a larger part of that community by teaching several courses as a member of the college's department of sociology/anthropology, while also serving as president, a practice that he has continued, teaching a junior/senior colloquium on human rights every fall.

"You never leave your roots," he says of teaching. "You try to keep doing what nourishes you, and teaching has been at the center of my life. Also, a leader should exemplify the central vision of the institution, which is education. So I teach partly as an example to everyone else, that teaching is important enough for the President to give his time to it...and fortunately, my first student evaluations were very good!"[26]

Dr. Long moved to Elizabethtown at the beginning of August 1996, in order to spend time with President Spiegler and get acquainted with the people and the campus. At the president's retreat held at Masonic Homes, Long said that his objective in holding the function was "not to solve everything wrong with this school, but to identify some of the things we need to work on."[27]

One of Long's first tasks was to find a new provost. Frederick Ritsch, who had been provost for 13 years, had chosen to return to teaching. In 1997, Dr. Ronald J. McAllister succeeded Ritsch as provost.

The new president's admiration for the strength of the college community resulted in his holding two or three "town meetings" every year to gauge the opinions of students, faculty, and staff on various subjects. Long had participated in such meetings at Merrimack College. "I think it's good for the [campus] community to come together and have these chances to think about things," he said.[28]

The first such forum was held on October 16, 1996 as part of the Wednesday at 10 series. President Long discussed such subjects as revenues, campus housing, and plans for achieving more diversity in hiring, then answered open questions from those attending.

At his inauguration on October 26th, the new president said that the three things he intended to do for the College were to make "responsive reason" the center of education, teach civic professionalism, and focus on learning rather than on instruction. "Great presidents are expressions of great communities,"[29] Long stated, tying his future and his success to that of the college.

During President Long's first semester at Elizabethtown, a number of events tested his mettle. On October 2, 1996, the eyes of the entire country were on Elizabethtown College as Republican presidential candidate Bob Dole visited the campus. Dole, whose right arm had been badly injured during his service in World War II, had undergone many months of therapy, and his visit to one of the College's occupational therapy classes was an effective way to bring more voter attention to his sacrifice.

The College hosted a rally in Thompson Gym, and between 3000 and 3500 people attended, including Pennsylvania Governor Tom Ridge and Pennsylvania Senators Arlen Specter and Rick Santorum. At the end of the rally, 6000 balloons were dropped and streamers were shot into the air. "We had a great time," Dole said of the visit. "It's a great school with a lot of very nice people, a lot of enthusiasm, and a lot of good fun...particularly good fun in a Republican rally, and I was honored to be here."[30]

Ironically, conservative Alan Keyes, who had struggled to win the Republican nomination from Dole in 1996, gave a lecture the same day in Leffler Chapel as part of the Wednesday at 10 series. His appearance had been scheduled long before the Dole campaign had made the decision to visit the College. Juggling Dole, Keyes, and the horde of prominent Pennsylvania politicians, not to mention the press, the crowd, and several protestors, was a trial by fire for the new President, who came through the experience smiling and unscathed, having gotten a great deal of media attention for the College in the process.

The good news continued the following month, when it was announced that, due to more initial contributions than expected, the $20 million endowment fund goal was being raised to $25 million. However, that same month one of the college's strongest supporters stepped out of the spotlight when Wayne Nicarry stepped down from his office as chairman of the board of trustees due to health. He remained on the board as vice-president, and was succeeded by Daniel H. Raffensperger.

Raffensperger, who was born in Maytown, Pa. in 1934, lived across the street from the College when he was a boy. He had close contact with the school from his youth, serving as a batboy for Coach Ira Herr, and appearing in a Sock and Buskin play. Though his parents, a brother, and two sisters attended the Elizabethtown College, Raffensperger went to Juniata, from which he was graduated in 1956 with a degree in English. He received his master's degree in 1960 from Bucknell, where he remained as an instructor from 1960 to 1962.

In 1963 he joined his family's business, Continental Press, an Elizabethtown firm that specialized in educational publishing. He became president of the company in 1981, and chairman of the board in 1990.

Raffensperger's father, Horace E. Raffensperger, had been secretary of the College's board of trustees, and Daniel became a member of the board in 1978. He was elected as vice-chairman in 1992, and chaired the search committee that had brought Dr. Long to the campus. Raffensperger's tenure as chairman of the board lasted from 1997 to 1999.

The new President of the College continued to search for new ways to improve it, and in January of 1997 announced the creation of the Office of Marketing and Public Affairs. Long had realized that colleges often don't do a good job of marketing themselves, and that such an office with a concentration on marketing would give the school "the capacity to plan better and to sharpen its identity."[31]

President Long also announced the new President's Fund for Distinction, "a grant which will facilitate the development of innovative programs dedicated to strengthening the future of the College and setting it apart from other institutions."[32] The fund would distribute $100,000 every year to individuals or groups who developed and executed creative programs, focussing on the themes that Dr. Long had emphasized in his inaugural address: responsiveness, civic professionalism, and learning, as well as technology and new competencies. In its first year of existence, thirteen programs benefited from the fund.

While the College was greeting the ideas of its new President, it had to say goodbye to a familiar face. Dean of Student Life Richard Crocker was resigning after seven years in office. The reason, he said, was that he had accomplished the tasks he had set out to do, which was to restore the College's trust in the dean, and help integrate college life into the academic part of the college by reaching out and cooperating with the faculty.

As a tongue-in-cheek parting gift, Dean Crocker left the College a new *alma mater*. Of the old one he said, "It is somewhat funny to wait for the inevitable snickers that arise as we sing about the endless lays in storied halls. In another age, the song perhaps was an asset. Now it is a liability."[33]

Crocker's *alma mater*, however, leaves something to be desired. He rhymes "change" and "remains," "together" and "forever," and "praise" and "say," while the second verse begins: "To build a place where learning thrives, where peace and honor dwell / Where all the tasks of daily life a better world compel."[34] Needless to say, the original *alma mater* was not replaced by Crocker's offering.

While the traditional *alma mater* remained intact, another, less long-lived and less highly thought of tradition was put on hold in the spring of 1997. This was the seventh annual "Beer Golf Open," an event that let "of age" students and others make their way through several off-campus houses, each with a designated "par" of liquid refreshment. Both the Pennsylvania Liquor Control Board and Elizabethtown Police Chief Robert Ardner told the Beer Golf organizers that there would be arrests and penalties for dispensing alcohol without a license, and the 1997 Open found itself in an inextricable bunker.

During the summer of 1997, the campus said goodbye to another old building, but hardly reluctantly. Preservation Hall, one of the old army structures that had been placed on campus after World War II, was no longer worthy of preservation. A victim of termite damage and a shifting structure that threatened its survival, it finally fell victim to demolition. Few wept.

The new fall semester found the college with a new dean of college life, Dr. Lisa L. Koogle, and a new director of the Young

Center, Dr. David B. Eller, one of the most distinguished scholars in the Church of the Brethren.

That semester also introduced the first in a series of public meetings on the Strategic Planning Process. At that August 26th meeting, President Long said, "It is the future of the College that is at stake...strategic planning does not eliminate the risks and dangers of the world, but rather helps address them in the most productive way."[35] It was his hope that the new strategic plan would be presented to the board of trustees in October of 1998.

Dr. Long's hope was fulfilled. By the end of October 1998 the board had accepted the strategic plan "with great enthusiasm,"[36] according to Long. The board authorized the College to develop operational plans for the twenty-two implementing objectives, asking for cost estimates, and requesting that priorities be given to some.

Dr. Long continued to search for new ways to increase the sense of community at the school. In the fall of 1997, the lunch program was restructured to make it easier for faculty, administration, and students to eat together. The College community joined the community at large that same autumn, when Elizabethtown College joined the "Adopt a Highway" program. During the first clean-up on September 21st, thirty-eight student senators spent three hours cleaning trash from a two-mile stretch of Route 283, gathering six bags of recyclable material and more than fifty bags of trash.

The College continued to put its house in order. Because interest rates had dropped in 1997, it refinanced 38% of its $19 million debt, buying back bonds and using the savings to help fund an innovative technology initiative over the following three years.

In 1997, the College set up agreements with both Loyola College and Rutgers to allow Elizabethtown graduates to waive up to 21 credits of graduate course work, earning an MBA in about a year. The college had made such previous agreements with Penn State and Lehigh.

The efforts of the new President, the faculty, administration, and trustees, as well as the attitude and performance of the students, continued to burnish the school's reputation. In 1998, for the fifth year in a row, *U. S. News and World Reports* ranked Elizabethtown College as one of the top five regional liberal arts colleges, a ranking it has continued to hold, just as it has continued to develop academically and in other ways.

In March 1999, President Long told a community forum of many changes ahead: an increase in the number of minorities interviewed for faculty positions, the creation of the office of Coordinator of Multicultural Affairs, a vast increase in the school's information technology budget, major changes in the way that students evaluate professors, called I.D.E.A, and an honors program for freshman in the fall of 2000.

The Hershey Foods Honors Program would be the fourth new program during President Long's term, in addition to art, biotechnology, and invasive cardiovascular technology majors. The honors program admitted students who were in the top 10% of their graduating class and had a 1200+ SAT. Honors students would be expected to maintain a 3.5 GPA throughout their college career, and would be taught special honors program courses.

As the College prepared to enter the twenty-first century, it would do so with a new chairman at the helm of the board of trustees. After three years as chairman, Daniel Raffensperger decided to step down, but remained on the board. His successor, elected in October 1999, was Ken Bowers, a 1959 graduate of Elizabethtown College.

Bowers, a resident of Hershey, retired from the Hershey Foods Corporation in 1993 as Vice-President of Corporate Communications. He had been honored by the Pennsylvania Public Relations Society with its Ernest R. McDowell Award for Excellence for Lifetime Achievement. He served the College as chairman of the board's development committee, which oversaw the completion of the $25 million endowment campaign, and was a member of the Strategic Planning Steering Committee. Bowers received an honorary degree from the college in May 1999, as well as two "Educate for Service" awards.

Among the changes scheduled to take place during Ken Bowers' chairmanship is a master land use and facilities plan with $58 million in new construction and campus improvements. The project includes a new science center, the renovation of the Baugher Student Center and Annenberg Center to create a "Campus Crossroads," a new business building, renovations to Thompson Gym and construction of an auxiliary gym, new garden apartments for students, and much more.

By the fall of 2000, the garden apartments, housing 92 students and named after Vera Hackman, were already a reality, as was a two-story addition to the Steinman Center, the renovation of Brinser Residence Hall, new athletic facilities, and a Centennial Garden. The College remained, as always, in the midst of change.

✑﹘✑

The students who attended Elizabethtown College during the 1990s saw a number of other changes as well, both on and off campus. By 1990, students were able to purchase several forms of birth control at the Health Center on campus. There was a continued emphasis on AIDS prevention, and on February 11, 1991, Jeanne White, the mother of young AIDS victim Ryan White, spoke at the College as part of the Student Senate AIDS education effort.

The AIDS Quilt came to campus in 1994. A display of 65 units made of 520 panels was shown for three days, raising $11,000 in donations and merchandise sales.

Another AIDS-related event, however, was not welcomed as warmly. In March 1994, two paintings by an HIV-positive Harrisburg artist were removed from exhibit in the Baugher Student Center after some complaints were heard. The Campus Appearance and Arts Committee reviewed the action, decided it was inappropriate, and had the paintings put back up, to President Spiegler's dismay. "The issue," Spiegler said, "is what is appropriate and it's not appropriate to force people involuntarily into a situation they find troublesome. The message that comes through to me is that we don't care about some people [those who criticized the paintings]."[37]

Another subject that held the attention of many students in the early 90s was the Gulf War, the United States' reaction to Iraqi leader Saddam Hussein's invasion and annexation of Kuwait. Some disapproved of the decision of America to gather and lead a multinational coalition to oust Saddam's troops from the beleaguered county, but in November 1990, President Spiegler spoke at a candlelight vigil held outside the Bucher Meetinghouse to honor the troops in the Middle East. "We need to recognize the fact," Spiegler said, "that our people are over there representing our country, and we need to show respect for our men and women stationed there."[38]

One soldier soon to be stationed there was senior student and Marine reservist Douglass A. Wells, who was called to duty on December 3rd. He trained for three weeks at Camp LeJeune, then went to Saudi Arabia, where he became one of the first Americans to enter Kuwait City after the American victory.

There were those on campus who protested the war. On January 27, 1991, professors Eugene Clemens and Kenneth Kreider organized two dozen college students and joined the march in Washington, D. C. to protest American involvement in the war. Senior Scott Campanella, one of the participating students, said, "I have 100 percent support for the troops, but I have zero percent for this war."[39]

The successful outcome of the war was not enough for President George Bush to win reelection, not even on the predominantly Republican Elizabethtown College campus. In September 1992, a debate between the Young Republicans and the College Democrats favoring challenger Bill Clinton was won by the Democrats, and a pre-election campus poll found Clinton with 58% of the vote, while Bush trailed at 25% and Ross Perot garnered 14%.

Diversity, or the lack thereof, also claimed attention. Student population was 96% Caucasian in the mid-90s. Along with increased administrative attempts to draw minority students and faculty members, the International Club attempted to spread diversity by holding the first International Fest in March 1998. The week-long festivities headlined the Stars of the Shanghai Theatre, as well as The Steel Kings, a Caribbean steel drum band, and international dancers. Foreign students modeled their native dress, foreign films were shown, and an international brunch was held, with food, teas, and coffee from around the world, including a traditional Japanese tea ceremony. The fest has become an annual event.

By the mid-90s, the definition of diversity had grown to include those who were physically disabled. In a 1997 *Etownian* article on freshman Kelly Berlin, the college was made to realize the difficulties faced on campus by those with disabilities. Kelly, confined to a motorized cart by a form of muscular dystrophy, still faced problems even after a number of changes were made to accommodate the disabled. At that time, stairs were the only access to the basement of the Learning Center, there were no elevators in dormitories, Alpha Hall had no elevators or ramps, and sections of the student bookstore were separated by steps. The effort continues to make every area of the campus accessible to Kelly and others with disabilities.

Student compassion for others only increased in the mid to late 90s. Two new Student Directed Learning Community programs appeared in 1995–96. Teens In Elizabethtown (TIE) focused on working to keep teens off the streets and in school, while Helping Hands increased awareness of physically and mentally handicapped citizens, and held seminars of interest to parents of handicapped children.

1995 also saw the first Hunger Banquet. On April 5th, over 100 students and staff members attended the Social Work Student Association's banquet, eating only rice and beans and drinking water. The function raised $200 for Oxfam America.

Clubs and organizations also continued to keep students busy. In 1998, the Activities Fair boasted 65 clubs. The quality of musical and theatre groups continued to grow, and a 1998 production of the musical, *Jesus Christ Superstar*, proved to be one of the most innovative and successful — and controversial — productions ever staged on campus. Directed by Michael Sevareid, an associate professor of theater, the production used a mostly female cast, with freshman Vicky Brewer cast as Jesus, a fact which in itself caused some complaints.

⁓§—§⁓

During the 1990s, athletics continued to thrive at Elizabethtown College. The men's soccer team won the MAC championship in 1991, and reached their 500th win on September 25, 1992. That year the Harrisburg Heat, a professional indoor soccer team, drafted senior Tim Jones, former All-American. The Blue Jays reached their 600th win in September of 1998, beating Concordia 2–0.

The women's soccer team became the 1996 MAC champions with a 7–1 win over Drew, and in the fall of 1997 played in their first national tournament match. They got to the semi-final round of the NCAA National Tournament, losing in overtime to William Smith, a loss that went down as a tie because it was decided on penalty kicks.

Coach Yvonne Kauffman reached her 400th win in women's basketball on February 11, 1993, and the Blue Jays beat Susquehanna in March 1995 to become the MAC champions. Nearly five years later, Coach Kauffman chalked up her 500th win, and on February 11, 1999, reached her 523rd win.

That game against Western Maryland marked an even more significant milestone for the team, as they reached the 800-win mark, defeating their opponent 68–49. In doing so, they became the first women's basketball program in NCAA history to win 800 games. Coach Kauffman said, "The win itself isn't as important as the people who have been there throughout the years."[40]

Women's tennis made its mark on the decade as well. The doubles team of Amy Jo Lutz and Amy Hite were not even seeded in 1992, but still managed to capture the MAC Women's Individual Championship. The women's team won the MAC Championship in 1993 and 1995.

The 1993 men's swim team posted a 17–0 record, breaking by a wide margin the previous record of 11 wins in 1971. In 1995 the team won its first MAC title in 25 years, while the women's swim team's Kim Lotts captured the MAC 100 yard freestyle title.

The women continued their wins. In 1996, freshman Jackie Zimmerman became Elizabethtown College's first All-American woman swimmer, finishing second nationally in the 100 breaststroke and third in the 200 breaststroke. She became the most decorated athlete in the college's history. By the time she graduated in 1999, she was a six-time All-American and the winner of 17 MAC gold medals.

In 1997, the women's swimming team won the MAC Champion Medley Relay, and won back to back MAC crowns in 1998 and 1999. They collected eight gold medals in 18 events in 1998, and increased the gold count to 11 medals in 1999.

Baseball also flourished. The team captured the 1993 MAC crown, setting a standard of excellence. By 1999, they had won the Commonwealth League title for the fourth time in the past six years.

In wrestling, the most notable event was the loss, not of a match, but of D. Kenneth Ober, the college's Athletic Director for 15 years and wrestling coach for 29 years. Ober retired in 1995, with a total record of 305–219–9, making him one of only 13 collegiate wrestling coaches to garner over 300 wins.

His 1979–80 team won the college's only MAC team crown, but he coached 27 individual MAC champions, 11 NCAA All-Americans, and two-time NCAA Division III champion Eric Mast, who succeeded him in 1993 as wrestling coach. He was inducted into the Pennsylvania Coaches Hall of Fame and the NCAA Division III Wrestling Hall of Fame.

≈§—§≈

Athletics continued to provide much of the excitement to be found on the Elizabethtown campus. But what caused even more excitement was the rapidly approaching centennial of the College's founding.

In early 1998, a centennial steering committee was formed, chaired by Gale E. Martin, associate director of college relations. In September the official centennial logo, designed by the Centennial Committee and the firm of Rice and Rice, Ltd., appeared with its slogan, "Making Our Mark on the World."

President Long's charge for the centennial was, "To lift up the achievements and heritage of our first hundred years; to envision new possibilities for the future; and to reposition ourselves in the context of history, society, and the educational marketplace."[41]

The centennial kickoff was announced at a special press conference in Leffler Chapel on February 10, 1999. David Eller portrayed I. N. H. Beahm, who discussed the college's history; President Long spoke of the values of peace, justice, non-violence, and human dignity first adopted by the founders of the school; Shirley Deichert talked about the key projects and events of the centennial; Janice Ruhl '54 talked about the plans for the kickoff; and Dylan Gadino, president of the class of 1999, announced the class's gift of a centennial garden, with flowers popular at the turn of the last century, and a bridge symbolizing the merging of past and future generations. The work on a centennial quilt was announced, and the official banner was unveiled and hung on the façade of Leffler Chapel.

The kickoff celebration took place on April 17, 1999, during the combined Reunion and Spring Arts Festival. A centennial parade marched through the streets of Elizabethtown to the campus. Its grand marshals were Louise Baugher Black '46, retired professor of English *emerita*, and John Leaman, the College's first Rhodes Scholar. The parade wound its way past the Rice & Rice building, on the side of which was painted a new mural by artist Wayne Fettro celebrating the centennial.

Once on campus, the celebration continued with horse-drawn carriage tours given by guides dressed as early Brethren personalities, including J. G. Francis. A midway held strolling entertainers, characters, and clowns, as well as carnival games, penny candy, and door prizes. In Leffler Chapel, professional singer Carolyn Black-Sotir, granddaughter of A. C. Baugher and the daughter of Louise Baugher Black, performed in *Just a Song at Twilight*, a solo concert of turn of the century songs.

An old-fashioned community picnic lunch was served in Thompson Gym, and the afternoon was also filled with activity, including the spring theatre production of *The Children's Hour*, concerts by Phalanx, an *a cappella* vocal group, and the Heritage Singers in the Bucher Meetinghouse. There was storytelling, several art shows, and a dance performance by the College dance troupe, E-Motion. The day concluded with the Centennial Ball at the Radisson Penn Harris Hotel in Camp Hill.

Another highlight of the weekend was the display of the as yet unfinished Centennial Quilt. The project was coordinated by associate professor of art Lou Ellen Schellenberg and Tana Parrett '69, assistant controller of the College. Fittingly, over 100 people had a hand in creating the quilt, which depicted scenes of the campus, such as Alpha Hall, the steeple of Leffler Chapel, the swans on Lake Placida, and the gazebo in The Dell, as well as small touches like J. G. Francis's bicycle. The final stitches were completed on September 9, 1999, and the quilt was dedicated and permanently hung in Leffler Chapel on October 2nd. It was a perfect symbol of the "hand-crafted" education received at the College.

Centennial activities continued through the next fourteen months. At the May 1999 commencement, members of the class of 1949 joined with the current graduating class in the processional. An innovative hundred-year tie-in took place with a showing of art by centenarian Ed Praediger in September. A centennial archival photograph exhibition was put together by Dr. Patricia Ricci, depicting 100 years of teaching and learning at the college.

The College's bonds with the Church were highlighted on September 19th, when an outdoor concert of antiphonal singing was presented near Lake Placida, performed by volunteers from the Centennial Church Partnership Committee and various Church of the Brethren congregations. There were many other college/church presentations. Six vesper services, as well as a Love Feast, were held throughout the year in the Bucher Meetinghouse. There was a symposium on the future of church relatedness and a field trip to Brethren heritage sites in October. A Brethren Heritage Quilt Exhibition was held in November and December, and the Young Center hosted a number of lectures, including the Durnbaugh Lectures that brought Dr. Donald Kraybill back to campus to speak.

In a more secular vein, the centennial homecoming on October 2, 1999, was the most spectacular ever. Traditional homecoming activities concluded with the premiere of the official centennial video, followed by a laser light centennial celebration presented by Sprint.

⇛—⇰

Perhaps the most meaningful moment of the centennial celebration came on February 2, 2000, which was designated Founders' Day. Looking back at an entire century of Elizabethtown College, there were hundreds of people who helped to make the school what it has become. From those honored ranks of faculty, staff, alumni, trustees, and friends who had a profound impact on the institution, thirteen were selected, one for each of the thirteen presidents who have served Elizabethtown College.

At a morning assembly, President Long bestowed the Centennial Medal on the following people or their representatives. All are mentioned elsewhere in this history, for they helped to make the history of Elizabethtown College:

* Edgar T. Bitting '50
* Shirley A. Deichert '66
* Charles S. Farver-Apgar
* Vera Hackman '25

* Ira R. Herr
* S. Dale High '63
* Yvonne E. "Yonnie" Kauffman
* Otis D. Kitchen
* Donald B. Kraybill
* Carlos R. Leffler
* Benjamin G. Musser '42
* Wayne A. Nicarry
* John P. Ranck '58

The gathering of such luminaries, their spouses, descendants, or representatives reminded the campus community of what had brought their college through the storms of the previous century. It was not only buildings or textbooks or land or money that turned a Brethren college with six students and half as many teachers into a world class institution offering 65 majors and minors to over 1500 students, and more than 600 courses taught by over 100 faculty members. People had done that, the kind of people who stood on the stage that morning.

All of these people and hundreds more like them had been willing to take the finest lessons from the past and use them to create a future, not only for themselves, but for Elizabethtown College. They had built on heritage while always looking forward. They were the ushers, the guides, those who would show the way by acts and by example.

As the world enters a new millennium, Elizabethtown College enters its second century from the greatest position of strength it has ever known, ready to address the new realities that await it. As President Ted Long said in June 2000, "Born of necessity and our continuing commitment to excellence, we have charted the course for our journey into this new century, using historic values in new ways to renew the College for a dramatic new age."[42]

---

1 *The Etownian*, May 8, 1992, p. 1
2 *The Etownian*, September 17, 1993, p. 5
3 *Mutual Expectations Committee Basic Understandings*, p. 1
4 op. cit. p. 4
5 op. cit. p. 6

6 *The Etownian*, November 5, 1993, p. 1
7 *The Etownian*, September 13, 1991, p. 1
8 *Elizabethtown*, Winter, 1989, p. 3
9 *The Etownian*, April 16, 1993, p. 1
10 *The Etownian*, April 23, 1993, p. 16
11 Ibid.
12 *The Etownian*, February 2, 1996, p. 1
13 *The Etownian*, September 25, 1992, p. 4
14 *The Etownian*, March 22, 1991, p. 1
15 *The Etownian*, April 5, 1991, p. 1
16 *The Etownian*, March 22, 1991, p. 1
17 *The Etownian*, October 23, 1992, p. 1
18 *The Etownian*, February 12, 1993, p. 1
19 *The Etownian*, January 27, 1995, p. 1
20 *The Etownian*, February 9, 1996, p. 1
21 Ibid.
22 op. cit. p. 3
23 *The Etownian*, September 6, 1996, p. 1
24 *Elizabethtown Magazine*, Summer 1996, p. 6
25 Interview, Dr. Theodore E. Long, August 10, 1999
26 Ibid.
27 *The Etownian*, September 6, 1996, p. 5
28 *The Etownian*, September 13, 1996, p. 3
29 *The Etownian*, November 1, 1996, p. 1
30 *The Etownian*, October 4, 1996, p. 1
31 *The Etownian*, January 24, 1997, p. 3
32 Ibid.
33 *The Etownian*, February 21, 1997, p. 7
34 Ibid.
35 *The Etownian*, September 5, 1997, p. 4
36 *The Etownian*, October 30, 1998, p. 1
37 *The Etownian*, March 25, 1994, p. 1
38 *The Etownian*, November 9, 1990, p. 1
39 *The Etownian*, February 1, 1991, p. 1
40 *Elizabethtown College: The First Hundred Years*, p. 99
41 *Elizabethtown Magazine*, Fall 1998, p. 23
42 *Beginning the Second Century*, p. 3

Epilogue
March 17, 2000

"A bundle of life..."

To the sound of "Oh God, Our Help In Ages Past," President Ted Long and a diminutive African man dressed in clerical garb and using a cane walked toward the stage in Thompson Gymnasium while an audience of over 3000 people and the College Concert Choir sang the hymn under the direction of Dr. John F. Harrison.

When the music ended, the two men were on the stage, the African man nearly dwarfed by the high-backed chair in which he sat. Dr. Long stood and welcomed the audience, then said:

> One hundred years ago, members of the Church of
> the Brethren, one of the historic peace churches, founded
> this college on the premise that the purpose of education
> was to unite the world of the spirit with the world of
> work, in an education for service. We remain true to
> that mission, affirming our heritage of peace, non-

*violence, human dignity and social justice, the central
values of Elizabethtown College. In the most recent elab-
oration of our mission, we have indicated our intent to
make those values manifest in the global community.*

*Our speaker tonight has given eloquent expression
to the values of this college in his own life of service, of
peacemaking and advocacy for justice. All of us who
cherish the mission of this college can learn from his
struggle. For his experience is not so distant from our
lives here today. We too face issues of racial justice and
the reconciliation of peoples, and the struggles of others
around the world affect us here today as well.*

Dr. Long then introduced the guest speaker, and Archbishop
Desmond M. Tutu, recipient of the 1984 Nobel Peace Prize for his
role in the triumph over apartheid in South Africa, stepped slowly to
the lectern. He smiled gently, acknowledging the standing ovation
that greeted him with small waves and murmurs of thanks.

Then he began to speak. For an hour he enthralled the audience, amusing them with his winsome humor and horrifying them
with his stories of the mind-numbing atrocities that occurred during
his people's struggle for freedom.

But what he talked about most was his experiences as Chair of
South Africa's Commission of Truth and Reconciliation, and of how
black Africans, after the defeat of apartheid, went beyond retributive
justice to restorative justice, granting clemency to those who admitted their crimes and forgiving those who had committed acts that
many would deem unforgivable. He partially credited his country's
attitude to *ubuntu*, a word that he said was difficult to render into
English:

> *...the essence of being human, where we see our
> humanity is caught up in one another. We form a bun-
> dle of life. A person is a person to other persons. The
> solitary human being is a contradiction. We are created
> for family, for togetherness. We are created for interde-*

pendence. We are created to exist in a delicate network of togetherness.

When your humanity is undermined, whether I like it or not, mine is inexorably undermined. When your humanity is enhanced, I benefit in an enhancement as well. So I need you to be you, so that I can be me. And in this understanding of our cooperative existence, communal harmony is the summum bonum, *the great good. And anger and resentment and revenge are corrosive of this great good.*

So to forgive is not to be altruistic. To forgive is the best form of self-interest. To forgive is to nurture this harmony that is so crucial for my continued existence, so crucial for your continued existence.

By the time Archbishop Tutu concluded, his address had taken on the rhythm and beauty of a poem. Looking about the huge audience, his arms stretched wide in inclusion, he spoke not only of God's dream, but of the dream of every person to whom the world of the spirit and service to humanity were more than mere words.

As he spoke, envisioning a future filled with Elizabethtown College's heritage of peace, non-violence, human dignity and social justice, it was not difficult to imagine, close by, the shades of those who had come before, of the founders and nurturers of the College, of those who had loved and served it throughout its first century:

God said:
I have a dream.
I have a dream of a new kind of society.
I have a dream of a world where there will be more compassion, more laughter, more joy, more caring, more sharing.
I have a dream of a new world, where they will beat their swords into plowshares and their spears into pruning hooks.
I have a dream of a world where the lion is going to lie again with the lamb, where they will know war no more, where they won't spend obscene amounts of

money on things they call defense budgets when they know that a very small fraction of this will ensure that my children everywhere have enough to eat and clean water.

I have a dream of a world where my children will know that they are my children, that all belong to this family, my family, our family, the human family in which there are no outsiders.

All, all are insiders.

Jesus said I, if I be lifted up, will draw — he didn't say some *— will draw* all.

All, all will be held in the embrace of a love that will not let us go.

All, all. Black, white, red, yellow, rich, poor, educated, not educated, young, old.

All, all will know that they belong — gay, lesbian, straight, all, all, all will belong.

And I have no one, except you, and you, and you to help me realize my dream.

Will you help me?

Please?

The answer came, loud and unmistakable. Three thousand people shook the building with their applause. Three thousand people stood in respect and solidarity, forming "a bundle of life."

The small man with the heart of a giant had finished. The heart of Elizabethtown College beat on.

Chairs of the Board of Trustees

Jesse C. Ziegler, 1900–18
Samuel H. Hertzler, 1918–36
Henry K. Ober, 1936–39
Rufus P. Bucher, 1939–54
Joseph W. Kettering, 1954–68
Aaron G. Breidenstine, 1960–74
Clifford B. Huffman, 1975–81
V. Lester Schreiber, 1982–91
Wayne A. Nicarry, 1991–96
Daniel H. Raffensperger, 1997–99
Kenneth L. Bowers, 2000–

College Principals and Presidents

I.N.H. Beahm, Principal, 1900–01; President, 1904–08
George N. Falkenstein, Principal, 1901–02
Daniel. C. Reber, Acting Principal, 1902–03; Principal, 1903–04;
    President, 1908–18
Henry K. Ober, President, 1918–21, 1924–28
Jacob. G. Meyer, President, 1921–24
Ralph W. Schlosser, President, 1928–29, 1930–41
Harry H. Nye, President, 1929–30
A.C. Baugher, President, 1941–61
Roy E. McAuley, President, 1961–66
Morley J. Mays, President, 1966–77
Mark C. Ebersole, President, 1977–85
Gerhard E. Spiegler, President, 1985–96
Theodore E. Long, President, 1996–

Centennial Celebration Steering Committee

Gale E. Martin, Chair
Louise Baugher Black '46
Kenneth L. Bowers '59
Jay R. Buffenmyer '59
Shirley A. Deichert '66
David C. Downing
Dylan Gadino '99
Jerry L. Garland '59
Conrad L. Kanagy
Carl B. Kaufman '52
Lisa L. Koogle
Carroll L. Kreider '60
M. Caroline Lalvani
Deborah Lee
Theodore E. Long
Lisa Marshall '00
Edward A. Novak III
Wanda Reid
Janice L. Ruhl '54
Lou Ellen Schellenberg
James E. Shreiner '73
Edward E. White, Jr.

Etown College Index

CHET WILLIAMSON

Chet Williamson has previously published fifteen novels, as well as a children's book. Nearly a hundred of his short stories have appeared in such magazines as *The New Yorker*, *Playboy*, *Esquire*, *The Magazine of Fantasy and Science Fiction*, and many other magazines and anthologies. A collection of his short fiction will be published in 2002. He has been a final nominee for the World Fantasy Award, the Mystery Writers of America's Edgar Award, and a six-time nominee for the Bram Stoker Award. He also writes book and music criticism for a variety of venues. His work has been adapted for television, radio, and recorded books. He is a graduate of Indiana University of Pennsylvania.

Williamson has been a lifelong resident of the Elizabethtown area. His wife Laurie is a second grade teacher in the Lower Dauphin School District, and his son Colin currently works and studies in Japan.